AUGUSTANA
DUCERE ET SERVIRE

Masters of the French Art Song:

Translations of the complete songs of Chausson, Debussy, Duparc, Fauré & Ravel

Timothy Le Van

The Scarecrow Press, Inc.
Lanham, Maryland, and London
2001

SCARECROW PRESS, INC.

Published in the United States of America
by Scarecrow Press, Inc.
4720 Boston Way, Lanham, Maryland 20706
www.scarecrowpress.com

4 Pleydell Gardens, Folkestone
Kent CT20 2DN, England

First paperback edition 2001

British Library Cataloguing in Publication Information Available

The hardback edition of this book was previously cataloged by the Library of Congress as follows:

Masters of the French art song : translations of the complete songs of
Chausson, Debussy, Duparc, Fauré & Ravel / by Timothy LeVan.
p. cm
Includes indexes.
ISBN 0-8108-2522-8 (acid-free paper)
1. Songs—France—Texts. I. Le Van, Timothy, 1961- .
ML54.6.M33 1991 <Case>
782.42168'026'8—dc20 91-41123

ISBN: 0-8108-4212-2 (paper)

Manufactured in the United States of America.

The paper used in this publication meets the minimum requirements of American National Standard for Information Sciences—Permanence of Paper for Printed Library Materials, ANSI/NISO Z39.48-1992.

To

Robert & Lois

My Loving and Ever-Supportive Parents

Contents

Acknowledgements

With greatest thanks to the valiant service,
exacting knowledge, and inexhaustible spirit of

Eric Lien

And with sincere thanks and appreciation to

David McCarthy

Preface

It is the hope of the author to provide an aid to all students of language by presenting precise word-by-word and poetic translations of the texts of the complete songs for voice and piano of Chausson, Debussy, Duparc, Fauré and Ravel.

The author encourages ongoing thoughtful evaluation of the relative strength, color, explicit and implicit meaning of each word, phrase, sentence and poem. It is his intent to use cognates wherever possible as a learning tool for the English-speaking artist.

Timothy LeVan is the founder and artistic director of the Opera Training Company of Charlotte, and was a pianist/vocal coach from 1987 to 1991 in the Masters of Opera Degree program offered jointly through the Tri-Cities Opera Company and the State University of New York at Binghamton. Previously he has been a pianist/coach at the Pittsburgh Opera, Pittsburgh Opera Theatre, Ithaca Opera, C.W. Post Summer Opera, was a pianist/coach at the Chautauqua Institution for three summers, and was a free-lance pianist/vocal coach in New York City for three seasons.

Mr. LeVan works with many singers from the Metropolitan Opera and the New York City Opera Companies and tours Asia, North Africa, Europe and North America as an accompanist.

The author of three translation texts, Masters of the Italian Art Song, Masters of the French Art Song and 24 Italian Art Songs, Mr. LeVan is now working on a fourth volume, Masters of the Early Italian Art Song.

Mr. LeVan holds a B.F.A. Degree in Piano from Carnegie-Mellon University, and has done graduate studies at the University of Lausanne and the Conservatory of Fribourg, Switzerland. He resides and teaches in Charlotte, North Carolina.

Introduction

This text is organized alphabetically, first by composer and second by song title.

Each song text is in a three-line format:

Line 1: The original-language text.

Line 2: A word-by-word, vertically accurate translation in the original word order, e.g.,

> J'oublierai les douleurs passées,...
> I-will-forget the sorrows past,...
> (I will forget past sorrows,...)

The number of English "words" is consistent with the number of original-language words, e.g., "J'oublierai les douleurs passées" (four French words) is translated as: "I-will-forget the sorrows past" (four English "words"). Hyphenation is used to accomplish this.

Line 3: A reconstruction of line #2 into more standard English. This line is not a freely poetic translation of the original-language text. Rarely has the author taken the liberty of translating beyond the literal meaning.

This three-line format is designed to help the reader in a translational process from original language, to word-by-word translation, to more standard English translation, and to a final artistic interpretation based upon the reader's knowledge gained from this step-by-step process.

Chausson

Amour d'Antan

Love of-Yesteryear

(Yesteryear's Love)

Mon amour d'antan, vous souvenez-vous?
My love of-yesteryear, yourself remember-you?
(My love of yesteryear, do you remember?)

Nos coeurs ont fleuri tout comme deux roses
Our hearts have flowered all like two roses
(Our hearts have flowered just like two roses)

Au vent printanier des baisers si doux.
To-the wind spring-like of-the kisses so sweet.
(in the springlike wind of kisses so sweet.)

Vous souvenez-vous de ces vieilles choses?
Yourself remember-you of these old things?
(Do you remember these old things?)

Voyez-vous toujours en vos songes d'or Les horizons bleus,
See-you always in your dreams of-gold The horizons blue,
(Do you still see in your golden dreams The blue horizons,)

la mer soleilleuse Qui baisant vos pieds lentement s'endort?
the sea sunny Which kissing your feet slowly itself-slumbers?
(the sunny sea Which, slowly kissing your feet, slumbers?)

En vos songes d'or peut-être oublieuse? Au rayon pâli
In your dreams of-gold perhaps forgetful? To-the ray paled
(In your golden, perhaps forgetful dreams? In the pale light)

des avrils passés Sentez-vous s'ouvrir la fleur
from-the Aprils past Feel-you itself-to-open the flower
(of Aprils past do you Feel the flower of your dreams opening,)

de vos rêves, bouquet d'odorants et de frais pensers?
of your dreams, bouquet of-fragrant and of fresh thoughts?
(bouquet of fragrant and fresh thoughts?)

Beaux avrils passés là-bas, sur les grêves!
Beautiful Aprils past there, on the shores!
(Beautiful past Aprils there, on the shores!)

Chausson

Apaisement

Appeasement

La lune blanche Luit dans les bois.
The moon white Shines in the woods.
(The white moon Shines in the woods.)

De chaque branche Part une voix Sous la ramée
From every branch Parts a voice Under the branch
(From every branch Parts a voice Under the branch)

O bien aimée L'étang reflète, Profond miroir,
Oh well loved The-pond reflects, Deep mirror,
(Oh beloved The pond reflects, Deep mirror)

La silhouette Du saule noir Où le vent pleure.
The silhouette Of-the willow black Where the wind weeps.
(The silhouette Of the black willow Where the wind weeps.)

Rêvons, c'est l'heure. Un vaste et tendre Apaisement
Let-us-dream, it-is the-hour. A vast and tender Appeasement
(Let us dream, it is time. A vast and tender Appeasement)

Semble descendre Du firmament Que l'astre irise.
Seems to-descend From-the firmament That the-star illuminates.
(Seems to descend From the firmanent That the star illuminates.)

C'est l'heure exquise!
It-it the-hour exquisite.
(It is an exquisite hour.)

Chausson

Ballade

Ballad

Quand les anges se sont perdus
When the angels themselves are lost
(When the angels)

Qui s'en venaient sur la mer
Who they-from-it came on the sea
(who came across the sea became lost)

Les oiseaux les ont attendus
The birds them have awaited
(The birds awaited them)

En criant éperdus Dans le vent amer.
In crying bewildered In the wind bitter.
(Crying bewilderedly in the bitter wind.)

Quand les vaisseaux se sont perdus
When the vessels themselves are lost
(When the ships that came across the sea)

Qui s'en venaient sur la mer,
Who they-from-it came on the sea,
(became lost,)

Les oiseaux les ont attendus,
The birds them have awaited,
(The birds awaited them,)

Puis, s'en sont allés dans le vent amer
Then, themselves-from-it are gone in the wind bitter
(Then, in the bitter wind)

S'en sont allés jusqu'aux chaumières
Themselves-from-it are gone until-to-the cottages
(They went to the cottages)

Qui dorment au bord de la mer;
Which sleep at-the border of the sea;
(Which sleep at the edge of the sea;)

Et ils ont dit qu'étaient perdus Les anges attendus.
And they have said that-were lost The angels awaited.
(And they said that the awaited angels were lost.)

S'en sont allés aux clochers des églises
Themselves-from-it are gone to-the belfries of-the churches
(They have gone to the belfries of the churches)

Qui chantent selon la brise,
Which sing according-to the breeze,
(Which sing according to the breeze,)

Et ils ont dit qu'étaient perdus Les vaisseaux attendus.
And they have said that-were lost The vessels awaited.
(And they said that the awaited ships were lost.)

Et la nuit les enfants étranges
And the night the children strange
(And at night the strange children)

Ont vu les ailes des anges
Have seen the wings of-the angels
(Saw the wings of angels)

Comme des vaisseaux flotter au ciel,
Like the vessels to-float in-the sky,
(Like ships floating in the sky,)

Ont vu des voiles comme des ailes
Have seen the sails like some wings
(Have seen the sails like wings)

Planer vers les étoiles.
To-glide toward the stars.
(Gliding toward the stars.)

Et mêlant les ailes, les voiles,
And mixing the wings, the sails,
(And mixing the wings, the sails,)

Et les navires et les anges,
And the vessels and the angels,
(And the vessels and the angels,)

Ils ont prié, les enfants frêles,
They have prayed, the children frail
(They prayed, the frail children)

Dans une ignorance blanche.
In an ignorance white.
(In a white ignorance.)

Chausson
Cantique à l'Epouse
Canticle to the-Spouse
(Canticle to the Wife)

Epouse au front lumineux, Voici que le soir descend,
Spouse with-the brow luminous, Here that the evening descends,
(Wife with the luminous brow, Here the evening descends,)

Et qu'il jette dans tes yeux Des rayons couleur de sang.
And that-it throws in your eyes Some rays color of blood.
(And casts in your eyes blood-red rays.)

Le crépuscule féerique T'environne d'un feu rose,
The twilight fairy-like You-circles with-a fire rose,
(The fairy-like twilight encircles you with a rosy fire,)

Viens me chanter un cantique Beau comme une sombre rose.
Come to-me to-sing a canticle Beautiful like a somber rose.
(Come sing me a song Beautiful as a somber rose.)

Ou plutôt ne chante pas, Viens te coucher sur mon coeur,
Or rather not sing not, Come yourself to-rest on my heart,
(Or rather do not sing, Come rest on my heart,)

Laisse-moi baiser tes bras Pâles comme l'aube en fleur.
Let-me to-kiss your arms Pale like the-dawn in flower.
(Let me kiss your arms Pale as the dawn in flower.)

La nuit de tes yeux m'attire, Nuit frémissante, mystique,
The night of your eyes me-attracts, Night trembling, mystic,
(The night of your eyes attracts me, Trembling, mystic night,)

Douce comme ton sourire Heureux et mélancolique.
Sweet like your smile Happy and melancholic.
(Sweet as your Happy and melancholy smile.)

Et soudain la profondeur Du passé religieux,
And suddenly the profundity Of-the past religious,
(And suddenly the depth Of the religious past,)

Le mystère et la grandeur, De notre amour sérieux,
The mystery and the grandeur, Of our love serious,
(The mystery and grandeur, Of our true love,)

S'ouvre au fond de nos pensées, Comme une vallée immense
Itself-opens in-the bottom of our thoughts, Like a valley immense
(Opens-up in the depth of our thoughts, Like an immense valley)

Où des forêts délaissées Rêvent dans un grand silence.
Where some forests deserted Dream in a great silence.
(Where deserted forests Dream in great silence.)

Chausson

Chanson d'Amour

Song of-Love

Loin de moi, loin de moi ces lèvres que j'adore
Far from me, far from me these lips that I-adore
(Far from me, far from me take the lips that I adore)

Et dont le mensonge, hélas! fut si doux.
And of-which the lying, alas! was so sweet.
(And whose lying, alas! was so sweet.)

Ces beaux yeux que le ciel de moi prend pour l'aurore
Those beautiful eyes that the heaven from me takes for the dawn
(Those beautiful eyes which my heaven takes for dawn)

Ces yeux qui rendraient le matin jaloux.
Those eyes that would-render the morning jealous.
(Those eyes that would make the morning jealous.)

Mais si malgré tout ma douleur te touche Ah!
But if in-spite-of all my sorrow you touches Ah!
(But if in spite of all my sorrow touches you Ah!)

rends-moi, rends-moi mes baisers,
return-me, return-me my kisses,
(return to me, return to me my kisses,)

Sceaux d'amour qui furent posés
Seals of-love that were placed
(Seals of love that were placed)

En vain sur tes yeux, tes yeux et ta bouche.
In vain on your eyes, your eyes and your mouth.
(In vain on your eyes, your eyes and your mouth.)

Chausson

Chanson d'Ophélie

Song of-Ophelia

Il est mort ayant bien souffert, Madame;
He is dead having well suffered, Madame;
(He is dead having greatly suffered, Madame;

Il est parti; c'est une chose faite.
He is left; it-is a thing done.
(He has left; it is done.)

Une pierre à ses pieds et pour poser sa tête, Un tertre vert.
A stone at his feet and for to-pose his head, A knoll green.
(A stone at his feet and a green knoll to rest his head.)

Sur le linceul de neige à pleines mains semées,
On the shroud of snow to full hands sown,
(On the shroud of snow plentifully strewn,)

Mille fleurs parfumées, Avant d'aller sous terre avec lui
1000 flowers perfumed, Before to-go under earth with him
(1000 perfumed flowers, Before going underground with him)

sans retour Dans leur jeunesse épanouie Ont bu,
without return In their youth in-full-bloom Have drunk,
(never to return In their full bloom of youth Have drunk,)

comme une fraiche pluie, Les larmes du sincère amour.
like a fresh rain, The tears of-the sincere love.
(like a fresh rain, The tears of sincere love.)

Chanson Perpétuelle
Song Perpetual
(Perpetual Song)

Bois frissonants, ciel étoilé,
Woods quivering, heaven starry,
(Quivering woods, starry heaven,)

Mon bien-aimé s'en est allé,
My well-loved himself-from-here has gone,
(My beloved has gone,)

Emportant mon coeur désolé.
Carrying my heart desolate.
(Carrying away my desolate heart.)

Vents, que vos plaintives rumeurs,
Winds, that your plaintive rumors,
(Winds, may your plaintive sounds,)

Que vos chants, rossignols charmeurs,
That your songs, nightingales charmers,
(May your songs, charming nightingales,)

Aillent lui dire que je meurs.
Go him to-tell that I am-dying.
(Go tell him that I am dying.)

Le premier soir qu'il vint ici,
The first evening that-he came here,
(The first evening that he came here,)

Mon âme fût à sa merci,
My soul was at his mercy,
(My soul was at his mercy,)

De fierté je n'eus plus souci.
For pride I not-had more care.
(I had no more care for pride.)

Mes regards étaient pleins d'aveux,
My glances were full of-avowals,
(My glances were full of consent,)

Il me prit dans ses bras nerveux,
He me took in his arms vigorous,
(He took me in his vigorous arms,)

Et me baisa près des cheveux.
And me kissed close to-the hair.
(And kissed my forehead.)

J'en eus un grand frémissement.
(I-of-it had a great trembling.
(I was taken with a great trembling.)

Et puis, je ne sais plus comment,
And then, I not know more how,
(And then, I know no longer how,)

Il est devenu mon amant.
He is become my lover.
(He became my lover.)

Je lui disais: "Tu m'aimeras
I to-him said: "You me-will-love
(I said to him: "You will love me)

Aussi longtemps que tu pourras."
As longtime as you can."
(As long as you can.")

Je ne dormais bien qu'en ses bras.
I not slept well but-in his arms.
(I slept well only in his arms.)

Mais lui, sentant son coeur éteint,
But he, feeling his heart put-out,
(But he, feeling dull in his heart,)

S'en est allé, l'autre matin,
Himself-from-here is gone, the-other morning,
(Went away the other morning.)

Sans moi, dans un pays lointain.
Without me, in a land faraway.
(Without me, to a faraway land.)

Puisque je n'ai plus mon ami,
Since I not-have more my lover,
(Since I no longer have my lover,)

Je mourrai dans l'étang parmi
I will-die in the-pond among
(I will die in the pond among)

Les fleurs, sous le flot endormi;
The flowers, under the tide sleeping;
(The flowers, sleeping under the water;)

Sur le bord arrivée, au vent,
On the bank arrived, to-the wind,
(When I have reached the bank, to the wind,)

Je dirai son nom en rêvant
I will-speak his name in dreaming
(I will speak his name in dreaming)

Que là je l'attendis souvent.
That there I him-awaited often.
(That there I awaited him often.)

Et comme en un linceul doré,
And as in a shroud gilded,
(And as in gilded shroud,)

Dans mes cheveux défaits, au gré
In my hair undone, to-the will
(In my flowing hair, to the will)

Du vent je m'abandonnerai.
Of-the wind I myself-will-abandon.
(Of the wind I will abandon myself.)

Les bonheurs passés verseront
The goodnesses past will-pour-out
(Past goodness will pour out)

Leur douce lumière sur mon front,
Their sweet light on my brow,
(Their sweet light onto my brow,)

Et les joncs verts m'enlaceront,
And the rushes green me-will-enlace
(And the green rushes will enlace me,)

Et mon sein croira, frémissant
And my breast will-believe, trembling
(And my breast will believe, trembling)

Sous l'enlacement caressant,
Under the-interlacing caressing,
(Under the caressing enlacement,)

Subir l'étreinte de l'absent!
To-submit the-embrace of the-absent-one!
(That it submits to the embrace of the absent one!)

Dans la Forêt du Charme
et de l'Enchantement
In the Forest of-the Charm
and of the-Enchantment
(In the Forest of Charm and Enchantment)

Sous vos sombres chevelures petites fées.
Under your dark tresses little fairies.
(Under your dark tresses are little fairies.)

Vous chantâtes sur mon chemin bien doucement
You sang on my path very softly
(You sang on my path very softly)

Sous vos sombres chevelures, petites fées
Under your dark tresses, little fairies
(Under your dark tresses, little fairies)

Dans la forêt du charme et de l'enchantement
In the forest of-the charm and of the-enchantment
(In the forest of charm and enchantment)

Dans la forêt du charme et des merveilleux rites
In the forest of-the charm and of-the marvelous rites
(In the forest of charm and marvelous rites)

gnômes compatissants, pendant que je dormais, de votre main,
gnomes compassionate, while that I slept, from your hand
(compassionate gnomes, while I slept, from your hand,)

honnêtes gnômes vous m'offrites un sceptre d'or hélas!
honest gnomes you me-offered a sceptre of-gold alas!
(honest gnomes you offered me a golden sceptre alas!)

pendant que je dormais J'ai su depuis ce temps
while that I slept I-have known since that time
(while I slept I have learned since that time)

que c'est mirage et leurre Les sceptres
that it-is mirage and lure The sceptres
(that the golden sceptres and the songs of the forest)

d'or et les chansons dans la forêt, Pourtant comme
of-gold and the songs in the forest, Yet like
(are a mirage and illusion, Yet like)

un enfant crédule, je les pleure
a child credulous, I them cry
(a credulous child, I cry for them)

et je voudrais dormir encor dans la forêt
and I would-like to-sleep still in the forest
(and would still like to sleep in the forest)

Qu'importe si je sais que c'est mirage et leurre.
What-import if I know that it-is mirage and lure.
(What does it matter that I know it is a mirage and illusion.)

Hébé
Hebe

Les yeux baissés, rougissante et candide,
The eyes lowered, reddening and candid,
(The lowered eyes, blushing and candid,)

Vers leur banquet quand Hébé s'avançait,
Toward their banquet when Hebe herself-advanced,
(When Hebe advanced toward their banquet,)

Les Dieux charmés tendaient leur coupe vide,
The Gods charmed tendered their cup empty,
(The charmed Gods held out their empty cup,)

Et de nectar l'enfant la remplissait.
And of nectar the-infant it refilled.
(And the child refilled it with nectar.)

Nous tous aussi, quand passe la jeunesse,
Us all also, when passes the youth,
(Also, we all, when youth passes,)

Nous lui tendons notre coupe à l'envie,
We to-her tender our cup to the-envy,
(Hold out our cup to her with longing,)

Quel est le vin qu'y verse la Déese?
What is the wine that-there pours the Goddess?
(What is the wine that the Goddess pours there?)

Nous l'ignorons; il enivre et ravit.
We it-do-not-know; it enibriates and intoxicates.
(We do not know it; it enibriates and intoxicates.)

Ayant souri dans sa grâce immortelle
Having smiled in her grace immortal
(Having smiled in her immortal grace)

Hébé s'éloigne; on la rappelle en vain.
Hebe herself-goes-away; one her calls-back in vain.
(Hebe goes away; one calls her back in vain.)

Longtemps encor, sur la route éternelle,
Longtime still, on the route eternal,
(For a long time still, on the eternal path,)

Notre oeil en pleurs suit l'échanson divin.
Our eye in tears follow the-cup-bearer divine.
(Our eyes in tears follow the divine cup-bearer.)

Chausson
Lassitude
Weariness

Ils ne savent plus où se poser ces baisers,
They not know more where themselves to-place these kisses,
(They no longer know where to place these kisses,)

Ces lèvres sur des yeux aveugles et glacés;
These lips on some eyes blind and frozen;
(These lips on blind and frozen eyes;)

Désormais endormis en leur songe superbe,
Henceforth asleep in their dream superb,
(Henceforth asleep in their superb dream,)

Ils regardent rêveurs comme des chiens dans l'herbe,
They look-at dreamy like some dogs in the-grass,
(They gaze dreamily like dogs in the grass,)

La foule des brebis grises à l'horizon
The crowd of-the ewes grey at the-horizon
(At the crowd of grey ewes on the horizon)

Brouter le clair de lune épars sur le gazon.
To-graze the light of moon scattered on the grass.
(Grazing the moonlight scattered on the grass.)

Aux caresses du ciel, vague comme leur vie,
To-the caresses of-the sky, vague like their life,
(To the caresses of the sky, vague like their life,

Indifférent et sans une flamme d'envie
Indifferent and without a flame of-envy
(Indifferent and without a flame of desire)

Pour ces roses de joie écloses sous leurs pas
For these roses of joy open under their steps
(For these roses of joy open under their steps)

Et ce long calme vert qu'ils ne comprennent pas.
And this long calm green that-they not understand not.
(And this long green calm that they do not understand.)

Chausson

L'Aveu

The-Vow

J'ai perdu la forêt, la plaine, Et les frais avrils
I-have lost the forest, the plain, And the fresh Aprils
(I have lost the forest, the plain, And the fresh Aprils)

d'autrefois. Donne tes lèvres, Leur haleine
of-othertimes. Give your lips, Their breath
(of old. Give your lips, Their breath)

Ce sera le souffle des bois. J'ai perdu l'océan morose,
This will-be the breath of-the woods. I-have lost the-ocean morose,
(will be the breath of the woods. I have lost the morose ocean,)

Son deuil, ses vagues, ses échos; Dis-moi n'importe
Its mourning, its waves, its echoes; Tell-me not-imports
(Its mourning, its waves, its echoes; Tell me any)

quelle chose, Ce sera la rumeur des flots.
what thing, This will-be the rumor of-the waves.
(thing, This will be the murmuring of the waves.)

Lourd d'une tristesse royale Mon front songe
Heavy from-a sadness royal My brow dreams
(Heavy from a royal sadness My brow dreams)

aux soleils enfuis. Oh! cache-moi dans ton sein pâle!
of-the suns escaped. Oh! hide-me in your breast pale!
(of escaped suns. Oh! hide me in your pale breast!

Ce sera le calme des nuits.
This will-be the calm of-the nights.
(This will be the calm of night.)

Chausson
La Caravane
The Caravan

La caravane humaine, au Sahara du monde,
The caravan human, in-the Sahara of-the world,
(The human caravan, in the Sahara of the world,)

Par ce chemin des ans qui n'a plus de retour,
By this path of-the years which not-have more of return,
(On this path of the years which has no return,)

S'en va, traînant le pied, brùlée aux feux du jour,
Itself-from-it goes, dragging the foot, burned by-the fires of-the day,
(Goes, dragging its feet, burned by the fire of the day,)

Et buvant sur ses bras la sueur qui l'inonde.
And drinking on its arms the sweat which it-inundates.
(And drinking on its arms the sweat which inundates it.)

Le grand lion rugit, et la tempête gronde:
The great lion roars, and the tempest rumbles:
(The great lion roars, and the storm rumbles:)

A l'horizon fuyard, ni minaret, ni tour.
To the-horizon fugitive, neither minaret, nor tower.
(On the fugitive horizon, neither minaret, nor tower.)

La seule ombre qu'on ait c'est l'ombre
The only shadow that-one has it-is the shadow
(The only shadow that one has is the shadow)

du vautour qui traverse le ciel, cherchant sa proie
of-the vulture who traverses the sky, searching its prey
(of the vulture who crosses the sky, searching for its unclean)

immonde. L'on avance toujours, Et voici que l'on voit
unclean. The-one advances always, And here that one sees
(prey. One always advances, And here one sees)

quelque chose de vert que l'on se montre du doigt!
some thing of green that one itself shows from-the finger!
(something green that you point out with your finger!)

C'est un bois de cyprès semé de blanches pierres.
It-is a wood of cypress sown with white stones.
(It is a cypress wood strewn with white stones.)

Dieu, pour vous reposer, dans le désert
God, for you to-rest, in the desert
(God, in order for you to rest, in the desert)

du temps, Comme des oasis a mis les cimetières.
of-the time, Like some oases has put the cemeteries.
(of time, Has placed cemeteries like oases.)

Couchez-vous, et dormez, Voyageurs haletants!
Lie-down-you, and sleep, Voyagers panting!
(Lie down, and sleep, panting Voyagers!)

Chausson

La Chanson Bien Douce

The Song Very Sweet

(The Very Sweet Song)

Ecoutez la chanson bien douce Qui ne pleure que pour vous plaire.
Hear the song well sweet Which not cries but for you to-please.
(Hear the very sweet song Which cries only to please you.)

Elle est discrète, elle est légère:
It is discreet, it is happy:
(It is discreet, it is happy:)

Un frisson d'eau sur de la mousse.
A shiver of-water on of the moss.
(A shiver of water on some moss.)

La voix vous fut connue et chère,
The voice to-you was known and dear,
(The voice was known and dear to you,)

Mais à présent elle est voilée Comme une veuve désolée
But at present it is veiled Like a widow desolated
(But now it is veiled Like a desolate widow)

Pourtant comme elle encore fière Et dans les longs plis
Nevertheless as she still proud And in the long folds
(But still as proud as she And in the long folds)

de son voile Qui palpite aux brises d'automne
of her veil Which palpitates with-the breezes of-autumn
(of her veil Which palpitates with the autumn breezes)

Cache et montre au coeur qui s'étonne
Hides and shows to-the heart which itself-surprises
(Hides and shows the surprised heart)

La vérité comme une étoile. Elle dit, la voix reconnue
The truth like a star. It said, the voice recognized
(The truth like a star. It said, the voice recognized)

Que la bonté c'est notre vie Que de la haine
That the goodness it-is our life That from the hate
(That goodness is our life That of hate)

et de l'envie Rien ne reste, la mort venue.
and from the-envy Nothing not remains, the death come.
(and envy Nothing remains, once death has come.)

Accueillez la voix qui persiste Dans son naïf épithalame
Welcome the voice that persists In its naive epithalamium
(Welcome the voice that persists in its naive nuptial song)

Allez, rien n'est meilleur à l'âme
Go, nothing not-is better for the-soul
(Go on, nothing is better for the soul)

Que de faire une âme moins triste.
Than to to-make a soul less sad.
(Than to make a soul less sad.)

Elle est en peine et de passage L'âme qui souffre sans colère
It is in pain and of passage The-soul that suffers without anger
(The soul which suffers without anger is in pain and in passing)

Et comme sa morale est claire...Ecoutez la chanson bien sage.
And since its moral is clear...Listen-to the song very sage.
(And since its moral is clear...Listen to the very wise song.)

Chausson
La Cigale
The Cicada

O cigale, née avec les beaux jours,
O cicada, born with the beautiful days,
(O cicada, born in happy days,)

Sur les verts rameaux, dès l'aube posée,
On the green branches, since the-dawn posed,
(Perched on the green branches since dawn,)

Contente de boire un peu de rosée,
Content to to-drink a little of dew,
(Content to drink a little dew,)

Et telle qu'un roi, tu chantes toujours.
And such that-a king, you sing always.
(And like a king, you always sing.)

Innocente à tous, paisible et sans ruses,
Innocent to all, peaceful and without ruses,
(Totally innocent, peaceful and guileless,)

Le gai laboureur, du chêne abrité,
The gay laborer, by-the oak sheltered,
(The happy laborer, sheltered by the oak,)

T'écoute de loin annoncer l'Eté.
You-hears from far to-announce the-Summer.
(Hears you from afar announcing Summer.)

Apollon t'honore autant que les Muses,
Apollo you-honors as-much as the Muses,
(Apollo honors you as much as the Muses,)

Et Zeus t'a donné l'Immortalité!
And Zeus you-has given the-Immortality!
(And Zeus has given you immortality!)

Salut, sage enfant de la terre antique,
Hail, sage infant of the earth antique,
(Hail, wise child of the ancient earth,)

Dont le chant invite à clore les yeux,
Whose the song invites to to-close the eyes,
(Whose song invites the eyes to close,)

Et qui, sous l'ardeur du soleil attique,
And who, under the-ardor of-the sun Attic,
(And who, under the heat of the Attic sun,)

N'ayant chair ni sang, vis semblable aux Dieux!
Not-having flesh nor blood, lives like the Gods!
(Having neither flesh nor blood, lives like the Gods!)

La Dernière Feuille
The Last Leaf

Dans la forêt chauve et rouillée
In the forest bald and rusted
(In the bald and rusted forest)

Il ne reste plus au rameau Qu'une pauvre feuille oubliée,
It not remains more on-the branch But-a poor leaf forgotten
(Nothing but a poor forgotten leaf remains on the branch)

Rien qu'une feuille et qu'un oiseau.
Nothing but-a leaf and but-a bird.
(Nothing but a leaf and a bird.)

Il ne reste plus en mon âme
It not remains more in my soul
(Nothing remains in my soul)

Qu'un seul amour pour y chanter;
But-a single love to there sing;
(But a single love to sing there;)

Mais le vent d'automne, qui brame,
But the wind of-autumn, that wails,
(But the autumn wind, that wails,)

Ne permet pas de l'écouter.
Not permits not to it-to-listen.
(Does not permit to listen to it.)

L'oiseau s'en va, la feuille tombe,
The-bird itself-of-it goes, the leaf falls,
(The bird flies away, the leaf falls,)

l'amour s'éteint, car c'est l'hiver.
the-love itself-extinguishes, because it-is the-winter.
(love extinguishes itself, because it is winter.)

Petit oiseau, viens sur ma tombe Chanter quand l'arbre sera vert.
Little bird, come on my tomb To-sing when the-tree will-be green.
(Little bird, come to my tomb To sing when the trees are green.)

Chausson
Le Charme
The Charm

Quand ton sourire me surprit,
When your smile me surprised,
(When your smile surprised me,)

Je sentis frémir tout mon être,
I felt to-tremble all my being,
(I felt all my being tremble,)

Mais ce qui domptais mon esprit
But that which subdued my spirit
(But that which subdued my spirit)

Je ne pus d'abord le connaître.
I not could at-first it to-know.
(At first I could not know.)

Quand ton regard tomba sur moi,
When your glance fell on me,
(When your glance fell upon me,)

Je sentis mon âme se fondre.
I felt my soul itself melt.
(I felt my soul melt.)

Mais ce que serait cet émoi,
But that which might-be this emotion,
(But what this emotion might be,)

Je ne pus d'abord en répondre.
I not could at-first of-it respond.
(At first I could not answer.)

Ce qui me vainquit à jamais,
That which me vanquished to never,
(That which vanquished me forever,)

Ce fut un plus douloureux charme,
That was a more sorrowful charm,
(Was a more sorrowful charm,)

Et je n'ai su que je t'aimais,
And I not-have known that I you-loved,
(And I did not know that I loved you,)

Qu'en voyant ta première larme.
But-upon seeing your first tear.
(Until I saw your first tear.)

Chausson

Le Colibri

The Humming-Bird

Le vert colibri, le roi des collines,
The green humming-bird, the king of-the hills,
(The green humming bird, the king of the hills,)

Voyant la rosée et le soleir clair
Seeing the dew and the sun bright
(Seeing the dew and the bright sun)

Luire dans son nid tissé d'herbes fines,
To-shine in its nest woven of-grasses fine,
(Shine in its nest woven of fine grasses,)

Comme un frais rayon s'échappe dans l'air.
Like a fresh ray itself-escapes in the-air.
(Like a fresh ray escapes into the air.)

Il se hâte et vole aux sources voisines,
It itself hastens and flies to-the springs neighboring,
(It hurries and flies to the neighboring springs,)

Où les bambous font le bruit de la mer,
Where the bamboos make the noise of the sea,
(Where the bamboos make a noise like the sea,)

Où l'açoka rouge aux odeurs divines
Where the-hibiscus red to-the odors divine
(Where the red hibiscus with its divine fragrance)

S'ouvre et porte au coeur un humide éclair.
Itself-opens and carries to-the heart a humid flash.
(Opens and carries a humid spark to the heart.)

Vers la fleur dorée il descend, se pose,
Toward the flower gilded it descends, itself poses,
(To the gilded flower it descends, alights,)

Et bois tant d'amour dans la coupe rose,
And drinks so-much of-love in the cup rosy,
(And drinks so much love from the rosy cup,)

(cont.)

Qu'il meurt ne sachant s'il l'a pu tarir!
That-he dies not knowing if-he it-has was-able to-exhaust!
(That he dies not knowing if he exhausted it!)

Sur ta lèvre pure, ô ma bien-aimée,
On your lip pure, o my well-loved,
(On your pure lip, o my beloved,)

Telle aussi mon âme eut voulu mourir,
Likewise also my soul had wanted to-die,
(Likewise my soul would have liked to die,)

Du premier baiser qui l'a parfumée.
Of-the first kiss that it-had perfumed.
(Of the first kiss which perfumed it.)

Chausson
Le Temps des Lilas
The Time of-the Lilacs

Le temps des lilas et le temps des roses
The time of-the lilacs and the time of-the roses
(The time of lilacs and the time of roses)

Ne reviendra plus à ce printemps-ci,
Not will-return more to this spring-here,
(Will return no more to this spring,)

Le temps des lilas et le temps des roses
The time of-the lilacs and the time of-the roses
(The time of lilacs and the time of roses)

Est passé, le temps des oeillets aussi.
Has passed, the time of-the carnations also.
(Has passed, the time of the carnations too.)

Le vent a changé, les cieux sont moroses,
The wind has changed, the skies are morose,
(The wind has changed, the skies are gloomy,)

Et nous n'irons plus courir, et cueillir
And we not-will-go more to-run, and to-gather
(And we will go no more to run, and to gather)

Les lilas en fleur et les belles roses;
The lilacs in flower and the beautiful roses;
(Lilacs in flower and beautiful roses;)

Le printemps est triste et ne peut fleurir.
The spring is sad and not can to-flower.
(Spring is sad and cannot flower.)

O joyeux et doux printemps de l'année,
O joyous and sweet spring of the-year,
(O joyous and sweet spring of the year,)

Qui vins, l'an passé, nous ensoleiller,
That came, the-year past, us to-shine-on,
(That came, last year, to shine on us,)

(cont.)

Notre fleur d'amour est si bien fanée,
Our flower of-love is so well faded,
(Our flower of love has faded so,)

Las! que ton baiser ne peut l'éveiller!
Alas! that your kiss not can it-to-awaken!
(Alas! that your kiss cannot awaken it!)

Et toi, que fais-tu? pas de fleurs écloses,
And you, what do-you? not of flowers blooming,
(And you, what are you doing? no blooming flowers,)

Point de gai soleil, ni d'ombrages frais;
No of gay sun, nor of-shadows cool;
(No happy sun, nor cool shadows;)

Le temps des lilas et le temps des roses,
The time of-the lilacs and the time of-the roses,
(The time of lilacs and the time of roses,)

Avec notre amour est mort, à jamais.
With our love is dead, to never.
(With our love is dead, forever.)

Chausson
Les Couronnes
The Crowns

C'est la fillette aux yeux cernés,
It-is the little-girl with-the eyes dark-circled,
(It is the little girl with the dark-circled eyes,)

Avec son air étonné Et ses trois frêles couronnes:
With her air astonished And her three frail crowns:
(With her astonished air And her three frail crowns:)

L'une de fraiche pimprenelle, L'autre de vigne en dentelle,
The-one of fresh burnet-herb, The-other of vine in lace,
(One of fresh burnet herb, Another of vine in lace,)

Dans la troisième une rose d'automne.
In the third a rose of-autumn.
(In the third an autumn rose.)

La pimprenelle est pour son âme, La vigne est pour l'amuser,
The burnet-herb is for her soul, The vine is for her-to-amuse,
(The burnet herb is for her soul, The vine is to amuse her,)

La rose à qui voudra l'aimer.
The rose to who will-want her-to-love.
(The rose for whoever will want to love her.)

Beau chevalier! Beau chevalier!
Beautiful knight! Beautiful knight!
(Handsome knight! Handsome knight!)

Mais il ne passe plus personne,
But it not passes more person,
(But no one passes by anymore,)

Et la fillette aux yeux cernés
And the young-girl with-the eyes dark-circled
(And the girl with the dark-circled eyes)

A laissé tomber les couronnes.
Has left to-fall the crowns.
(Has dropped her crowns.)

Chausson

Las Fauves

Weary Wild-Animals

O les passions en allées, Et les rires et les sanglots!
Oh the passions from-there went, And the laughs and the tears!
(Oh the passions, and laughs and tears have gone!)

Malades et les yeux miclos Parmi les feuilles effeuillées,
Sick and the eyes half-closed Among the leaves fallen,
(Sick, their half-closed eyes Among the fallen leaves,)

Les chiens jaunes de mes péchés, Les hyènes louches de mes haines
The dogs yellow of my sins, The hyenas sordid of my hates
(The yellow dogs of my sins, The sordid hyenas of my hatred)

Et sur l'ennui pâle des haines
And on the-boredom pale of-the hates
(And on the pale boredom of hate)

Les lions de l'amour couchés!
The lions of the-love crouched!
(The lions of love crouched!)

En l'impuissance de leur rêve Et languides sous la langueur
In the-powerlessness of their dream And languid under the languor
(In the inability of their dream And languishing under the languor)

De leur ciel morne et sans couleur Elles regarderont sans trêve
Of their sky gloomy and without color They will-see without respite
(Of their gloomy and colorless sky They will watch without respite)

Les brebis des tentations S'éloigner lentes une à une
The ewes of-the temptations Themselves-to-leave slow one by one
(The ewes of temptation go away slowly, one by one)

En l'immobile clair de lune Mes immobiles passions!
In the-immobile light of moon My immobile passions!
(In the immobile moonlight My immobile passions!)

Chausson

Les Heures

The Hours

Les pâles heures, sous la lune, En chantant jusqu'à mourir,
The pale hours, under the moon, While singing until to-die,
(The pale hours, under the moon, singing until death,)

Avec un triste sourire, Vont une à une,
With a sad smile, Go one by one,
(With a sad smile, Go, one by one,)

Sur un lac baigné de lune, Où, avec un sombre sourire,
On a lake bathed in moon, Where, with a somber smile,
(On a lake bathed in moonlight, Where with a somber smile,)

Elles tendent, une à une, Les mains qui mènent à mourir;
They stretch-out, one by one, The hands that lead to to-die;
(They stretch out, one by one, Hands that lead to death;)

Et certains, blêmes sous la lune,
And certain-ones, pallid under the moon,
(And some, pallid under the moon,)

Aux yeux d'iris sans sourire, Sachant
With-the eyes of-irises without smile, Knowing
(With unsmiling iris-like eyes, Knowing)

Que l'heure est de mourir, Donnent leurs mains une à une;
That the-hour is of to-die, Give their hands one by one;
(That it is the hour of death, Give their hands one by one;)

Et tous s'en vont dans l'ombre et dans la lune,
And all themselves-from-there go in the-shadow and in the moon,
(And they all go into the shadow and into the moonlight,)

Pour s'alanguir et puis mourir,
For themselves-to-languish and then to-die,
(To languish and then to die,)

Avec les heures une à une, Les heures au pâle sourire.
With the hours one by one, The hours with-the pale smile.
(With the hours one by one, The hours with the pale smile.)

Chausson

Les Papillons

The Butterflies

Les papillons couleur de neige Volent par essaim sur la mer;
The butterflies color of snow Fly by swarms over the sea;
(The snowy butterflies Fly in swarms over the sea;)

Beaux papillons blancs, quand pourrai-je
Beautiful butterflies white, when will-be-able-I
(Beautiful white butterflies, when will I be able)

Prendre le bleu chemin de l'air?
To-take the blue path of the-air?
(To take the blue path of the air?)

Savez-vous, o belle des belles,
Know-you, o beautiful of-the beautifuls,
(Do you know, o most beautiful,)

Ma bayadère aux yeux de jais,
My bayadere with-the eyes of jet,
(My dancing girl with jet-black eyes,)

S'ils me voulaient prêter leurs ailes,
If-they me would-like to-lend their wings,
(If they would lend me their wings,)

Dites, savez-vous, où j'irais?
Say, know-you, where I-would-go?
(Tell me, do you know, where I would go?)

Sans prendre un seul baiser aux roses,
Without to-take a single kiss from-the roses,
(Without taking a single kiss from the roses,)

A travers vallons et forêts, J'irais à vos lèvres mi-closes,
To traverse valleys and forests, I-would-go to your lips half-closed,
(Across valleys and forests, I would go to your half-closed lips,)

Fleur de mon âme, et j'y mourrais.
Flower of my soul, and I-there would-die.
(Flower of my soul, and there I would die.)

Chausson
Nanny
Nanny

Bois chers aux ramiers, pleurez, doux feuillages,
Woods dear to-the doves, weep, gentle leaves,
(Woods dear to the doves, weep, gentle leaves,)

Et toi, source vive, et vous frais sentiers,
And you, spring living, and you cool paths,
(And you, flowing spring, and you cool paths,)

Pleurez, o bruyères sauvages, Buissons de houx et d'églantiers.
Weep, o heather wild, Bushes of holly and of-wild-roses.
(Weep, o wild heather, Holly bushes and wild roses.)

Printemps, roi fleuri de la verte année,
Spring, king flowered of the green year,
(Spring, king beflowered with the green year,)

O jeune dieu, pleure! Eté mûrissant,
O young god, weep! Summer ripening,
(O young god, weep! Ripening summer,)

Coupe ta tresse couronnée, Et pleure, automne rougissant.
Cut your tresses crowned, And weep, autumn reddening.
(Cut your crowned tresses, And weep, reddening autumn.)

L'angoisse d'aimer brise un coeur fidèle,
The-anguish to-love breaks a heart faithful,
(Love's anguish breaks a faithful heart,)

Terre et ciel, pleurez! Oh! que je l'aimais!
Earth and heaven, weep! Oh! that I her-loved!
(Heaven and earth, weep! Oh! how I loved her!)

Cher pays, ne parle plus d'elle;
Dear land, not speak more of-her;
(Dear land, speak no more of her;)

Nanny ne reviendra jamais!
Nanny not will-return never!
(Nanny will never return!)

Chausson
Nocturne
Nocturne

La nuit était pensive et ténébreuse; à peine
The night was pensive and gloomy; to pain
(The night was pensive and gloomy; faintly)

Quelques épingles d'or scintillaient dans l'ébène
Some pins of-gold sparkled in the-ebony
(Some pins of gold sparkled in the ebony)

De ses grands cheveux déroulés,
Of her great hair uncoiled,
(Of her long uncoiled hair,)

Qui, sur nous, sur la mer lointaine, et sur la terre
Which, on us, on the sea far-away, and on the earth
(Which, on us, on the faraway sea, and on earth)

Ensevelie en un sommeil plein de mystère,
Shrouded in a sleep full of mystery,
(Shrouded in a sleep full of mystery,)

Secouaient des parfums ailés.
Scattered some perfumes winged.
(Scattered winged perfumes.)

Et notre jeune amour, naissant de nos pensées,
And our young love, born of our thoughts,
(And our young love, born of our thoughts,)

S'éveillait sur le lit de cent roses glacées
Itself-awoke on the bed of hundred roses frozen
(Awoke on a bed of a hundred frozen roses)

Qui n'avaient respiré qu'un jour;
Which not-had breathed but-a day;
(Which had not breathed but a day;)

Et moi, je lui disais, pâle et tremblant de fièvre,
And me, I to-her said, pale and trembling of fever,
(And I, I told her, pale and trembling with fever,)

Que nous mourrions tous deux, le sourire à la lèvre,
That we would-die all two, the smile on the lip,
(That we would die together, a smile on our lips,)

En même temps que notre amour.
In same time as our love.
(At the same time as our love.)

Chausson
Nos Souvenirs
Our Memories

Nos souvenirs, toutes ces choses
Our memories, all those things
(Our memories, all those things)

Qu'à tous les vents nous effeuillons
That-to all the winds we pick
(That to all the winds we throw off)

Comme des pétales de roses Ou des ailes de papillons,
Like some petals of roses Or some wings of butterflies,
(Like rose petals Or butterfly wings,)

Ont d'une joie évanouie Gardé tout le parfum secret,
Have of-a joy fainted Kept all the perfume secret,
(Have kept all the secret perfume of a vanished joy,)

Et c'est une chose inouïe Comme le passé reparaît.
And it-is a thing extraordinary Like the past reappears.
(And it is an extraordinary thing How the past reappears.)

A de certains moments il semble Que le rêve dure toujours
At of certain moments it seems That the dream lasts always
(At certain moments it seems That the dream still lasts)

Et que l'on soit encore ensemble Comme au temps
And that the-one is still together Like in-the time
(And we are still together As in the time)

des défunts amours; Pendant qu'à demi l'on sommeille,
of-the dead loves; While that-to half the-one slumbers,
(of former loves; While we doze,)

Bercé par la vague chanson D'une voix qui charme l'oreille,
Rocked by the vague song Of-a voice which charms the-ear,
(Rocked by the faint song Of a voice which charms the ear,)

Sur les lèvres voltige un nom.
On the lips flutters a name.
(a name floats on the lips.)

Et cette heure où l'on se rappelle
And this hour where the-one itself remembers
(And that hour when we remember)

Son coeur follement dépensé,
Its heart foolishly spent,
(Our foolishly wasted heart,)

Est comme un frissonnement d'aile
Is like a shivering of-wing
(Is like a shivering wing)

Qui s'en vient du joyeux passé.
Which itself-from-there comes from-the joyful past.
(Which comes from the joyful past.)

Chausson

Oraison

Oration

Vous savez, Seigneur, ma misère!
You know, Lord, my misery!
(You know, Lord, my misery!)

Voyez ce que je vous apporte Des fleurs mauvaises de la terre
See that which I you bring Some flowers bad of the earth
(See that which I bring you: Some bad flowers of the earth)

Et du soleil sur une morte Voyez aussi ma lassitude,
And some sun on a corpse See also my lassitude,
(And sun on a corpse See also my weariness,)

La lune éteinte et l'aube noire;
The moon extinguished and the-dawn black;
(The faded moon and black dawn;)

Et fécondez ma solitude
And make-fruitful my solitude
(And make my solitude fruitful)

En l'arrosant de votre gloire.
By it-sprinkling of your glory.
(By sprinkling it with your glory.)

Ouvrez-moi, Seigneur, votre voie,
Open-to-me, Lord, your way,
(Open to me, Lord, your way,)

Eclairez mon âme lasse Car la tristesse de ma joie
Enlighten my soul weary Because the sadness of my joy
(Enlighten my weary soul Because the sadness of my joy)

Semble de l'herbe sous la glace.
Resembles of the-grass under the ice.
(Resembles grass under ice.)

Chausson

Printemps Triste

Spring Sad

(Sad Spring)

Nos sentiers aimés s'en vont refleurir
Our paths loved themselves-from-there go to-reflower
(Our beloved paths begin to reflower)

Et mon coeur brisé ne peut pas renaître.
And my heart broken not can not to-be-reborn.
(And my broken heart cannot be reborn.)

Aussi chaque soir me voit accourir
Also each evening me sees to-run
(Thus each evening sees me hasten)

Et longuement pleurer sous ta fenêtre.
And long to-cry under your window.
(And cry for a long time under your window.)

Ta fenêtre vide où ne brille plus
Your window empty where not shines more
(Your empty window where shines no more)

Ta tête charmante et ton doux sourire;
Your head charming and your sweet smile;
(Your charming head and your sweet smile;)

Et comme je pense à nos jours perdus,
And as I think of our days lost,
(And as I think of our lost days,)

Je me lamente, et je ne sais que dire.
I myself lament, and I not know what to-say.
(I lament, and I know not what to say.)

Et toujours les fleurs, et toujours le ciel,
And always the flowers, and always the heavens,
(And always the flowers, and always the sky,)

Printintemps Triste
(cont.)

Et l'âme des bois dans leur ombre épaisse
And the-soul of-the woods in their shade thick
(And the soul of the woods in their thick shade)

Murmurant en choeur un chant éternel
Murmuring in choir a song eternal
(Murmuring together an eternal song)

Qui se répand dans l'air chargé d'ivresse!
Which itself pours-out in the-air charged with-inebriation!
(Which pours out into the drunken air!)

Et la mer qui roule au soleil levant,
And the sea which rolls to-the sun rising,
(And the sea which rolls to the rising sun,)

Emportant bien loin toutes mes pensées...
Removing well far all my thoughts...
(Carrying all my thoughts far away...)

Qu'elles aillent donc sur l'aile du vent
May-they go then on the-wing of-the wind
(May they go then on the wing of the wind)

Jusques à toi, ces colombes blessées!
Until to you, these doves wounded!
(to you, these wounded doves!)

Chausson
Sérénade
Serenade

Tes grands yeux doux semblent des îles
Your large eyes sweet resemble some islands
(Your large sweet eyes resemble islands)

Qui nagent dans un lac d'azur;
That swim in a lake of-azure;
(That swim in an azure lake;)

Aux fraîcheurs de tes yeux tranquilles, Fais-moi tranquille
To-the freshness of your eyes tranquil, Make-me tranquil
(With the freshness of your tranquil eyes, Make me tranquil)

Et fais-moi pur. Ton corps a l'adorable enfance
And make-me pure. Your body has the-adorable infancy
(And make me pure. Your body has the adorable infancy)

Des clairs paradis de jadis; Enveloppe-moi de silence,
Of-the bright paradises of old; Envelope-me with silence,
(Of bright paradises of old; Envelope me with silence,)

Du silence argenté des lys. Alangui par les yeux tranquilles
With-the silence silvery of lilies. Made-lifeless by the eyes tranquil
(With the silvery silence of lilies. Made lifeless by the tranquil eyes)

des étoiles caressant l'air,
of-the stars caressing the-air,
(of stars caressing the air,)

J'ai tant rêvé la paix des îles,
I-have so-much dreamed the peace of the islands,
(I dreamed so much of the peace of the islands,)

sous un soir frissonnant et clair!
under an evening shivering and clear!
(under a shivering and clear evening!)

Chausson

Sérénade Italienne
Serenade Italian
(Italian Serenade)

Partons en barque sur la mer
Let-us-leave in boat on the sea
(Let us leave by boat on the sea)

Pour passer la nuit aux étoiles.
For to-pass the night to-the stars.
(To pass the night under the stars.)

Vois, il souffle juste assez d'air
See, it blows just enough of-air
(See, there is just enough breeze)

Pour enfler la toile des voiles.
For to-inflate the canvas of-the sails.
(To fill the canvas of the sails.)

Le vieux pêcheur italien
The old fisherman Italian
(The old Italian fisherman)

Et ses deux fils, qui nous conduisent,
And his two sons, who us steer,
(And his two sons, who steer us,)

Ecoutent mais n'entendent rien
Listen but not-understand nothing
(Listen, but understand none)

Aux mots que nos bouches se disent.
Of-the words that our mouths themselves say.
(Of the words we speak.)

Sur la mer calme et sombre, vois,
On the sea calm and dark, see,
(On the calm and dark sea, see,)

Nous pouvons échanger nos âmes,
We can to-exchange our souls,
(We can tell of our souls,)

Et nul ne comprendra nos voix,
And no-one not will-understand our voices,
(And no one will understand our voices,)

Que la nuit, le ciel et les lames.
But the night, the heaven and the waves.
(But the night, heaven and the waves.)

Chausson
Serre Chaude
Greenhouse Hot
(Hot Greenhouse)

O serre au milieu des forêts!
Oh greenhouse in-the middle of-the forests!
(Oh greenhouse in the midst of the forests!)

Et vos portes à jamais closes!
And your doors to never closed!
(And your doors forever closed!)

Et tout ce qu'il y a sous votre coupole!
And all this that-it there has under your cupola!
(And all there is under your canopy!)

Et dans mon âme en vos analogies!
And in my soul in your analogies!
(And in my soul in your analogies!)

Les pensées d'une princesse qui a faim,
The thoughts of-a princess who has hunger,
(The thoughts of a princess who is hungry,)

L'ennui d'un matelot dans le désert, Une musique de cuivre
The-boredom of-a sailor in the desert, A music of copper
(The boredom of a sailor in the desert, Brass music)

Aux fenêtres des incurables. Allez aux angles
At-the windows of-the incurables. Go to-the corners
(At the windows of the incurables. Go to the mildest corners!)

les plus tièdes! On dirait une femme évanouie
the most tepid! One would-say a woman fainted
(One would say a fainted woman)

un jour de moisson, Il y a des postillons dans la cour
a day of harvest, It there has of-the messengers in the courtyard
(at harvest time, there are messengers in the courtyard)

de l'hospice.
of the-hospice.
(of the hospice.)

Au loin passe un chasseur d'élan devenu infirmier
To-the far passes a hunter of-elk become nurse
(In the distance an elk hunter, turned nurse,)

Examinez au clair de lune. Oh! rien n'y est à sa place.
Examine to-the light of moon. Oh! nothing not-there is at its place.
(Look in the moonlight. Oh! nothing here is in its place.)

On dirait une folle devant les juges, Un navire de guerre
One would-say a mad-woman before the judges, A vessel of war
(One might say a mad-woman before judges, A warship)

à pleines voiles Sur un canal Des oiseaux de nuit sur des lis
at full sails On a canal Some birds of night on some lilies
(at full sail On a canal Birds of night on lilies)

Un glas vers midi (Làbàs sous ces cloches!)
A tolling toward noon (Over-there under those bells!)
(A tolling around noon [Over there under those bells!])

Une étape de malades dans la prairie Une odeur d'éther
A stopping-place for sick-people on the prairie An odor of-ether
(A stopping place for sick people on the prairie An scent of ether)

un jour de soleil Mon Dieu! Mon Dieu!
one day of sun My God! My God!
(on a sunny day My God! My God!)

Quand aurons-nous la pluie Et la neige
When will-have-we the rain And the snow
(When will we have rain And snow)

Et le vent dans la serre!
And the wind in the greenhouse!
(And wind in the greenhouse!)

Chausson

Serre d'Ennui

Greenhouse of-Boredom

O cet ennui bleu dans le coeur! Avec la vision meilleure,
Oh this boredom blue in the heart! With the vision best,
(Oh this blue boredom in my heart! With the best vision,)

Dans le clair de lune qui pleure, De mes rêves bleus de languer!
In the light of moon that cries, Of my dreams blue of languor!
(In the weeping moonlight, Of my blue dreams of languor!)

Cet ennui bleu comme la serre, Où l'on voit
This boredom blue like the greenhouse, Where the-one sees
(This blue boredom like the greenhouse, Where one sees)

closes à travers Les vitrages profonds et verts,
closed to traverse The windows deep and green,
(shut across the deep and green windows,)

Couvertes de lune et de verre Les grandes végétations
Covered with moon and with glass The great vegetation
(Covered with moon and glass The great vegetation)

Dont l'oubli nocturne s'allonge,
Whose the-oblivion nocturnal itself-lengthens,
(Whose nightly oblivion lengthens,)

Immobilement Comme un songe Sur les roses des passions.
Immovably As a dream On the roses of-the passions.
(Immovably As a dream On the roses of passion.)

Où de l'eau très lente s'élève En mélant la lune
Where from the-water very slow itself-rises In mixing the moon
(Where the water very slowly rises Mixing with the moon)

et le ciel. En un sanglot glauque éternel
and the sky. In a sob sea-green eternal
(and the sky. In a sea-green eternal sob)

Monotonement comme un rêve.
Monotonously like a dream.
(Monotonously like a dream.)

Debussy
Ariettes Oubliées
Airs Forgotten
(Forgotten Airs)

C'est l'extase...
It-is the-ecstasy...

C'est l'extase langoureuse, C'est la fatigue
It-is the-ecstasy langourous, It-is the fatigue
(It is the langourous ecstasy, It is the loving fatigue)

amoureuse, C'est tous les frissons des bois
loving, It-is all the shivers of-the woods
(It is all the shivering of the woods)

Parmi l'étreinte des brises, C'est, vers
Among the-embrace of-the breezes, It-is, toward
(Among the embrace of the breezes, It is, near)

les ramures grises, Le choeur des petites voix.
the branches gray, the choir of-the little voices.
(the gray branches, the choir of small voices.)

O le frêle et frais murmure! Cela gazouille et susurre.
Oh the frail and fresh murmur! That twitters and whispers.
(Oh frail and fresh murmur! That twitters and whispers.)

Cela ressemble au cri doux Que l'herbe agitée
That resembles to-the cry sweet That the-grass agitated
(That resembles the sweet cry That the agitated grass)

expire...Tu dirais, sous l'eau qui vire,
exhales ... You would-say, under the-water that swirls,
(exhales ... You might say, under the swirling water,)

Le roulis sourd des cailloux. Cette âme qui se
The rolling deaf of-the pebbles. This soul which itself
(The soft rolling of pebbles. This soul which)

lamente En cette plainte dormante, C'est la nôtre,
laments In this complaint sleeping, It-is the ours,
(laments In this sleeping complaint, Is ours,)

n'est-ce pas? La mienne, dis, et la tienne,
not-is-it not? The mine, say, and the yours,
(is it not? Mine, say, and yours,)

Dont s'exhale l'humble antienne
From-which itself-exhales the-humble refrain
(From which exhales the humble refrain)

Par ce tiède soir, tout bas?
By this tepid evening, all soft.
(In this warm evening, very softly.)

Debussy
Ariettes Oubliées
Airs Forgotten
(Forgotten Airs)

Il pleure dans mon coeur...
It weeps in my heart...

Il pleure dans mon coeur Comme il pleut sur la ville.
It weeps in my heart Like it rains on the city.
(It weeps in my heart Like it rains on the city.)

Quelle est cette langueur Qui pénètre mon coeur?
What is this languor That penetrates my heart?
(What is this languor That penetrates my heart?

O bruit doux de la pluie Par terre et sur les toits,
Oh noise sweet of the rain On earth and on the roofs,
(Oh sweet noise of the rain On the ground and on the roofs,)

Pour un coeur qui s'ennuie, O le bruit de la pluie!
For a heart that itself-wearies, Oh the noise of the rain!
(For a heart that is weary, Oh the noise of the rain!)

Il pleure sans raison Dans ce coeur qui
It weeps without reason In this heart which
(It weeps without reason In this heart which)

s'écoeure. Quoi! nulle trahison?
itself-disheartens. What! no treason?
(is dejected. What! no treason?)

Ce deuil est sans raison. C'est bien la pire peine
This mourning is without reason. It-is well the worst pain
(This sorrow is without reason. It is indeed the worst pain)

De ne savoir pourquoi, Sans amour et sans haine,
Of not to-know why, Without love and without hate,
(to not know why, Without love and without hate,)

Mon coeur a tant de peine.
My heart has so-much of pain.
(My heart has so much pain.)

Debussy

Ariettes Oubliées

Airs Forgotten

(Forgotten Airs)

L'ombre des arbres...

The-shadow of-the trees...

L'ombre des arbres dans la rivière embrumée
The-shadow of-the trees in the river misty
(The shadow of the trees in the misty river)

Meurt comme de la fumée, Tandis qu'en l'air,
Dies like of the smoke, While that-in the-air,
(Dies like smoke, While in the air,)

parmi les ramures réelles, Se plaignent
among the branches real, Themselves complain
(among the real branches, The turtle doves)

les tourterelles. Combien, ô voyageur,
the turtle-doves. How-much, oh voyager,
(complain. How much, oh voyager,)

ce paysage blême Te mira blême toi-même,
this landscape pale You mirrored pale your-self,
(this pale landscape mirrored your own pale self,)

Et que tristes pleuraient dans les hautes feuillées,
And how sadly cried in the high foliage,
(And how sadly cried in the high foliage,)

Tes espérances noyées.
Your hopes drowned.
(Your drowned hopes.)

Debussy
Ariettes Oubliées
Airs Forgotten
(Forgotten Airs)

Chevaux de Bois
Horses of Wood
(Merry-Go-Round)

Tournez, tournez, bons chevaux de bois,
Turn, turn, good horses of wood,
(Turn, turn, good wooden horses,)

Tournez cent tours, tournez mille tours;
Turn a-hundred turns, turn a thousand turns;
(Turn a hundred turns, turn a thousand turns;)

Tournez souvent et tournez toujours,
Turn often and turn always,
(Turn often and turn always,)

Tournez, tournez au son des hautbois.
Turn, turn to-the sound of-the oboes.
(Turn, turn to the sound of the oboes.)

L'enfant tout rouge et la mêre blanche,
The-child all red and the mother white,
(The child all red and the mother white,)

Le gars en noir et la fille en rose,
The fellow in black and the girl in pink,
(The fellow in black and the girl in pink,)

L'une à la chose et l'autre à la pose,
The-one at the thing and the-other at the pose,
(The one natural and the other in a pose,)

Chacun se paie un sou de dimanche.
Each himself paying a penny of Sunday.
(Each one spending his Sunday penny.)

Tournez, tournez, chevaux de leur coeur,
Turn, turn, horses of their heart,
(Turn, turn, horses of their heart,)

Tandis qu'autour de tous vos tournois,
While of-around of all your tournaments,
(While around all your games,)

Clignote l'oeil du filou sournois,
Winks the-eye of-the rogue sly,
(Winks the eye of the sly rogue,)

Tournez au son du piston vainqueur.
Turn to-the sound of-the cornet victorious.
(Turn to the sound of the victorious cornet.)

C'est étonnant comme ça vous soûle
It-is astonishing how that you intoxicates
(It is astonishing how it intoxicates you)

D'aller ainsi dans ce cirque bête,
To-go thus in this circus silly,
(To go about thus in this silly circus,)

Rien dans le ventre et mal dans la tête,
Nothing in the stomach and ache in the head,
(Nothing in the stomach and an ache in the head,)

Du mal en masse et du bien en foule.
Of-the bad in mass and of-the good in crowd.
(A lot of bad and a crowd of good.)

Tournez, dadas, sans qu'il soit besoin
Turn, hobby-horses, without that-it be need
(Turn, hobby horses, without there being need)

D'user jamais de nuls éperons
To-use never of any spurs
(To ever use spurs)

Pour commander à vos galops ronds,
For to-control your gallops round,
(To control your round gallops,)

Tournez, tournez, sans espoir de foin.
Turn, turn, without hope of hay.
(Turn, turn, without hope of hay.)

Et dépéchez, chevaux de leur âme,
And hurry, horses of their soul,
(And hurry, horses of their soul,)

Déjà voici que sonne à la soupe
Already here that sounds to the supper
(Already here supper sounds)

La nuit qui tombe et chasse la troupe
The night which falls and chases the crowd
(The falling night and chases the crowd)

De gais buveurs que leur soif affame. Tournez, tournez!
Of gay drinkers that their thirst famishes. Turn, turn!
(Of happy drinkers whose thirst famishes. Turn, turn!)

Le ciel en velours D'astres en or se vêt lentement.
The heaven in velvet Of-stars in gold itself vests slowly.
(The velvet heaven dresses itself slowly with golden stars.)

L'église tinte un glas tristement.
The-church chimes a knell sadly.
(The church chimes a knell sadly.)

Tournez au son joyeux des tambours, tournez.
Turn to-the sound joyous of-the drums, turn.
(Turn to the joyous sound of the drums, turn.)

Debussy
Ariettes Oubliées
Airs Forgotten
(Forgotten Airs)

Green
Green

Voici des fruits, des fleurs, des feuilles
Here-are some fruits, some flowers, some leaves
(Here are some fruits, flowers, leaves)

et des branches, Et puis voici mon coeur,
and some branches, And then here-is my heart,
(and branches, And then here is my heart,)

qui ne bat que pour vous. Ne le déchirez
which not beats but for you. Not it tear-apart
(which beats only for you. Do not tear it apart)

pas avec vos deux mains blanches, Et qu'à vos yeux
not with your two hands white, And may-to your eyes
(with your two white hands, And may the humble present)

si beaux l'humble présent soit doux. J'arrive tout
so beautiful the-humble present be sweet. I-arrive all
(be sweet to your beautiful eyes. I arrive still)

couvert encore de rosée Que le vent du matin
covered still of dew That the wind of-the morning
(all covered with dew That the morning wind)

vient glacer à mon front. Souffrez que ma fatigue,
comes to-freeze at my face. Suffer that my fatigue,
(freezes on my face. Allow my fatigue)

à vos pieds reposée, Rêve des chers instants
at your feet repose, Dream of-the dear instants
(resting at your feet, to Dream of the dear moments)

qui la délasseront. Sur votre jeune sein
which it will-refresh. On your young breast
(which will refresh it. On your young breast)

laissez rouler ma tête, Toute sonore encore
let to-roll my head, All sonorous still
(let my head roll, Still all ringing)

de vos derniers baisers; Laissez-la s'apaiser
of your last kisses; Let-it itself-to-calm
(from your last kisses; Let it be calmed)

de la bonne tempête, Et que je dorme un peu
from the good tempest, And may I sleep a little
(from the good tempest, And, let me sleep a little)

puisque vous reposez.
since you repose.
(since you are resting.)

Debussy

Ariettes Oubliées

Airs Forgotten

(Forgotten Airs)

Spleen

Spleen

Les roses étaient toutes rouges, Et les lierres étaient tout noirs.
The roses were all red, And the ivies were all black.
(The roses were all red, And the ivies were all black.)

Chère, pour peu que tu te bouges, Renaissent
Dear, for little that you yourself budge, Are-reborn
(Dear, with your slightest movement, all my desperation)

tous mes désespoirs. Le ciel était trop bleu, trop tendre,
all my despairs. The heaven was too blue, too tender,
(is reborn. The heaven was too blue, too tender,)

La mer trop verte et l'air trop doux.
The sea too green and the-air too mild.
(The sea too green and the air too mild.)

Je crains toujours, ce qu'est d'attendre!
I fear always, this which-is to-await!
(I always fear, that this is to be awaited!)

Quelque fuite atroce de vous. Du houx à la feuille
Some flight atrocious of you. Of-the holly to the leaf
(Some atrocious flight of yours. Of the holly and the varnished)

vernie Et du luisant buis, je suis las,
varnished And of-the shining box-tree, I am weary,
(leaf And of the shining box tree, I am weary,)

Et de la campagne infinie, Et de tout,
And of the country infinite, And of all,
(And of the infinite country, And of everything,)

fors de vous, hélas!
except of you, alas!
(except you, alas!)

Debussy

Beau Soir

Beautiful Night

Lorsqu'au soleil couchant les rivières sont roses,
When-in-the sun setting the rivers are rosy,
(When in the setting sun the rivers are pink,)

Et qu'un tiède frisson court sur les champs de blé,
And when-a tepid shiver runs over the fields of wheat,
(And when a warm shiver runs over the wheat fields,)

Un conseil d'être heureux semble sortir des choses
A counsel of-to-be happy seems to-emerge from-the things
(A counsel to be happy seems to emerge)

Et monter vers le coeur troublé. Un conseil de goûter
And to-mount toward the heart troubled. A counsel of to-taste
(And rise toward the troubled heart. A counsel to taste)

le charme d'être au monde Cependant qu'on est jeune
the charm of-to-be in the world While that-one is young
(the charm of existing in the world While one is young)

et que le soir est beau, Car nous nous
and that the evening is beautiful, Because we ourselves
(and the evening is beautiful, Because we)

en allons, comme s'en va cette onde:
from-it go, like itself-from-it goes this wave:
(go from it, like this wave goes from it:)

Elle à la mer, nous au tombeau.
It to the sea, us to-the tomb.
(It to the sea, we to the grave.)

Dans le Jardin
In the Garden

Je regardais dans le jardin, Furtif au travers
I was-looking into the garden, Furtively to-the breadth
(I was looking into the garden, Furtively across)

de la haie; Je t'ai vue, enfant! et soudain,
of the hedge; I you-have seen, child! and suddenly,
(the hedge; I saw you, child! and suddenly,)

Mon coeur tressaillit: je t'aimais!
My heart trembled: I you-loved!
(My heart trembled: I loved you!)

Je m'égratignais aux épines, Mes doigts saignaient
I myself-scratched on-the thorns, My fingers bled
(I scratched myself on the thorns, My fingers bled)

avec les mures, Et ma souffrance était divine:
with the berries, And my suffering was divine:
(with the berries, And my suffering was divine:)

Je voyais ton front de gamine, Tes cheveux d'or
I saw your face of girl, Your hair of-gold
(I saw your girlish face, Your golden hair)

et ton front pur! Grandette et pourtant puérile,
and your brow pure! Grown and yet childlike,
(and your pure face! Grown and yet childlike,)

Coquette d'instinct seulement, Les yeux bleus ombrés de longs
Coquette by-instinct only, The eyes blue shaded by long
(A flirt by instinct only, Blue eyes shaded by long)

cils, Qui regardent tout gentiment, Un corps un peu frêle et
lashes, Which look all gracefully, A body a little frail and
(lashes, Which gaze so prettily, A body a little frail and)

charmant, Une voix de mai, des gestes d'avril!
charming, A voice of May, some gestures of-April!
(charming, A voice of May, with gestures of April!)

Debussy

Fleur des Blés

Flower of the Wheats

(Wheat Flowers)

Le long des blés que la brise Fait onduler
The length of-the wheats that the breeze Makes to-undulate
(All along the wheat fields, which the breeze ripples)

puis défrise En un désordre coquet, J'ai trouvé
then to-uncurl In a disorder flirtatious, I-have found
(and uncurls In playful disorder, I have found)

de bonne prise De t'y cueillir un bouquet.
of good taking To you-here to-gather a bouquet.
(a good opportunity to gather a bouquet for you.)

Mets-le vite à ton corsage, Il est fait à ton image
Place-it quickly at your bodice, It is made to your image
(Place it quickly at your bodice, it is made in your image)

En même temps que pour toi...Ton petit doigt,
In same time as for you...Your little finger,
(As well as for you...A little bird,)

je le gage, T'a déjà soufflé pourquoi: Ces épis dorés,
I it wager, You-has already breathed why: These stalks golden
(I wager, has already told you why: These golden clusters)

c'est l'onde De ta chevelure blonde Toute d'or et
it-is the-wave Of your hair blond All of-gold and
(are the waves Of your blond hair All golden and)

de soleil; Ce coquelicot qui fronde, C'est
of sun; This poppy that sways, It-is
(sunny; This poppy that sways, Is)

ta bouche au sang vermeil. Et ces bluets,
your mouth to-the blood red. And these cornflowers,
(your crimson mouth. And these cornflowers,)

beau mystère! Points d'azur que rien n'altère,
beautiful mystery! Points of-blue that nothing not-alters,
(beautiful mystery! Specks of blue that nothing can alter,)

Ces bluets ce sont tes yeux, Si bleus qu'on dirait,
These cornflowers they are your eyes, So blue that-one would-say,
(These cornflowers are your eyes, So blue that one might say,)

sur terre, Deux éclats tombés des cieux.
on earth, Two flashes fallen from-the skies.
(on earth, Two flashes fallen from the skies.)

Debussy

Le Balcon

The Balcony

Mère des souvenirs, maîtresse des maîtresses,
Mother of-the memories, mistress of-the mistresses,
(Mother of memories, mistress of mistresses,)

O toi, tous mes plaisirs! ô toi, tous mes devoirs!
O you, all my pleasures! O you, all my duties!
(O you, all my pleasures! O you, all my duties!)

Tu te rappelleras la beauté des caresses,
You yourself will-recall the beauty of-the caresses,
(You will remember the beauty of caresses,)

La douceur du foyer et le charme des soirs,
The sweetness of-the home and the charm of-the evenings,
(The sweetness of home and the charm of evenings,)

Les soirs illuminés par l'ardeur du charbon,
The evenings illuminated by the-ardor of-the coal,
(Evenings illuminated by the ardor of coal,)

Et les soirs au balcon, voilés de vapeur rose.
And the evenings on-the balcony, veiled of vapor rosy.
(And evenings on the balcony, veiled by rosy vapor.)

Que ton sein m'était doux! Que ton coeur m'était
How your breast to-me-was sweet! How your heart to-me-was
How sweet to me was your breast! How good to me was your

bon! Nous avons dit souvent d'impérissables choses.
good! We have said often of-imperishable things.
(heart! We often said everlasting things.)

Que les soleils sont beaux par les chaudes soirées!
How the suns are beautiful by the warm evenings!
(How beautiful are the suns on warm evenings!)

Que l'espace est profond! que le coeur est puissant!
How the-space is profound! how the heart is powerful!
(How profound is space! how powerful the heart!)

En me penchant vers toi, reine des adorées,
On myself leaning toward you, queen of-the adored,
(Leaning toward you, queen of the adored,)

Je croyais respirer le parfum de ton sang.
I thought to-breath the perfume of your blood.
(I thought I was breathing the perfume of your blood.)

La nuit s'épaississait ainsi qu'une cloison,
The night itself-thickened thus that-a partition,
(The night thickened like a partition,)

Et mes yeux dans le noir devinaient tes prunelles,
And my eyes in the black, guessed your pupils,
(And my eyes in the blackness sensed your pupils,)

Et je buvais ton souffle, ô douceur, ô poison!
And I drank your breath, o sweetness, o poison!
(And I drank your breath, o sweetness, o poison!)

Et tes pieds s'endormaient dans mes mains fraternelles,
And your feet themselves-fell-asleep in my hands brotherly,
(And your feet fell asleep in my brotherly hands,)

Je sais l'art d'évoquer les minutes heureuses,
I know the-art of-to-evoke the minutes happy,
(I know the art of evoking small pleasures,)

Et revis mon passé blotti dans tes genoux.
And relive my past buried in your knees.
(And relive my past buried in your knees.)

Car à quoi bon chercher tes beautés langoureuses
Because to what good to-seek your beauties languorous
(Because what good is seeking your languorous beauties)

Ailleurs qu'en ton cher corps et qu'en ton coeur
Elsewhere than-in your dear body and than-in your heart
(Outside of your dear body and your heart)

si doux? Ces serments, ces parfums, ces baisers infinis.
so sweet? These oaths, these perfumes, these kisses infinite.
(so sweet? These oaths, these perfumes, these infinite kisses.)

Renaîtront-ils d'un gouffre interdit à nos sondes
Will-be-reborn-they from-a gulf forbidden to our probings
(Will they be reborn from an abyss forbidden to our probings)

Comme montent au ciel les soleils rajeunis
Like rise to-the heaven the suns rejuvenated
(Like rejuvenated suns rise to the heaven)

Après s'être lavés au fond des mers profondes?
After themselves-to-be washed at-the bottom of-the seas deep?
(After washing themselves at the bottom of the deep seas?)

Debussy

Harmonie du Soir

Harmony of-the Evening

Voici venir les temps où vibrant sur sa tige,
Here-is to-come the times where vibrating on its stem,
(Here comes the time when vibrating on its stem,)

Chaque fleur s'évapore ainsi qu'un encensoir;
Each flower itself-evaporates thus that-an incensor;
(Each flower exhales like an incensor;)

Les sons et les parfums tournent dans l'air du soir,
The sounds and the perfumes turn in the-air of-the evening,
(The sounds and the perfumes turn in the evening air,)

Valse mélancolique et langoureux vertige.
Waltz melancholy and langourous dizziness.
(Melancholy waltz and langourous giddiness.)

Le violon frémit comme un coeur qu'on afflige,
The violin quivers like a heart that-one afflicts,
(The violin quivers like an afflicted heart,)

Le ciel est triste et beau comme un grand reposoir;
The sky is sad and beautiful like a great altar-of-repose;
(The heavens are sad and beautiful like a great resting place;)

Un coeur tendre, qui hait le néant vaste et noir!
A heart tender, that hates the nothingness vast and black!
(A tender heart, that hates the vast and black nothingness!)

Le soleil s'est noyé dans son sang qui se fige...
The sun itself-is drowned in its blood which itself congeals...
(The sun has drowned in its congealed blood...)

Du passé lumineux recueille tout vestige.
From-the past luminous gather all vestige.
(Recall all vestiges Of the luminous past.)

---Ton souvenir en moi luit comme un ostensoir.
---Your memory in me shines like an ostensory.
(---Your memory in me shines like an ostensory.)

Jane

Jane

Je pâlis et tombe en langueur: Deux beaux yeux
I grow-pale and fall into languor: Two beautiful eyes
(I grow pale and fall into languorousness: Two beautiful eyes)

m'ont blessé le coeur. Rose pourprée et tout humide
me-have wounded the heart. Rose purple and all humid
(have wounded my heart. Purple rose all dewy)

Ce n'était pas sa lèvre en feu; C'étaient ses yeux
This not-was not her lips in fire; Those-were her eyes
(It was not her lips afire; It was those eyes)

d'un si beau bleu Sous l'or de sa tresse fluide.
of-a so beautiful blue Under the-gold of her tress flowing.
(of so beautiful a blue Under the gold of her flowing tresses.)

Je pâlis et tombe en langueur: Deux beaux yeux
I grow-pale and fall into languor: Two beautiful eyes
(I grow pale and fall into languorousness: Two beautiful eyes)

m'ont brisé le coeur. Toute mon âme fut ravie,
me-have broken the heart. All my soul was ravished,
(have broken my heart. All my soul was ravished,)

Doux étaient son rire et sa voix;
Sweet were her laughter and her voice;
(Sweet were her laughter and her voice;)

Mais ses deux yeux bleus, je le vois
But her two eyes blue, I it see
(But her two blue eyes, I see it)

Ont pris mes forces et ma vie. Hélas, la chose
Have taken my forces and my life. Alas, the thing
(Have taken my powers and my life. Alas, this thing)

est bien certaine: Si Jane repousse mon voeu,
is well certain: If Jane repulses my vow,
(is quite certain: If Jane rejects my vow,)

Jane
(cont.)

Dans ses deux yeux d'un si beau bleu
In her two eyes of-a so beautiful blue
(In her two eyes of a so beautiful blue)

J'irai puiser ma mort prochaine.
I-will-go to-draw my death next.
(I will go in search of my approaching death.)

Debussy

Le Jet d'Eau

The Jet of-Water

(The Fountain)

Tes beaux yeux sont las, pauvre amante!
Your beautiful eyes are weary, poor lover!
(Your beautiful eyes are weary, poor lover!)

Reste longtemps sans les rouvrir, Dans cette
Remain long-time without them to-reopen, In this
(Stay for a long time without reopening them, In this)

pose nonchalante Où t'a surprise le plaisir.
pose nonchalant Where you-has surprised the pleasure.
(nonchalant pose In which pleasure has surprised you.)

Dans la cour le jet d'eau qui jase Et
In the courtyard the jet of-water which chatters And
(In the courtyard the chattering fountain And)

ne se tait ni nuit ni jour, Entretient doucement
not itself is-silent neither night nor day, Prolongs sweetly
(which never stops talking day or night, Prolongs sweetly)

l'extase Où ce soir m'a plongé l'amour.
the-ecstasy Where this evening me-has plunged the-love.
(the ecstasy Into which love has plunged me tonight.)

La gerbe d'eau qui berce Ses mille fleurs,
The spray of-water which cradles Its thousand flowers,
(The spray of water which cradles Its thousand flowers,)

Que la lune traverse De ses pâleurs, Tombe comme
That the moon traverses With its pallid-lights, Falls like
(That the moon crosses with its pallid lights, Falls like)

une averse De larges pleurs. Ainsi ton âme
a shower Of large tears. Thus your soul
(a shower Of large tears. Thus your soul)

qu'incendie L'éclair brûlant des voluptés
that-burns The-flash burning of-the voluptuousnesses
(that the burning flash of voluptousness sets afire)

S'élance, rapide et hardie, Vers les vastes
Itself-darts, rapid and bold, Toward the vast
(Darts rapidly and boldly, Toward the vast)

cieux enchantés. Puis, elle s'épanche, mourante,
heavens enchanted. Then, it itself-pours-out, dying,
(enchanted heavens. Then, it pours out, dying)

En un flot de triste langueur, Qui par une
In a wave of sad languor, Which by an
(In a wave of sad languor, Which on an)

invisible pente Descend jusqu'au fond de mon coeur.
invisible slope Descends until-to-the depth of my heart.
(invisible slope Descends to the depth of my heart.)

O toi, que la nuit rend si belle, Qu'il m'est doux,
O you, that the night renders so beautiful, How-it me-is sweet,
(O you, that night makes so beautiful, How sweet it is to me,)

penché vers tes seins, D'écouter la plainte
bent toward your breasts, To-hear the complaint
(bent toward your breasts, To hear the eternal)

éternelle Qui sanglote dans les bassins!
eternal That sobs in the basins!
(complaint Sobbing in the basins!)

Lune, eau sonore, nuit bénie, Arbres qui frissonnez
Moon, water sonorous, night blessed, Trees that quiver
(Moon, sonorous water, blessed night, quivering Trees)

autour, Votre pure mélancolie Est le miroir de mon amour.
around, Your pure melancholy Is the mirror of my love.
(all around, Your pure melancholy Is the mirror of my love.)

Debussy

Recueillement

Meditation

Sois sage, ô ma Douleur, et tiens-toi plus tranquille.
Be sage, o my Sorrow, and hold-yourself more tranquil.
(Be wise, o my Sorrow, and be more tranquil.)

Tu réclamais le Soir; il descend; le voici:
You called the Evening; it descends; it here-is:
(You called the Evening; it descends; here it comes:)

Une atmosphère obscure enveloppe la ville,
An atmosphere obscure envelops the city,
(An obscure atmosphere envelops the city,)

Aux uns portant la paix, aux autres le souci.
To-the ones bringing the peace, to-the others the worry.
(To some bringing peace, to others worry.)

Pendant que des mortels la multitude vile,
While that of-the mortals the multitude vile,
(While the vile multitude of mortals,)

Sous le fouet du Plaisir, ce bourreau sans merci,
Under the whip of-the Pleasure, that executioner without mercy,
(Under the whip of Pleasure, that merciless executioner,)

Va ceuillir des remords dans la fête servile,
Goes to-gather some remorse in the feast servile,
(Goes to gather remorse in the servile feast,)

Ma Douleur, donne-moi la main; viens par ici,
My Sorrow, give-me the hand; come by here,
(Sorrow, give me your hand; come over here,)

Loin d'eux. Vois se pencher les défuntes Années,
Far from-them. See themselves to-lean the defunct Years,
(Far from them. See the dead Years leaning,)

Sur les balcons du ciel, en robes surannées;
On the balconies of-the sky, in robes old-fashioned;
(Over the balconies of heaven, in old-fashioned robes;)

Surgir du fond des eaux le Regret souriant;
To-surge from-the depth of-the waters the Regret smiling;
(Surging from the depths of the water smiling Regret;)

Le Soleil moribond s'endormir sous une arche,
The Sun dying itself-to-fall-asleep under an arch,
(The dying Sun going to sleep under an arch,)

Et, comme un long linceul traînant à l'Orient,
And, like a long shroud trailing to the-Orient,
(And, like a long shroud trailing toward the Orient,)

Entends, ma chère, entends la douce Nuit qui marche.
Hear, my dear, hear the sweet Night that walks.
(Hear, my dear, hear the sweet Night walking.)

Debussy

La Mort des Amants

The Death of-the Lovers

Nous aurons des lits pleins d'odeurs légères,
We will-have some beds full of-odors light,
(We will have beds full of light fragrances,)

Des divans profonds comme des tombeaux;
Some divans deep like some tombs;
(Divans deep as tombs;)

Et d'étranges fleurs sur des étagères,
And some-strange flowers on some shelves,
(And strange flowers on shelves,)

Ecloses pour nous sous des cieux plus beaux,
Unclosed for us under the skies more beautiful,
(Open for us under more beautiful skies,)

Usant à l'envie leurs chaleurs dernières;
Using at the-wish their ardors final;
(Using at will their final ardors;)

Nos deux coeurs seront deux vastes flambeaux,
Our two hearts will-be two vast torches,
(Our two hearts will be two large torches,)

Qui réfléchiront leurs doubles lumières
Which will-reflect their double lights
(Which will reflect their double lights)

Dans nos deux esprits, ces miroirs jumeaux.
In our two spirits, these mirrors twin.
(In our two spirits, these twin mirrors.)

Un soir fait de rose et de bleu mystique
An evening made of rose and of blue mystical
(On an evening made of rose and mystical blue)

Nous échangerons un éclair unique, Comme un long
We will-exchange a flash-of-lightning single, Like a long
(We will exchange a single flash of lightning, Like a long)

sanglot tout chargé d'adieu, Et plus tard un ange,
sob all charged with-farewell, And more late an angel,
(sob all charged with parting, And later an angel,)

entrouvrant les portes, Viendra ranimer, fidèle et joyeux,
opening the doors, Will-come to-reanimate, faithful and joyous,
(opening the doors, Will come to reanimate, faithful and joyous,)

Les miroirs ternis et les flammes mortes.
The mirrors tarnished and the flames dead.
(The tarnished mirrors and the dead flames.)

Debussy

Deux Rondels de Charles d'Orléans

Two Rondels of Charles d'Orléans

Le temps a laissé son manteau...

The time has left its cloak...
(Time has left its cloak...)

Le temps a laissé son manteau De vent de froidure
The time has left its cloak Of wind of cold
(Time has left its cloak Of wind, cold)

et de pluie Et s'est vêtu de broderie, De
and of rain And itself-is vested with embroidery, With
(and rain And clothed itself with embroidery, With)

soleil rayant, clair et beau. Il n'y a bête
sun shining, bright and beautiful. It not-there has beast
(shining sun, bright and beautiful. There is neither bird)

ni oiseau Qui en son jargon ne chante ou crie:
nor bird Which in its jargon not sings or cries:
(nor beast Which in its jargon neither sings nor cries:)

Le temps a laissé son manteau. Rivière, fontaine
The time has left its cloak. River, fountain
(Time has left its cloak. River, fountain)

et ruisseau Portent en livrée jolie Gouttes
and stream Wear in livery fine Drops
(and stream Wear as fine livery Drops)

d'argent d'orfèvrerie. Chacun s'habille de nouveau.
of-silver of-silversmith. Each itself-clothes of new.
(of hand wrought silver. Each clothes itself anew.)

Le temps a laissé son manteau!
The time has left its cloak!
(Time has left its cloak!)

Deux Rondels de Charles d'Orléans

Two Rondels of Charles d'Orléans

Pour ce que plaisance est morte...

For this that pleasure is dead...
(Because pleasure is dead...)

Pour ce que Plaisance est morte Ce mai,
For this that Pleasure is dead This May,
(Because Pleasure is dead This May,)

suis vêtu de noir; C'est grand pitié de véoir
I-am vested of black; It-is great pity to to-see
(I am clothed in black; It is a great pity to see)

Mon coeur qui s'en déconforte.
My heart which itself-of-it is-discomforted.
(My discomforted heart.)

Je m'habille de la sorte Que dois, pour faire devoir,
I myself-dress of the sort That I-must, for to-make to-owe,
(I cloth myself in the way That I must, out of duty,)

Pour ce que Plaisance est morte Ce mai,
For this that Pleasure is dead This May,
(Because Pleasure is dead This May,)

suis vêtu de noir. Le temps ces nouvelles porte
I-am vested of black. The time these news brings
(I am clothed in black. Time brings this news)

Qui ne veut déduit avoir; Mais par force du plouvoir
That not wants diversion to-have; But by force of-the rain
(That wants to have no diversion; But by force of rain)

Fait des champs clore la porte. Pour ce que Plaisance est morte.
Makes of-the fields to-close the door. For this that Pleasure is dead.
(Closes the door to the fields. Because Pleasure is dead.)

Debussy

Fêtes Galantes I

Festivals Galant I

(Galant Festivals)

En Sourdine

In Sourdine

(Muted)

Calmes dans le demi-jour Que les branches hautes font,
Calm in the half-day That the branches high make,
(Calm in the twilight That the high branches make,)

Pénétrons bien notre amour De ce silence profond.
Let-us-Penetrate well our love Of this silence profound.
(Let us Penetrate well our love with this profound silence.)

Fondons nos âmes, nos coeurs Et nos sens extasiés,
Let-us-melt our souls, our hearts And our senses ecstatic,
(Let us melt together our souls, our hearts And our ecstatic senses)

Parmi les vagues langueurs Des pins et des arbousiers.
Among the vague languors Of-the pines and of-the arbutus.
(Among the mild languors Of the pines and arbutus.)

Ferme tes yeux à demi, Croise tes bras sur ton sein,
Close your eyes to half, Cross your arms on your breast,
(Half-close your eyes, Cross your arms on your breast,)

Et de ton coeur endormi Chasse à jamais tout dessein.
And from your heart sleeping Chase to never all design.
(And from your sleeping heart Chase away all design forever.)

Laissons-nous persuader Au souffle berceur et doux
Let-us-ourselves to-persuade To-the breeze cradling and soft
(Let us be persuaded by the cradling and soft breeze)

Qui vient à tes pieds rider les ondes de gazon roux.
That comes to your feet to-ripple the waves of grass reddish.
(That comes to your feet rippling the waves of reddish grass.)

Et quand, solennel, le soir Des chênes noirs tombera,
And when, solemn, the evening From-the oaks black will-fall,
(And when solemnly, the evening falls From the black oaks,)

Voix de notre désespoir, Le rossignol chantera.
Voice of our despair, The nightingale will-sing.
(Voice of our despair, The nightingale will sing.)

Debussy
Fêtes Galantes I
Festivals Galant I
(Galant Festivals)

Fantoches
Marionettes

Scaramouche et Pulcinella Qu'un mauvais dessein
Scaramouche and Pulcinella Who-an evil design
(Scaramouche and Pulcinella Who an evil design)

rassembla Gesticulent, noirs sous la lune.
brought-together Gesticulate, black under the moon.
(brought together Gesticulate, black under the moon.)

Cependant l'excellent docteur Bolognais cueille avec lenteur
While the-excellent doctor from-Bologna gathers with slowness
(While the excellent doctor from Bologna slowly gathers)

Des simples parmi l'herbe brune.
Some medieval-plants among the-grass dark.
(Medieval-plants among the dark grass.)

Lors sa fille, piquant, minois,
Then his daughter, piquant, pretty-faced,
(Then his piquant, pretty-faced daughter,)

Sous la charmille en tapinois
Under the hedge in slyly
(slyly Under the hedge)

Se glisse demi-nue, en quête
Herself-glides half-nude, in quest
(Slips half-nude, in search)

De son beau pirate espagnol;
Of her handsome pirate Spanish;
(Of her handsome Spanish pirate;)

Dont un amoureux rossignol Clame la détresse à tue-tête.
Whose an amorous nightingale Proclaims the distress at top-voice.
(Whose distress an amorous nightingale Proclaims loudly.)

Debussy

Fêtes Galantes I
Festivals Galant I
(Galant Festivals)

Clair de Lune
Light of Moon
(Moonlight)

Votre âme est un paysage choisi
Your soul is a landscape chosen
(Your soul is a chosen landscape)

Que vont charmant masques et bergamasques,
Which goes charming masks and bergamasks,
(Which is charmed by masks and bergamasks,)

Jouant du luth, et dansant, et quasi
Playing of-the lute, and dancing, and almost
(Playing the lute, and dancing, and almost)

Tristes sous leurs déguisements fantasques.
Sad under their disguises fantastic.
(Sad under their fantastic disguises.)

Tout en chantant sur le mode mineur
All in singing on the mode minor
(All the while singing in the minor mode of)

L'amour vainqueur et la vie opportune,
The-love victorious and the life opportune,
(victorious love and the opportune life,)

Ils n'ont pas l'air de croire à leur bonheur
They not-have not the-air of to-believe to their happiness
(They don't seem to believe in their happiness)

Et leur chanson se mêle au clair de lune.
And their song itself mixes with-the light of moon.
(And their song mixes with the moonlight.)

Au calme clair de lune triste et beau,
In-the calm light of moon sad and beautiful,
(In the calm moonlight, sad and beautiful,)

Qui fait rêver les oiseaux dans les arbres
Which makes to-dream the birds in the trees
(Which makes the birds dream in the trees)

Et sangloter d'extase les jets d'eau,
And to-sob from-ecstasy the jets of-water,
(And the fountains sob from ecstasy,)

Les grands jets d'eau sveltes parmi les marbres.
The great jets of-water slender among the marbles.
(The great slender jets of water among the marbles.)

Debussy

Fêtes Galantes II

Festivals Galant II

(Galant Festivals)

Les Ingénus

The Ingenuous-Ones

(The Unsophisticated Ones)

Les hauts talons luttaient avec les longues jupes,
The high heels were-struggling with the long skirts,
(The high heels struggled with the long skirts,)

En sorte que, selon le terrain et le vent,
In sort that, according-to the terrain and the wind,
(In such a way that, according to the terrain and the wind,)

Parfois luisaient des bas de jambes,
Sometimes were-gleaming some bottom of legs,
(Sometimes the lower legs gleamed,)

Trop souvent interceptés!
Too often intercepted!
(Too often intercepted!)

Et nous aimions ce jeu de dupes.
And we loved this game of dupes.
(And we loved this game of dupes.)

Parfois aussi le dard d'un insecte jaloux
Sometimes also the dart of-an insect jealous
(Sometimes too the sting of a jealous insect)

Inquiétait le col des belles sous les branches,
Disquieted the neck of-the beauties under the branches,
(Disquieted the neck of the beauties under the branches,)

Et c'étaient des éclairs soudains des nuques blanches,
And these-were some flashes sudden of-the napes white,
(And these were sudden flashes of white napes,)

Et ce régal comblait nos jeunes yeux de fous.
And this delight gratified our young eyes of foolish-ones.
(And this delight gratified our foolish young eyes.)

Le soir tombait, un soir equivoque d'automne:
The evening was-falling, an evening equivocal of-autumn:
(The evening fell, an equivocal autumn evening:)

Les belles se pendant rêveuses à nos bras,
The beauties themselves hanging dreamily on our arms,
(The beauties hanging dreamily on our arms,)

Dirent alors des mots si spéciaux, tout bas,
Said then some words so special, all low,
(Then said words so special, very softly,)

Que notre âme depuis ce temps tremble et s'étonne.
That our soul since that time trembles and itself-astonishes.
(That since that time our soul trembles and is astonished.)

Debussy
Fêtes Galantes II
Festivals Galant II
(Galant Festivals)

Le Faune
The Faun

Un vieux faune de terre cuite
An old faun of terra cotta
(An old faun of terra-cotta)

Rit au centre des boulingrins,
Laughs in-the center of-the bowling-green,
(Laughs in the middle of the bowling green,)

Présageant sans doute une suite
Presaging without doubt a sequel
(Doubtlessly predicting)

Mauvaise à ces instants sereins,
Evil to these instants serene,
(an Evil sequel to these serene moments,)

Qui m'ont conduit et t'ont conduite, Mélancoliques pèlerins,
Which me-have led and you-have led, Melancholy pilgrims,
(Which have led me and led you, Melancholy pilgrims,)

Jusqu'à cette heure dont la fuite
Until-to this hour of-which the flight
(To this hour whose flight)

Tournoie au son des tambourins.
Turns to-the sound of-the tambourins.
(Turns to the sound of tambourins.)

Debussy
Fêtes Galantes II
Festivals Galant II
(Galant Festivals)

Colloque Sentimental
Colloquium Sentimental
(Sentimental Colloquium)

Dans le vieux parc solitaire et glacé
In the old park solitary and icy
(In the old park, solitary and bitter cold,)

Deux formes ont tout à l'heure passé.
Two forms have all to the-hour passed.
(Two forms just passed.)

Leurs yeux sont morts et leurs lèvres sont molles,
Their eyes are dead and their lips are soft,
(Their eyes are dead and their lips are weak,)

Et l'on entend à peine leurs paroles.
And the-one hears to pain their words.
(And one hardly hears their words.)

Dans le vieux parc solitaire et glacé
In the old park solitary and icy
(In the old park, solitary and bitter cold,)

Deux spectres ont évoqué le passé.
Two specters have evoked the past.
(Two specters have evoked the past.)

Te souvient-il de notre extase ancienne?
You remind-it of our ecstasy former?
(Do you remember our former ecstasy?)

Pourquoi voulez-vous donc qu'il m'en souvienne?
Why wish-you then that-it me-of-it remind?
(Why do you want me to remember it?)

Ton coeur bat-il toujours à mon seul nom?
Your heart beats-it always to my single name?
(Does your heart still beat to my name alone?)

Toujours vois-tu mon âme en rêve? Non.
Always see-you my soul in dream? No.
(Do you still see my soul in your dreams? No.)

Ah! les beaux jours de bonheur indicible
Ah! the beautiful days of happiness unspeakable
(Ah! the beautiful days of unspeakable happiness)

Où nous joignions nos bouches! C'est possible.
Where we joined our mouths! It-is possible.
(When our lips joined! It is possible.)

Qu'il était bleu le ciel, et grand, l'espoir!
How-it was blue the sky, and large, the-hope!
(How blue was the sky, and how large, the hope!)

L'espoir a fui, vaincu, vers le ciel noir.
The-hope has fled, vanquished, toward the sky black.
(Hope has fled, vanquished, toward the black heaven.)

Tels ils marchaient dans les avoines folles,
Such they walked in the oats wild,
(Thus they walked in the wild oats,)

Et la nuit seule entendit leurs paroles.
And the night alone heard their words.
(And the night alone heard their words.)

L'Échelonnement des Haies
The-Row of-the Hedges
(The Hedgerow)

L'échelonnement des haies Moutonne à l'infini, mer
The-row of-the hedges Rolls to the-infinity, sea
(The rows of hedge Rolls into infinity, a)

Claire dans le brouillard clair,
Clear in the mist clear,
(Clear sea in the clear mist,)

Qui sent bon les jeunes baies.
Which smells good the young berries.
(Which smells good with young berries.)

Des arbres et des moulins Sont légers sur le vert tendre,
Some trees and some mills Are light on the green tender,
(Trees and mills Are light on the tender green,)

Où vient s'ébattre et s'étendre
Where come itself-to-frolic and itself-to-stretch-out
(Where the agility of colts)

L'agilité des poulains.
The-agility of-the colts.
(come to frolic and stretch.)

Dans ce vague d'un Dimanche, Voici se jouer aussi,
In this empty of-a Sunday, Here themselves to-play also,
(On this empty Sunday, Here play also,)

De grandes brebis, aussi Douces que leur laine blanche.
Of large sheep, as Soft that their wool white.
(Large sheep, as Soft as their white wool.)

Tout à l'heure déferlait, L'onde roulée en volutes
All at the-hour unfurled, The-wave rolled in volutes
(Presently unfurled, The wave, rolling in spirals)

De cloches comme des flutes Dans le ciel comme du lait.
Of bells like some flutes In the sky like some milk.
(Of bells like flutes In the milky sky.)

La Belle au Bois Dormant
The Beauty in-the Woods Sleeping
(Sleeping Beauty)

Des trous à son pourpoint vermeil, Un chevalier
Some holes to his doublet crimson, A knight
(With holes in his crimson doublet, A knight)

va par la brune, Les cheveux tout pleins de soleil,
goes by the dusk, The hairs all full of sun,
(comes at dusk, His sunlit hair,)

Sous un casque couleur de lune. Dormez toujours,
Under a helmet color of moon. Sleep always,
(Under a moon-colored helmet. Sleep still,)

dormez au bois, L'anneau, la Belle, à votre doigt.
sleep in-the woods, The-ring, the Beauty, on your finger.
(sleep in the woods, The ring, Beauty, on your finger.)

Dans la poussière des batailles, Il a tué loyal
In the dust of-the battles, He has killed loyal
(In the dust of battles, He has killed loyally)

et droit, En frappant d'estoc et de taille,
and just, In striking of-point and of blade,
(and justly, Striking with point and blade,)

Ainsi que frapperait un roi. Dormez au bois,
Thus that would-strike a king. Sleep in-the woods,
(As a king would fight. Sleep in the woods,)

où la verveine, Fleurit avec la marjolaine.
where the verbena, Flowers with the marjoram.
(where the verbena, Flowers with the marjoram.)

Et par les monts et par la plaine, Monté sur
And on the hills and on the plain, Mounted on
(And on the hills and on the plain, Mounted on)

son grand destrier, Il court, il court à perdre haleine,
his great steed, He races, he races to lose breath,
(his great steed, He races, he races breathlessly,)

Et tout droit sur ses étriers. Dormez la Belle
And all upright on his stirrups. Sleep the Beauty
(And upright in his stirrups. Sleep, Beauty)

au Bois, rêvez Qu'un prince vous épouserez.
in-the Woods, dream That-a prince you will-espouse.
(in the Woods, dream That a prince will marry you.)

Dans la forêt des lilas blancs, Sous l'éperon d'or
In the forest of-the lilacs white, Under the-spur of-gold
(In the forest of white lilacs, Under the golden spur)

qui l'excite, Son destrier perle de sang
which it-excites, His steed pearls with blood
(which excites it, His steed pearls with blood)

Les lilas blancs, et va plus vite. Dormez au bois,
The lilacs white, and goes more fast. Sleep in-the woods,
(The white lilacs, and goes faster. Sleep in the woods,)

dormez, la Belle Sous vos courtines de dentelle.
sleep, the Beauty Under your curtains of lace.
(sleep, Beauty Under your lace curtains.)

Mais il a pris l'anneau vermeil, Le chevalier qui
But he has taken the-ring crimson, The knight who
(But he has taken the crimson ring, The knight who)

par la brune, A des cheveux pleins de soleil,
by the dusk, Has some hairs full of sun,
(at dusk, Whose hair is full of sun,)

Sous un casque couleur de lune. Ne dormez plus,
Under a helmet color of moon. Not sleep more,
(Under a moon-colored helmet. Sleep no more,)

La Belle au Bois, L'anneau n'est plus à votre doigt.
The Beauty in-the Woods, The-ring not-is more on your finger.
(Beauty in the Woods, The ring is no longer on your finger.)

Debussy

La Grotte

The Grotto

Auprès de cette grotte sombre Où l'on respire
Near of that grotto dark Where the-one breathes
(Near that dark grotto Where one breathes)

air si doux, L'onde lutte avec les cailloux
air so sweet, The-wave struggles with the pebbles
(air so sweet, The wave struggles with the pebbles)

Et la lumière avecque l'ombre. Ces flots,
And the light with the-shade. These waves,
(And the light with the shade. These waves,)

lassés de l'exercise Qu'ils ont fait dessus
weary from the-exercise that-They have made upon
(weary from the exercise That they have made upon)

ce gravier, Se reposent dans ce rivier
this gravel, Themselves repose on this river
(this gravel, Rest on this brook)

Où mourût autrefois Narcisse...
Where died another-time Narcissus...
(Where once Narcissus died...)

L'ombre de cette fleur vermeille
The-shadow of this flower crimson
(The shadow of this crimson flower)

Et celle de ces joncs pendants
And that of these rushes hanging
(And of these hanging rushes)

Paraissent être là-dedans Les songes de l'eau qui sommeille.
Seem to-be there-within The dreams of the-water which sleeps.
(Seem to be there within The dreams of the sleeping water.)

La Mer est Plus Belle

The Sea is More Beautiful

La mer est plus belle Que les cathédrales;
The sea is more beautiful Than the cathedrals;
(The sea is more beautiful Than cathedrals;)

Nourrice fidèle, Berceuse de râles;
Nurse faithful, Soother of death-rattles;
(faithful Nurse, Soother of death rattles;)

La mer sur qui prie La Vierge Marie!
The sea on which prays The Virgin Mary!
(The sea over which prays The Virgin Mary!)

Elle a tous les dons, Terribles et doux,
She has all the gifts, Terrible and sweet,
(It has all the gifts, Terrible and sweet,)

J'entends ses pardons, Gronder ses courroux;
I-hear its pardons, To-growl its anger;
(I hear its pardons, And its anger rumbling;)

Cette immensité N'a rien d'entêté.
This immensity Not-has nothing of-hard-headed.
(This immensity has no stubborness.)

Oh! Si patiente, Même quand méchante!
Oh! So patient, Even when wicked!
(Oh! So patient, Even when wicked!)

Un souffle ami hante La vague, et nous chante:
A breath friend haunts The wave, and to-us sings:
(A loving breath haunts The wave, and sings to us:)

"Vous, sans espérance, Mourez sans souffrance!"
"You, without hope, Die without suffering!"
("You, without hope, Die without suffering!")

Et puis, sous les cieux
And then, under the skies
(And then, under the skies)

Qui s'y rient plus clairs,
Which themselves-there laugh more brightly,
(Which laugh here more brightly,)

Elle a des airs bleus, Roses, gris et verts...
It has some airs blue, Pink, gray and green...
(It seems blue, Pink, gray and green...)

Plus belle que tous, Meilleure que nous!
More beautiful than all, Better than we!
(More beautiful than all, Better than we!)

Debussy

Le Promenoir des Deux Amants

The Walk of-the Two Lovers

Auprès de cette grotte sombre...

Near of this grotto somber...

Auprès de cette grotte sombre Où l'on respire
Near of that grotto dark Where the-one breathes
(Near that dark grotto Where one breathes)

air si doux, L'onde lutte avec les cailloux
air so sweet, The-wave struggles with the pebbles
(air so sweet, The wave struggles with the pebbles)

Et la lumière avecque l'ombre. Ces flots,
And the light with the-shade. These wavess,
(And the light with the shade. These waves,)

lassés de l'exercise Qu'ils ont fait dessus
weary from the-exercise that-They have made upon
(weary from the exercise That they have made upon)

ce gravier, Se reposent dans ce rivier
this gravel, Themselves repose on this river
(this gravel, Rest on this river)

Où mourût autrefois Narcisse...
Where died another-time Narcissus...
(Where once Narcissus died...)

L'ombre de cette fleur vermeille
The-shadow of this flower rosy
(The shadow of this rosy flower)

Et celle de ces joncs pendants
And that of these rushes hanging
(And these hanging rushes)

Paraissent être là-dedans Les songes de l'eau qui sommeille.
Seem to-be there-within The dreams of the-water which sleeps.
(Seem to be there within The dreams of the sleeping water.)

Le Promenoir des Deux Amants
The Walk of-the Two Lovers

Crois mon conseil, chère Climène...
Believe my counsel, dear Climène...

Crois mon conseil, chère Climène; Pour laisser
Believe my counsel, dear Climene; For to-let
(Believe my advice, dear Climene; To allow)

arriver le soir, Je te prie, allons nous asseoir
to-arrive the evening, I you pray, let-us-go us to-sit
(evening to come, I pray you, let us sit)

Sur le bord de cette fontaine. N'ouis-tu pas
On the border of this fountain. Not-hear-you not
(On the edge of this fountain. Do you not hear)

soupirer Zéphire, De merveille et d'amour atteint,
to-sigh Zephyr, Of marvel and of-love stricken,
(the sighing west wind, Stricken by marvel and love,)

Voyant des roses sur ton teint Qui ne sont
Seeing some roses on your complexion Which not are
(Seeing the roses on your complexion Which are)

pas de son empire? Sa bouche d'odeur toute pleine
not of its empire? Its mouth of-odor all full
(not of its empire? Its mouth all full of fragrances)

A soufflé sur notre chemin, Mêlant un esprit de jasmin
Has breathed on our path, Mixing a spirit of jasmin
(Has breathed on our path, Mixing a spirit of jasmin)

A l'ambre de ta douce haleine.
To the-amber of your sweet breath.
(With the amber of your sweet breath.)

Le Promenoir des Deux Amants
The Walk of-the Two Lovers

Je tremble en voyant ton visage...
I tremble in seeing your visage...

Je tremble en voyant ton visage Flotter avecque mes désirs,
I tremble in seeing your visage To-Float with my desires,
(I tremble upon seeing your face Floating with my desires,)

Tant j'ai de peur que mes soupirs
So-much I-have of fear that my sighs
(So afraid am I that my sighs)

Ne lui fasse faire naufrage.
Not him make to-make shipwreck.
(Would shipwreck him.)

De crainte de cette aventure
Of fear of this adventure
(Out of fear of this adventure)

Ne commets pas si librement A cet infidèle élément
Not commits not so freely To this unfaithful element
(Do not commit so freely To this unfaithful element)

Tous les trésors de la Nature. Veux-tu, par un doux privilège,
All the treasure of the Nature. Wish-you, by a sweet privilege,
(All the treasures of Nature. Do you want, by a sweet privilege,)

Me mettre au-dessus des humains?
Me to-place to-the-on of-the humans?
(To place me above humans?)

Fais-moi boire au creux de tes mains,
Make-me to-drink in-the crux of your hands,
(Make me drink in the hollow of your hands,)

Si l'eau n'en dissout point la neige.
If the-water not-of-it dissolves none the snow.
(If the water dissolves none of the snow.)

Le Son du Cor
The Sound of-the Horn

Le son du cor s'afflige vers les bois,
The sound of-the horn itself-grieves toward the woods,
(The sound of the horn grieves near the woods,)

D'une douleur on veut croire orpheline
With-a sadness one wishes to-believe orphan
(With a sadness one wishes to believe an orphan)

Qui vient mourir au bas de la colline,
Who comes to-die at-the base of the hill,
(Which comes to die at the foot of the hill,)

Parmi la bise errant en courts abois.
Among the north-wind roving in short barks.
(Among the roving north wind in short gusts.)

L'âme du loup pleure dans cette voix,
The-soul of-the wolf cries in this voice,
(The soul of the wolf cries in that voice,)

Qui monte avec le soleil, qui décline
Which rises with the sun, which declines
(Which rises with the sun, which sets)

D'une agonie on veut croire câline,
With-an agony one wishes to-believe tender,
(With an agony one wishes to believe tender,)

Et qui ravit et qui navre à la fois.
And which ravishes and which distresses at the time.
(And which ravishes and distresses at once.)

Pour faire mieux cette plainte assoupie,
For to-make better this complaint sleepy,
(Better to make this sleepy complaint,)

La neige tombe à longs traits de charpie
The snow falls in long lines of shredded-linen
(The snow falls in long shreds of linen)

A travers le couchant sanguinolent,
To traverse the setting-sun blood-tinged,
(Across the blood-tinged setting sun)

Et l'air a l'air d'être un soupir d'automne,
And the-air has the-air of-to-be a sigh of-autumn,
(And the air seems like an autumn sigh,)

Tant il fait doux par ce soir monotone,
So-much it makes sweet by this evening monotonous,
(It sweetens so this dull evening,)

Où se dorlote un paysage lent.
Where itself pampers a landscape slow.
(Where a slow country indulges itself.)

Les Angélus

The Bells of Angelus

Cloches chrétiennes pour les matines,
Bells Christian for the matins,
(Christian morning bells,)

Sonnant au coeur d'espérer encore!
Sounding to-the heart of-to-hope again!
(Sounding the heart to hope again!)

Angelus angelisés d'aurore! Las! Où sont
Angelus made-angelic by-dawn! Alas! Where are
(Angelus made angelic by the dawn! Alas! Where are)

vos prières câlines? Vous étiez de si
your prayers tender? You were of so
(your tender prayers? You were such)

douces folies! Et chanterelles d'amours prochaines!
sweet follies! And decoys of-loves imminent!
(sweet follies! And decoys of coming loves!)

Aujourd'hui souveraine est ma peine, Et toutes matines
Today sovereign is my pain, And all matins
(Today my pain is sovereign, And all matins are)

abolies. Je ne vis plus que d'ombre et de soir;
abolished. I not live more than of-shadow and of evening;
(abolished. I live on nothing but shadow and evening;)

Les las angelus pleurent la mort, Et là,
The weary bells-of-Angelus weep the death, And there,
(The weary Angelus bells weep for death, And there,)

dans mon coeur résigné, dort La seule veuve de tout espoir.
in my heart resigned, sleeps The only widow of all hope.
(in my resigned heart, sleeps The only widow of all hope.)

Debussy
Les Cloches
The Bells

Les feuilles s'ouvraient sur le bord des branches,
The leaves themselves-were-opening on the edge of-the branches,
(The leaves were open on the edges of the branches,)

Délicatement, Les cloches tintaient, légères et franches,
Delicately, The bells were-ringing, light and frank,
(Delicately, The bells rang, lightly and clearly,)

Dans le ciel clément. Rythmique et fervent comme
In the heaven clement. Rhythmic and fervent like
(In the clement heaven. Rhythmic and fervent like)

une antienne, Ce lointain appel Me remémorait
an anthem, That distant call Me reminded
(an anthem, That distant call reminded Me)

la blancheur chrétienne Des fleurs de l'autel.
the whiteness Christian Of-the flowers of the-altar.
(of the Christian whiteness Of altar flowers.)

Ces cloches parlaient d'heureuses années, Et dans
These bells were-speaking of-happy years, And in
(These bells spoke of happy years, And in)

le grand bois Semblaient reverdir les feuilles
the great woods Seemed to-re-green the leaves
(the great woods Seemed to turn green again)

fanées Des jours d'autrefois.
faded Of-the days of-another-time.
(the faded leaves of days gone by.)

Mandoline
Mandolin

Les donneurs de sérénades Et les belles écouteuses,
The givers of serenades And the beautiful listeners,
(The givers of serenades And the beautiful listeners,)

Echangent des propos fades Sous les ramures chanteuses.
Exchange some words dull Under the branches singing.
(Exchange empty words Under the singing branches.)

C'est Tircis et c'est Aminte, Et c'est l'éternel
It-is Tircis and it-is Aminte, And it-is the-eternal
(It is Tircis and Aminte, And the eternal)

Clitandre, Et c'est Damis qui pour mainte
Clitandre, And it-is Damis who for many
(Clitandre, And Damis, who for many)

Cruelle fait maint vers tendre. Leurs courtes
Cruel-woman makes many verses tender. Their short
(a Cruel woman makes many a tender verse. Their short)

vestes de soie, Leurs longues robes à queues,
vests of silk, Their long dresses to tails,
(jackets of silk, Their long dresses with trains,)

Leur élégance, leur joie, Et leurs molles ombres bleues,
Their elegance, their joy, And their soft shadows blue,
(Their elegance, their joy, And their soft blue shadows,)

Tourbillonnent dans l'extase D'une lune rose et grise,
Whirl in the-ecstasy Of-a moon pink and gray,
(Whirl in the ecstasy Of a pink and gray moon,)

Et la mandoline jase Parmi les frissons de brise.
And the mandolin chatters Among the shivers of breeze.
(And the mandolin chatters Among the shivers of the breeze.)

Noël des enfants qui n'ont plus de maisons
Christmas of-the children who not-have more of homes
(Christmas of the children who have no homes)

Nous n'avons plus de maisons! Les ennemis
We not-have more of homes! The enemies
(We have no more homes! The enemies)

ont tout pris, jusqu'à notre petit lit!
have all taken, until-to our little bed!
(have taken everything, even our little bed!)

Ils ont brûlé l'école et notre maître aussi.
They have burned the-school and our teacher too.
(They have burned the school and our teacher too.)

Ils ont brûlé l'église et monsieur Jésus-Christ
They have burned the-church and mister Jesus-Christ
(They have burned the church and mister Jesus Christ)

et le vieux pauvre
and the old-man poor
(and the poor old man)

qui n'a pas pu s'en aller!
who not-has not been-able himself-from-there to-go!
(who could not get away!)

Bien sûr! Papa est à la guerre, Pauvre maman est morte
Of course! Papa is at the war, Poor mommy is dead
(Of course! Papa is at war, Poor mommy died)

Avant d'avoir vu tout ça. Qu'est-ce que l'on va
Before of-to-have seen all that. What-is-this that the-one goes
(Before having seen all this. What is one to do?)

faire? Noël! petit Noël!
to-do? Christmas! little Christmas!
(Christmas! little Christmas!)

n'aller pas chez eux,
not-to-go not to-the-home-of them,
(do not go to their homes,)

n'allez plus jamais chez eux. Punissez-les! Vengez
not-go more never to-the-home-of them. Punish-them! Avenge
(never go to their homes again. Punish them! Avenge)

les enfants de France! Les petits Belges,
the children of France! The little Belgians,
(the children of France! The little Belgians,)

les petites Serbes, et les petits Polonais aussi!
the little Serbians, and the little Poles also!
(the little Serbians, and the little Poles too!)

Si nous en oublions, pardonnez-nous. Noël! Noël!
If we of-them forget, pardon-us. Christmas! Christmas!
(If we have forgotten any forgive us. Christmas! Christmas!)

surtout, pas de joujoux, Tâchez de nous redonner
above-all, not of toys, Try to us to-re-give
(above all, no toys, Try to give us)

le pain quotidien. Noël! écoutez-nous, nous n'avons
the bread daily. Christmas! hear-us, we not-have
(our daily bread. Christmas! hear us, we have)

plus de petits sabots: Mais donnez la victoire
more of little wooden-shoes: But give the victory
(no more little wooden shoes: But give victory)

aux enfants de France!
to-the children of France!
(to the children of France!)

Debussy

Nuit d'Étoiles

Night of-Stars
(Starry Night)

Nuit d'étoiles, sous tes voiles, Sous ta brise
Night of-stars, under your veils, Under your breeze
(Starry night, under your veils, Under your breeze)

et tes parfums, Triste lyre qui soupire,
and your perfumes, Sad lyre which sighs,
(and your perfume, Sighing sad lyre,)

Je rêve aux amours défunts. La sereine mélancolie
I dream of-the loves defunct. The serene melancholy
(I dream of my past loves. The serene melancholy)

Vient éclore au fond de mon coeur.
Comes to-open at-the base of my heart.
(Opens up in the bottom of my heart.)

Et j'entends l'âme de ma mie Tressaillir
And I-hear the-soul of my love To-tremble
(And I hear the soul of my love Tremble)

dans le bois rêveur. Je revois à notre fontaine
in the woods dreaming. I re-see at our fountain
(in the dreaming woods. I see again in our fountain)

Tes regards bleus comme les cieux; Cette rose,
Your glances blue like the skies; This rose,
(Your glances blue as the skies; This rose)

c'est ton haleine, Et ces étoiles sont tes yeux.
it-is your breath, And these stars are your eyes.
(is your breath, And these stars are your eyes.)

Paysage Sentimental
Landscape Sentimental
(Sentimental Landscape)

Le ciel d'hiver, si doux, si triste, si dormant,
The sky of-winter, so gentle, so sad, so sleeping,
(The winter sky, so gentle, so sad, so sleepy,)

Où le soleil errait parmi des vapeurs blanches,
Where the sun wandered among some vapors white,
(Where the sun wandered among white vapors,)

Etait pareil au doux, au profond sentiment
Was equal to-the gentle, to-the profound sentiment
(Was equal to the gentle, to the profound sentiment)

Qui nous rendait heureux mélancoliquement
Which us rendered happy melancholically
(Which made us melancholically happy)

Par cet après-midi de baisers sous les branches.
By this afternoon of kisses under the branches.
(On this afternoon of kisses under the branches.)

Branches mortes qu'aucun souffle ne remuait,
Branches dead that-no breath not stirred,
(Dead branches that no breath stirred,)

Branches noires avec quelque feuille fanée.
Branches black with some leaf faded.
(Black branches with faded leaves.)

Ah! que ta bouche s'est à ma bouche donnée
Ah! how your mouth itself-is to my mouth given
(Ah! how your mouth yielded to mine)

Plus tendrement encore dans ce grand bois muet,
More tenderly still in this large wood mute,
(More tenderly still in this large silent wood,)

Et dans cette langueur de la mort de l'année,
And in this languor of the death of the-year,
(And in this languor of the year's death,)

La mort de tout sinon de toi que j'aime tant,
The death of all if-not of you whom I-love so-much,
(The death of all except you whom I love so much,)

Et sinon du bonheur dont mon âme est comblée,
And if-not of-the happiness of-which my soul is filled,
(And except the happiness which fills my soul,)

Bonheur qui dort au fond de cette âme isolée,
Happiness that sleeps in-the bottom of this soul isolated,
(Happiness that sleeps at the bottom of this isolated soul,)

Mystérieux, paisible et frais comme l'étang
Mysterious, peaceful and fresh like the-pond
(Mysterious, peaceful and fresh like the pond)

Qui pâlissait au fond de la pâle vallée.
Which paled at-the bottom of the pale valley.
(Which paled at the bottom of the pale valley.)

Proses Lyriques
Prose Lyrical
(Lyrical Prose)

De Rêve...
Of Dream...

La nuit a des douceurs de femme Et les vieux
The night has some tendernesses of woman And the old
(The night has the tenderness of woman And the old)

arbres sous la lune d'or, Songent! A celle qui
trees under the moon of-gold, Dream! To her who
(trees under the golden moon, Dream! She who)

vient de passer la tête emperlée, Maintenant
comes of to-pass the head empearled, Now
(just passed her head empearled, Now)

navrée, à jamais navrée, Ils n'ont pas su
distressed, to never distressed, They not-have not known
(distressed, forever distressed, They did not know)

lui faire signe... Toutes! elles ont passé:
her to-make sign... All! they have passed:
(how to call her... All! they have passed:)

les Frêles, les Folles, Semant leur rire
the Frail-ones, the Frantic-ones, Sowing their smile
(the Frail ones, the Frantic ones, Sowing their smile)

au gazon grêle, aux brises frôleuses la caresse
to-the grass thin, to-the breezes grazing the caress
(to the thin grass, to the grazing breezes the charming caress)

charmeuse des hanches fleurissantes. Hélas!
charming of-their hips flourishing. Alas!
(of their flourishing hips. Alas!)

de tout ceci, plus rien qu'un blanc frisson...
of all this, more nothing but-a white shiver...
(of all this, nothing more than a white shiver...)

Les vieux arbres sous la lune d'or pleurent
The old trees under the moon of-gold weep
(The old trees under the golden moon weep)

leurs belles feuilles d'or! Nul ne leur
their beautiful leaves of-gold! No-one not to-them
(their beautiful golden leaves! No one will)

dédiera plus la fierté des casques d'or
will-dedicate more the pride of-the helmets of-gold
(dedicate to them anymore the pride of golden helmets)

Maintenant ternis, à jamais ternis. Les chevaliers
Now tarnished, to never tarnished. The knights
(Now tarnished, forever tarnished. The knights)

sont morts Sur le chemin du Grâal! La nuit a
are dead On the path of-the Grail! The night has
(are dead On the path to the Grail! The night has)

des douceurs de femme, Des mains semblent
the tendernesses of woman, Some hands seem
(the tenderness of woman, Hands seem)

frôler les âmes, mains si folles, si frêles,
to-graze the souls, hands so frantic, so frail,
(to touch the souls, hands so frantic, so frail,)

Au temps où les épées chantaient pour Elles!
In-the time where the swords sang for Them!
(In the times when swords sang for Them!)

D'étranges soupirs s'élèvent sous les arbres.
Of-strange sighs themselves-rise under the trees.
(Strange sighs rise under the trees.)

Mon âme c'est du rêve ancien qui t'étreint!
My soul it-is some dream ancient that you-embraces.
(My soul is some ancient dream that embraces you.)

Debussy
Proses Lyriques
Prose Lyrical
(Lyrical Prose)

De Grève...
Of Shore...
(Of the Shore...)

Sur la mer les crépuscules tombent, Soie blanche effilée.
On the sea the twilights fall, Silk white frayed.
(On the sea twilights fall, Frayed white silk.)

Les vagues comme des petites folles Jasent,
The waves like some little fools Chatter,
(The waves like little fools Chatter,)

petites filles sortant de l'école, Parmi les froufrous
little girls leaving from the-school, Among the rustling
(little girls leaving school, Among the rustling)

de leur robe, Soie verte irisée! Les nuages, graves
of their dress, Silk green iridescent! The clouds, grave
(of their dresses, Iridescent green Silk! The clouds, grave)

voyageurs, Se concertent sur le prochain orage,
travelers, Themselves consult on the next storm,
(travelers, consult Themselves on the next storm,)

Et c'est un fond vraiment trop grave A cette
And it-is a background truly too grave To this
(And it is a background truly too solemn For this)

anglaise aquarelle. Les vagues, les petites vagues,
English watercolor. The waves, the little waves,
(English watercolor. The waves, the little waves,)

Ne savent plus où se mettre,
Not know more where themselves to-put,
(Know not where to go,)

Car voici la méchante averse,
Because here-is the wicked downpour,
(Because here is the wicked downpour,)

Froufrous de jupes envolées, Soie verte affolée.
Rustling of skirts flying, Silk green terrified.
(Rustling of flying skirts, Terrified green silk.)

Mais la lune, compatissante à tous! Vient apaiser
But the moon, compassionate to all! Comes to-appease
(But the moon, compassionate to all! Comes to appease)

ce gris conflit, Et caresse lentement ses
this gray conflict, And caress slowly its
(this gray conflict, And slowly caress)

petites amies Qui s'offrent comme lèvres aimantes
little friends Who themselves-offer like lips loving
(its little friends Who offer themselves like loving lips)

A ce tiède et blanc baiser. Puis, plus rien....
To this tepid and white kiss. Then, more nothing...
(To this warm, white kiss. Then, nothing more...)

Plus que les cloches attardées des flottantes églises!
More than the bells tardy of-the floating churches!
(Nothing but the tardy bells of the floating churches!)

Angélus des vagues, Soie blanche apaisée!
Angelus of-the waves, Silk white appeased!
(Angelus of the waves, Appeased white silk!)

Debussy
Proses Lyriques
Prose Lyrical
(Lyrical Prose)

De Fleurs...
Of Flowers...

Dans l'ennui si désolément vert de la serre de douleur,
In the-ennui so desolately green of the hothouse of sorrow,
(In the boredom so desolately green of the hothouse of sorrow)

Les fleurs enlacent mon coeur de leurs tiges méchantes.
The flowers enlace my heart with their stems wicked.
(The flowers entwine my heart with their wicked stems.)

Ah! quand reviendront autour de ma tête
Ah! when will-return around of my head
(Ah! when will they return around my head)

Les chères mains si tendrement désenlaceuses?
The dear hands so tenderly unbinding?
(The dear hands so tenderly unbinding?)

Les grands Iris violets Violèrent méchamment tes yeux
The great Irises violet Ravished wickedly your eyes
(The great violet Irises wickedly Ravished your eyes)

En semblant les refléter, Eux, qui furent
In seeming them to-reflect, They, that were
(In seeming to reflect them, They, that were)

l'eau du songe où plongèrent mes rêves
the-water of-the dream where plunged my dreams
(the water of the dream where my dreams plunged)

Si doucement enclos en leur couleur; Et les lys,
So sweetly enclosed in their color; And the lilies,
(So sweetly enclosed in their color; And the lilies,)

blancs jets d'eau de pistils embaumés, Ont perdu
white jets of-water of pistils fragrant, Have lost
(white fountains of fragrant pistils, Have lost)

leur grâce blanche Et ne sont plus que pauvres
their grace white And not are more than poor
(their white grace And are no more than poor)

malades sans soleil! Soleil! ami des fleurs mauvaises,
invalids without sun! Sun! friend of-the flowers bad,
(invalids without sun! Sun! friend of sick flowers,)

Tueur de rêves! Tueur d'illusions! Ce pain béni
Killer of dreams! Killer of-illusions! This bread blessed
(Killer of dreams! Killer of illusions! This blessed bread)

des âmes misérables! Venez! Venez!
of-the souls miserable! Come! Come!
(of miserable souls! Come! Come!)

Les mains salvatrices!
The hands of-saving!
(Hands of salvation!)

Brisez les vitres de mensonge,
Break the windows of falsehood,
(Break the windows of fasehood.)

Brisez les vitres de maléfice,
Break the windows of wickedness,
(Break the windows of wickedness,)

Mon âme meurt de trop de soleil! Mirages!
My soul dies of too-much of sun! Mirages!
(My soul dies from too much sun! Mirages!)

Plus ne refleurira la joie de mes yeux
More not will-reflower the joy of my eyes
(No more will the joy of my eyes reflower)

Et mes mains sont lasses de prier!
And my hands are weary of to-pray!
(And my hands are weary of praying!)

(cont.)

Eternellement ce bruit fou des pétales noirs de l'ennui
Eternally this noise mad of-the petals black of the-boredom
(Eternally this frantic noise of the black petals of boredom)

Tombant goutte à goutte sur ma tête Dans le vert
Falling drop to drop on my head In the green
(Falling drop by drop on my head In the green)

de la serre de douleur!
of the hothouse of sorrow!
(of the hothouse of sorrow!)

Debussy
Proses Lyriques
Prose Lyrical
(Lyrical Prose)

De Soir
Of Evening

Dimanche sur les villes, Dimanche dans les coeurs!
Sunday on the towns, Sunday in the hearts!
(Sunday in the towns, Sunday in the hearts!)

Dimanche chez les petites filles chantant d'une voix informée
Sunday at-the-home-of the little girls singing of-a voice unformed
(Sunday with the little girls singing in an unformed voice)

des rondes obstinées où de bonnes
some rounds obstinate where of good
(incessant roundelays where many)

Tours n'en ont plus que pour quelques jours!
Towers not-of-them have more than for some days!
(Towers have no more than a few days left!)

Dimanche, les gares sont folles!
Sunday, the depots are mad!
(Sunday, the train-stations are mad!)

Tout le monde appareille pour des banlieux d'aventure
All the world casts-off for the suburbs of-adventure
(Everyone casts off to the adventuresome suburbs)

en se disant adieu avec des gestes éperdus!
in themselves saying goodbye with some gestures distracted!
(saying goodbye with distracted gestures!)

Dimanche, les trains vont vite, dévorés par d'insatiables
Sunday, the trains go fast, devoured by the-insatiable
(Sunday, the trains go fast, devoured by insatiable)

tunnels; Et les bons signaux des routes échangent d'un
tunnels; And the good signals of-the routes exchange with-an
(tunnels; And the good route signals exchange)

oeil unique des impressions toutes mécaniques.
eye single some impressions all mechanical.
(mechanical impressions with a single eye.)

Dimanche, dans le bleu de mes rêves, où mes pensées
Sunday, in the blue of my dreams, where my thoughts
(Sunday, in the blue of my dreams, where my sad thoughts)

tristes de feux d'artifices manqués Ne veulent
sad of fire of-artifice missed Not want
(of not attended fireworks Never again)

plus quitter le deuil de vieux Dimanches trépassés.
more to-leave the grief of old Sundays departed.
(want to leave the grief of old departed Sundays.)

Et la nuit, à pas de velours, vient endormir le
And the night, to step of velvet, comes to-sleep the
(And the night, with velvet step, comes to put the beautiful)

beau ciel fatigué, et c'est Dimanche dans les avenues
beautiful heaven fatigued, and it-is Sunday in the avenues
(fatigued heaven to sleep, and it is Sunday in the avenues)

d'étoiles; la Vierge or sur argent laisse tomber
of-stars; the Virgin gold on silver lets to-fall
(of the stars; the golden Virgin on silver drops)

les fleurs de sommeil! Vite, les petits anges,
the flowers of sleep! Quickly, the little angels,
(the flowers of sleep! Quickly, little angels,)

dépassez les hirondelles afin de vous coucher,
overtake the swallows in-order-that of you to-sleep,
(overtake the swallows so you may sleep,)

forts d'absolution!
strong of-absolution!
(assured of absolution!)

Prenez pitié des villes,
Take pity of-the towns,
(Take pity on the towns,)

Prenez pitié des coeurs,
Take pity of-the hearts,
(Take pity on the hearts,)

Vous, la Vierge or sur argent!
You, the Virgin gold on silver!
(You, golden Virgin on silver!)

Debussy

Quatre Chansons de Jeunesse

Four Songs of Youth

Pantomime

Pantomime

Pierrot qui n'a rien d'un Clitandre Vide un flacon
Pierrot who not-has nothing of-a Clitandre Empties a flask
(Pierrot who is nothing like Clitandre Empties a flask)

sans plus attendre Et, pratique, entame un pâté.
without more to-wait And, practical, starts-upon a pâté.
(without waiting any longer And, practical, starts upon a pâté)

Cassandre, au fond de l'avenue,
Cassandre, at-the bottom of the-avenue,
(Cassandre, at the bottom of the avenue,)

Verse une larme méconnue Sur son neveu déshérité
Sheds a tear misunderstood On her nephew disinherited
(Shed a misunderstood tear Over her disinherited nephew)

Ce faquin d'Arlequin combine L'enlèvement de Colombine
That rascal of-Harlequin plans The-kidnapping of Colombine
(That rascal Harlequin plans The kidnapping of Colombine)

Et pirouette quatre fois. Colombine rêve, surprise
And pirouettes four times. Colombine dreams, surprised
(And pirouettes four times. Colombine dreams, surprised)

De sentir un coeur dans la brise
Of to-feel a heart in the breeze
(To feel a heart in the breeze)

Et d'entendre en son coeur des voix. Ah.
And of-to-hear in her heart some voices. Ah.
(And to hear voices in her heart. Ah.)

Quatre Chansons de Jeunesse
Four Songs of Youth

Clair de Lune
Light of Moon
(Moonlight)

Votre âme est un paysage choisi
Your soul is a landscape chosen
(Your soul is a chosen landscape)

Que vont charmant masques et bergamasques,
Which goes charming masks and bergamasks,
(Which is charmed by masks and bergamasks,)

Jouant du luth, et dansant, et quasi
Playing of-the lute, and dancing, and almost
(Playing the lute, and dancing, and almost)

Tristes sous leurs déguisements fantasques.
Sad under their disguises fantastic.
(Sad under their fantastic disguises.)

Tout en chantant sur le mode mineur
All in singing on the mode minor
(All the while singing in the minor mode of)

L'amour vainqueur et la vie opportune,
The-love victorious and the life opportune,
(victorious love and the opportune life,)

Ils n'ont pas l'air de croire à leur bonheur
They not-have not the-air of to-believe to their happiness
(They don't seem to believe in their happiness)

Et leur chanson se mêle au clair de lune.
And their song itself mixes with-the light of moon.
(And their song mixes with the moonlight.)

Au calme clair de lune triste et beau,
In-the calm light of moon sad and beautiful,
(In the calm moonlight, sad and beautiful,)

Qui fait rêver les oiseaux dans les arbres
Which makes to-dream the birds in the trees
(Which makes the birds dream in the trees)

Et sangloter d'extase les jets d'eau,
And to-sob from-ecstasy the jets of-water,
(And the fountains sob from ecstasy,)

Les grands jets d'eau sveltes parmi les marbres.
The great jets of-water slender among the marbles.
(The great slender jets of water among the marbles.)

Quatre Chansons de Jeunesse
Four Songs of Youth

Pierrot
Pierrot

Le bon Pierrot que la foule contemple
The good Pierrot whom the crowd contemplates
(The good Pierrot whom the crowd contemplates)

Ayant fini les noces d'Arlequin Suit en songeant
Having finished the wedding of-Harlequin Follows in dreaming
(Having finished the wedding of Harlequin dreamingly follows)

le boulevard du temple. Une fillette au souple casaquin.
the boulevard of-the temple. A young-girl to-the supple gown.
(the temple boulevard. A young girl in supple gown.)

En vain l'agace de son oeil coquin
In vain him-irritates with her eye roguish
(In vain irritates him with her roguish eye)

Et cependant mystérieuse et lisse
And meanwhile mysterious and smooth
(And meanwhile mysterious and smooth)

Faisant de lui sa plus chère délice
Making of him its most dear delight
(Making of him its dearest delight)

La blanche lune aux cornes de taureau
The white moon to-the horns of bull
(The white moon with bull's horns)

Jette un regard de son oeil en coulisse
Throws a glance of its eye in wings
(Throws a sideways glance)

A son ami Jean Gaspard Debureau. Ah. Ah.
To its friend Jean Gaspard Debureau. Ah. Ah.
(To its friend Jean Gaspard Debureau. Ah. Ah.)

Quatre Chansons de Jeunesse
Four Songs of Youth

Apparition
Apparition

La lune s'attristait. Des séraphins en pleurs
The moon itself-became-sad. Some seraphim in tears
(The moon became sad. The seraphim in tears)

Rêvant, l'archet aux doigts, dans le calme des fleurs
Dreaming, the-bow to-the fingers, in the calm of-the flowers
(Deaming, bow in their fingers, in the calm of the Vaporous)

Vaporeuses, tiraient de mourantes violes
Vaporous, plucked from mournful viols
(flowers, plucked from mournful viols)

De blancs sanglots glissants sur l'azur des corolles.
Some white sobs sliding on the-azure of-the corollas.
(White sobs sliding on the blue corollas.)

C'était le jour béni de ton premier baiser.
It-was the day blessed of your first kiss.
(It was the blessed day of your first kiss.)

Ma songerie aimant à me martyriser
My dreaming loving to myself to-martyr
(My dreaming which loved to martyr me)

S'enivrait savamment du parfum de tristesse
Itself-intoxicated knowingly with-the perfume of sadness
(Intoxicated itself skillfully with perfume of sadness)

Que même sans regret et sans déboire laisse
That likewise without regret and without doubt leaves
(That likewise without regret and without doubt leaves)

La cueillaison d'un Rêve au coeur qui l'a cueilli.
The harvest of-a Dream to-the heart that it-has gathered.
(The harvest of a Dream in the heart that gathered it.)

J'errais donc, l'oeil rivé sur le pavé vieilli
I-wandered then, the-eye fixed on the pavement aged
(Thus I wandered, my eye fixed on the aged pavement)

Quand avec du soleil aux cheveux, dans la rue
When with of-the sun to-the hair, in the street
(When with the sun in my hair, on the street)

Et dans le soir, Tu m'es en riant apparue
And in the night, You me-are in laughing appeared
(And in the night, You appeared laughing before me)

Et j'ai cru voir la fée au chapeau de clarté
And I-have believed to-see the fairy with-the hat of clarity
(And I thought I saw the fairy with the halo of light)

Qui jadis sur mes beaux sommeils d'enfant gâté
Which formerly on my beautiful slumbers of-child spoiled
(Which once on my beautiful slumbers of a spoiled child)

Passait, laissant toujours de ses mains mal fermées
Passed, leaving always from her hands badly closed
(Passed, leaving always from her half-closed hands)

Neiger de blancs bouquets d'étoiles parfumées.
To-snow some white bouquets of-stars perfumed.
(Snows of white bouquets of perfumed stars.)

Romance

Romance

L'âme évaporée et souffrante, L'âme douce,
The-soul evaporated and suffering, The-soul sweet,
(The soul, evaporated and suffering, The gentle soul,)

l'âme odorante Des lis divins que j'ai cueillis
the-soul frangrant Of-the lilies divine that I-have gathered
(the fragrant soul Of the divine lilies that I gathered)

Dans le jardin de ta pensée, Où donc les vents
In the garden of your thought, Where then the winds
(In the garden of your thought, Where then have the winds)

l'ont-ils chassée Cette âme adorable des lis?
it-have-they chased This soul adorable of-the lilies?
(chased it This adorable soul of the lilies?)

N'est-il plus un parfum qui reste
Not-is-it more a perfume that stays
(Is there no more perfume that remains)

De la suavité céleste,
Of the sweetness celestial,
(Of the celestial sweetness,)

Des jours où tu m'enveloppais
From-the days where you me-enveloped
(From the days when you enveloped me)

D'une vapeur surnaturelle,
With-a vapor supernatural,
(With a supernatural vapor,)

Faite d'espoir, d'amour fidèle,
Made of-hope, of-love faithful,
(Made of hope, of faithful love,)

De béatitude et de paix?
Of beatitude and of peace?
(Of blessedness and of peace?)

Trois Ballades de François Villon
Three Ballads of François Villon

Ballade de Villon à s'Amie
Ballad of Villon to His-Love

Fausse beauté, qui tant me coûte cher, Rude en effet,
False beauty, who so-much me costs dear, Harsh in effect,
(False beauty, who costs me so dearly, Harsh indeed,)

hypocrite douceur, Amour dur, plus que fer, à mâcher;
hypocritical sweetness, Love hard, more than iron, to chew;
(with hypocritical sweetness, Hard love, harder than iron, to chew,)

Nommer te puis de ma deffaçon soeur. Charme félon,
To-name you I-can of my undoing sister. Charm felonious,
(I can call you sister of my undoing. Treacherous charm,)

la mort d'un pauvre coeur, Orgueil mussé,
the death of-a poor heart, Pride dissembled,
(the death of a poor heart, Dissembled pride,)

qui gens met au mourir, Yeux sans pitié!
which people put to to-die, Eyes without pity!
(which people put to death, Pitiless eyes!)

ne veut droit de rigueur, Sans empirer,
not wish right of severity, Without to-worsen,
(From such severity will not justice, Without worsening,)

un pauvre secourir? Mieux m'eût valu avoir été crier
a poor-one to-assist? Better me-had valued to-have had to-cry
(assist a poor one? I'd have been better advised to cry)

Ailleurs secours, c'eût été mon bonheur:
Elsewhere help, that-would-have been my happiness:
(For help Elsewhere, that might have been my happiness:)

Rien ne m'eût su de ce fait arracher;
Nothing not me-would-have known from this fact to-tear-away;
(Nothing would have known how to tear me away from this;)

Trotter m'en faut en fuite à déshonneur.
To-trot me-of-it must in flight to dishonor.
(I must go in flight to my dishonor.)

Haro, haro, le grandet le mineur! Et qu'est ceci?
Harrow, harrow, the great the minor! And what-is this-here?
(Shame, shame, call great and small! And what is this?)

Mourrai sans coup férir, Ou pitié peut,
I-will-die without blow to-strike, Or pity can,
(I shall die without striking a blow, Or will pity,)

selon cette teneur, Sans empirer, un pauvre
according-to this tenor, Without to-worsen, a poor-one
(according to these terms, Without worsening, assist)

secourir? Un temps viendra, qui fera dessécher,
to-assist? A time will-come, that will-make to-dry-up
(a poor one? A time will come, that will dry up,)

Jaunir, flétrir, votre épanuie fleur: J'en risse
To-yellow, to-wither, your blooming flower: I-of-it laugh
(Yellow, wither, your blooming flower: I will laugh)

lors, se tant peusse marcher, Mais las! nenni:
then, if so-much can to-walk, But alas! not-at-all:
(then, if I can still walk, But alas! not at all:)

ce serait donc foleur, Vieil je serai;
this would-be thus folly, Old I will-be;
(this would be folly, I will be old;)

vous, laide et sans couleur, Or, buvez fort, tant
you, ugly and without color, But, drink strong, so-much
(you, ugly and colorless, But drink deep, while)

que ru peut courir. Ne donnez pas à tous cette douleur,
that brook can to-run. Not give not to all this sorrow,
(the brook can still run. Do not give to all this sorrow,)

Sans empirer, un pauvre secourir.
Without to-worsen, a poor-one to-assist.
(Without worsening, assist a poor one.)

Prince amoureux, des amants le greigneur,
Prince amorous, of-the lovers the greatest,
(Loving prince, of lovers the greatest,)

Votre mal gré ne voudrais encourir;
Your evil will not might-want to-incur;
(Your evil will I do not wish to incur;)

Mais tout franc coeur doit, par Notre Seigneur,
But all frank heart must, by Our Lord,
(But every honest heart must, by Our Lord,)

Sans empirer, un pauvre secourir.
Without to-worsen, a poor-one to-assist.
(Without worsening, assist a poor one.)

Trois Ballades de François Villon
Three Ballades of François Villon

Ballade que Villon fait à la requête de sa mère pour prier Notre-Dame
Ballad that Villon wrote at the request of his mother to pray Our-Lady

Dame du ciel, régente terrienne, Emperière des
Lady of-the heaven, regent earthly, Empress of-the
(Lady of heaven, Regent of earth, Empress of)

infernaux palus, Recevez-moi, votre humble chrétienne,
infernal swamps, Receive-me, your humble Christian-woman,
(infernal swamps, Receive me, your humble Christian woman,)

Que comprinse sois entre vos élus,
That included I-be among your elect,
(Let me be numbered among your elect,)

Ce nonobstant qu'onques rien ne valus.
This notwithstanding that-never nothing not was-worth.
(This notwithstanding that I have never been of any worth.)

Les biens de vous, ma Dame et ma Maîtresse,
The goodnesses of you, my Lady and my Mistress,
(Your goodness, my Lady and my Mistress,)

Sont trop plus grands que ne suis pécheresse,
Are too-much more great than not am sinner,
(Is far greater than my sinfulness,)

Sans lesquels biens, âme ne peut mérir N'avoir
Without which goodnesses, soul not can to-merit Not-to-have
(Without these goodnesses, no soul can merit Nor have)

les cieux, je n'en suis menteresse. En cette foi
the heavens, I not-of-it am liar. In this faith
(the heavens, I do not speak falsely. In this faith)

je veux vivre et mourir. A votre Fils dites que
I wish to-live and to-die. To your Son say that
(I wish to live and die. To your Son say that)

je suis sienne; De lui soient mes péchés abolus:
I am his; Of him be my sins absolved:
(I am his; Through him let my sins be absolved.)

Pardonnez-moi comme à l'Egyptienne, Ou comme il fit
Pardon-me like to the-Egyptian-woman, Or like he did
(Pardon me like the Egyptian woman, Or like he did)

au clerc Théophilus, Lequel par vous fût quitte et absolu,
to-the priest Theophilus, who by you was acquitted and absolved,
(the priest Theophilus, who by you was acquitted and absolved,)

Combien qu'il eût au diable fait promesse.
However that-he had to-the devil made promise.
(Even though he had made promise to the devil.)

Préservez-moi que je n'accomplisse ce! Vierge portant
Preserve-me that I not-accomplish that! Virgin carrying
(Preserve me from doing that! Virgin bearing)

sans rompure encourir Le sacrement qu'on célèbre
without blemish to-incur The sacrament that-one celebrates
(without blemish The sacrament that we celebrate)

à la messe. Femme je suis pauvrette et ancienne,
to the Mass. Woman I am poor and old,
(to Mass. I am a poor and old woman,)

Qui rien ne sait, onques lettre ne lu; Au moutier
Who nothing not knows, never lettered nor read; In-the church
(Who knows nothing, never lettered nor read; In the church)

vois, dont suis paroissienne, Paradis peint où sont
see, whose am parishioner, Paradise pictured where are
(I see, where I am a parishioner, a picture of Paradise with)

harpes et lus, Et un enfer où damnés sont boullus:
harps and lutes, And a hell where damned are boiled:
(harps and lutes, And hell where the damned are boiled:)

L'un me fait peur, l'autre joie et liesse.
The-one me makes fear, the-other joy and delight.
(The one gives me fear, the other joy and delight.)

La joie avoir fais moi, haute Déesse, A qui pécheurs
The joy to-have make me, high Goddess, To whom sinners
(Give me joy, exalted Goddess, To whom all sinners)

doivent tous recourir, Comblés de foi, sans feinte ne paresse.
must all to-resort, Full of faith, without pretense nor laziness.
(must resort, Full of faith, without pretense nor laziness.)

En cette foi je veux vivre et mourir.
In this faith I wish to-live and to-die.
(In this faith I wish to live and die.)

Debussy

Trois Ballades de François Villon

Three Ballads of François Villon

Ballade des Femmes de Paris

Ballad of-the Women of Paris

Quoiqu'on tient belles langagières Florentines,
Although-one holds beautiful talkers Florentines,
(Although they say Florentines are beautiful talkers,)

Vênitiennes, Assez pour être messagères,
Venetians, Enough for to-be messengers,
(Venetians, Enough to be messengers,)

Et mêmement les anciennes; Mais soit Lombardes,
And likewise the old-women; But be Lombardic,
(And likewise old women; But be they Lombardic,)

Romaines, Genevoises, à mes périls, Piémontaises,
Roman, Genevese, to my perils, Piedmontese,
(Roman, Genevese, or heaven help me, Piedmontese,)

Savoisiennes, Il n'est bon bec que de Paris.
Savoyard, It not-is good beak but of Paris.
(Savoyard, The only good chatter is Parisian.)

De beau parlé tiennent chayères, Ce dit-on,
Of beautiful spoken hold professorships, That says-one,
(They hold professorships in speaking well, they say,)

Napolitaines, Et que sont bonnes caquetières
Neapolitans, And that are good cacklers
(Neapolitans, And that are good cacklers)

Allemandes et Prussiennes, Soit Grecques,
Germans and Prussians, Be Greek,
(the Germans and Prussians, Be they Greek,)

Egyptiennes, De Hongrie ou d'autre pays,
Egyptians, From Hungary or from-other lands,
(Egyptians, From Hungary or other lands,)

Espagnoles ou Castellannes, Il n'est bon
Spaniards or Castilians, It not-is good
(Spaniards or Castilians, The only good)

bec que de Paris. Brettes, Suisses, n'y savent guère,
beak but of Paris. Bretons, Swiss, not-of-it know hardly,
(chatter is Parisian. Bretons, Swiss, know little about it,)

Ne Gasconnes et Toulousaines; Du Petit-Pont
Nor from-Gascony and from-Toulouse; From-the Petit-Pont
(Nor those from Gascony and Toulouse; From the Petit Pont)

deux harangères Les conclueront, et les Lorraines,
two harangers Them will-conclude, and those from-Lorraine,
(two harangers will conclude, and those from Lorraine,)

Anglèches ou Calaisiennes, (Ai-je beaucoup de lieux compris?)
from-England or from-Calais (Have-I many of lands included?)
(England or Calais [Have I included enough lands?])

Picardes, de Valenciennes...Il n'est bon bec que
From-Picardy, from Valenciennes...It not-is good beak but
(From Picardy, from Valenciennes...The only good chatter is
Parisian.)

de Paris. Prince, aux dames parisiennes, De bien
of Paris. Prince, to-the ladies Parisian, Of well
(Prince, to the Parisian ladies, give the prize)

parler donnez le prix; Quoi qu'on die d'Italiennes,
to-speak give the prize; What that-one says of-Italians,
(for speaking well; Whatever they say of Italians,)

Il n'est bon bec que de Paris.
It not-is good beak but of Paris.
(The only good chatter is Parisian.)

Debussy

Trois Chansons de Bilitis
Three Songs of Bilitis

La Flûte de Pan
The Flute of Pan

Pour le jour des Hyacinthes il m'a donné une syrinx
For the day of-the Hyacinthia he me-has given a pipe
(For Hyacinthia day he has given me a pipe)

faite de roseaux bien taillés, unis avec la blanche
made of reeds well tailored, united with the white
(made of well-cut reeds, joined with white)

cire qui est douce à mes lèvres comme le miel.
wax which is sweet to my lips like the honey.
(wax which is sweet as honey to my lips.)

Il m'apprend à jouer, assise sur ses genoux;
He me-teaches to to-play, seated on his knees;
(He teaches me to play, seated on his knees;)

mais je suis un peu tremblante. Il en joue
but I am a little trembling. He of-it plays
(but I tremble a bit. He plays it)

après moi, si doucement que je l'entends à peine.
after me, so softly that I him-hear to pain.
(after me, so softly that I hardly hear him.)

Nous n'avons rien à nous dire, tant nous
We not-have nothing to us to-say, so-much we
(We have nothing to say, we are so)

sommes près l'un de l'autre;
are close the-one to the-other;
(close to each other;)

mais nos chansons veulent se répondre,
but our songs want themselves to-answer,
(but our songs want to answer each other,)

et tour à tour nos bouches s'unissent sur la flûte.
and turn to turn our mouths themselves-unite on the flute.
(and by turns our mouths unite on the flute.)

Il est tard; voici le chant des grenouilles
It is late, here-is the song of-the frogs
(It is late; here is the song of the green)

vertes qui commence avec la nuit.
green which begins with the night.
(frogs which begins with nightfall.)

Ma mère ne croira jamais
My mother not will-believe ever
(My mother will never believe)

que je suis restée si longtemps à chercher ma ceinture perdue.
that I am stayed so longtime to to-seach-for my belt lost.
(that I stayed so long to look for my lost belt.)

Debussy
Trois Chansons de Bilitis
Three Songs of Bilitis

La Chevelure
The Hair

Il m'a dit: "Cette nuit, j'ai rêvé, J'avais
He me-has said: "This night, I-have dreamed, I-had
(He said to me: "Last night, I dreamed your hair)

ta chevelure autour de mon cou.
your hair around of my neck.
(was around my neck.)

J'avais tes cheveux comme un collier noir
I-had your hair like a necklace black
(I had your hair like a black necklace)

autour de ma nuque et sur ma poitrine.
around of my neck and on my chest.
(around my neck and on my chest.)

Je les caressais, et c'était les miens; et nous étions
I them caressed, and it-was the mine; and we were
(I caressed it, and it was mine; and we were)

liés pour toujours ainsi, par la même chevelure
linked for always thus, by the same hair
(joined forever thus, by the same hair)

la bouche sur la bouche, ainsi que deux lauriers
the mouth on the mouth, thus that two laurels
(mouth to mouth, as two laurels)

n'ont souvent qu'une racine. Et peu à peu,
not-have often but-one root. And little by little,
(often have only one root. And little by little,)

il m'a semblé, tant nos membres étaient confondus,
it me-has seemed, so-much our limbs were mingled,
(it seemed to me, our limbs were so mingled,)

que je devenais toi-même ou que tu entrais
that I was-becoming your-self or that you were-entering
(that I was becoming you or that you were entering)

en moi comme mon songe." Quand il eut achevé, il mit
in me like my dream." When he had finished, he put
(me like my dream." When he had finished, he softly put)

doucement ses mains sur mes épaules, et il me regarda d'un
softly his hands on my shoulders, and he me regarded with-a
(his hands on my shoulders, and looked at me with a)

regard si tendre, que je baissai les yeux avec un frisson.
glance so tender, that I lowered the eyes with a shiver.
(glance so tender, that I lowered my eyes with a shiver.)

Debussy

Trois Chansons de Bilitis

Three Songs of Bilitis

Le Tombeau des Naïdes

The Tomb of-the Naiads

Le long du bois couvert de givre, je marchais;
The length of-the wood covered with frost, I walked;
(Along the woods covered with frost, I walked;)

mes cheveux, devant ma bouche, se fleurissaient
my hair, before my mouth, itself flourished
(my hair, in front of my mouth, grew)

de petits glaçons, et mes sandales étaient lourdes
with little icicles, and my sandals were heavy
(icicles, and my sandals were heavy)

de neige fangeuse et tassée. Il me dit:
with snow muddy and packed. He to-me said:
(with muddy and packed snow. He said to me:)

"Que cherches-tu?" "Je suis la trace du satyre.
"What search-you?" "I follow the trace of-the satyr.
("What are you looking for?" "I am tracking the satyr.)

Ses petits pas fourchus alternent comme des trous
His little steps cloven alternate like some holes
(His little cloven steps alternate like the holes)

dans un manteau blanc." Il me dit: "Les satyres
in a cloak white." He to-me said: "The satyrs
(in a white cloak." He said to me: "The satyrs)

sont morts. Les satyres et les nymphes aussi.
are dead. The satyrs and the nymphs too.
(are dead. Satyrs and nymphs alike.)

Depuis trente ans il n'a pas fait un hiver
Since thirty years it not-has not made a winter
(For thirty years there has not been a winter)

aussi terrible. La trace que tu vois est celle
so terrible. The trace that you see is that
(so terrible. The trail that you see is that)

d'un bouc Mais restons ici, où est leur tombeau."
of-a goat But let-us-remain here, where is their tomb."
(of a goat But let's stay here, where their tomb is.")

Et avec le fer de sa houe il cassa la glace
And with the iron of his hoe he broke the ice
(And with the iron of his hoe he broke the ice)

de la source où jadis riaient les naïdes.
of the spring where once laughed the naiads.
(of the spring where naiads once laughed.)

Il prenait de grands morceaux froids,
He was-taking some large pieces cold,
(He took large cold pieces,)

et les soulevant vers le ciel
and them raising toward the sky
(and raising them toward the pale)

pâle il regardait au travers.
pale he looked to-the through.
(sky, he looked through them.)

Trois Poèmes de Stéphane Mallarmé
Three Poems of Stéphane Mallarme

Soupir
Sigh

Mon âme vers ton front où rêve, ô calme soeur,
My soul toward your face where dreams, oh calm sister,
(My soul toward your face in which dreams, oh calm sister,)

Un automne jonché de taches de rousseur
An autumn scattered with spots of redness
(An autumn scattered with freckles)

Et vers le ciel errant de ton oeil angélique Monte,
And toward the sky wandering of your eye angelic Rises,
(And toward the wandering sky of your angelic eye Rises,)

comme dans un jardin mélancolique, Fidèle, un blanc jet d'eau
like in a garden melancholy, Faithful, a white jet of-water
(like in a melancholy garden, Faithful, a white fountain)

soupire vers l'Azure! Vers l'Azure attendri d'Octobre
sighs toward the-Azur! Toward the-Azur made-tender of-October
(sighs to the Sky! The sky made tender by pale and)

pâle et pur Qui mire aux grands bassins
pale and pure Which mirrors in-the great basins
(pure October Which mirrors in the great basins)

sa langueur infinie Et laisse, sur l'eau morte
its languor infinite And leaves, on the-water dead
(its infinite languor And leaves, on the dead water)

où la fauve agonie Des feuilles erre au vent
where the wild agony Of-the leaves wanders in-the wind
(where the tawny agony Of leaves wanders in the wind)

et creuse un froid sillon,
and hollows-out a cold furrow,
(and hollows out a cold furrow,)

Se traîner le soleil jaune d'un long rayon.
Itself to-drag the sun yellow with-a long ray.
(the yellow sun dragging a long ray.)

Trois Poèmes de Stéphane Mallarmé
Three Poems of Stéphane Mallarmé

Placet Futile
Petition Futile
(Futile Petition)

Princesse! à jalouser le destin d'une Hébé
Princess! to to-envy the destiny of-a Hébé
(Princess! to envy the destiny of a Hébé)

Qui point sur cette tasse au baiser de vos lèvres,
Which rises on this cup to-the kiss of your lips,
(Which rises on this cup to the kiss of your lips,)

J'use mes feux mais n'ai rang discret que d'abbé
I-use my fires but not-have rank discreet only of abbé
(I wear-out my desires but have only the discreet rank of abbé)

Et ne figurerai même nu sur le Sèvres.
And not will-appear even nude on the Sèvres.
(And likewise will not appear nude on the Sèvres.)

Comme je ne suis pas ton bichon embarbé,
Like I not am not your lap-dog bearded,
(As I am not your bearded lap-dog,)

Ni la pastille ni du rouge, ni Jeux mièvres
Nor the lozenge nor of-the rouge, nor Games vapid
(Nor lozenge nor rouge, nor vapid Games)

Et que sur moi je sais ton regard clos tombé,
And that on me I know your glance closed fallen,
(And since I know that your closed glance has fallen on me,)

Blonde dont les coiffeurs divins sont des orfèvres!
Blond-one whose the hairdressers divine are some goldsmiths!
(Blond one whose divine hairdressers are goldsmiths!)

Nommez-nous...toi de qui tant de ris framboisés
Name-us...you of whom so-much of laughter raspberried
(Name us...you whose so many raspberried laughs)

Se joignent en troupeau d'agneaux apprivoisés
Themselves join in flock of-lambs tamed
(Join together in a flock of tamed lambs)

Chez tous broutant les voeux et bêlant aux délires,
At everyone grazing the wishes and bleating to-the deliriums,
(Grazing everywhere at their pleasure and bleating to delirium,)

Nommez-nous...pour qu'Amour ailé d'un éventail
Name-us...for that-Love winged of-a fan
(Name us...so that Love winged with a fan)

M'y peigne flûte aux doigts endormant ce bercail,
Me-there paints flute to-the fingers sleeping this sheepfold,
(Paints me there flute in fingers lulling this sheepfold,)

Princesse, nommez-nous berger de vos sourires.
Princess, name-us shepherd of your smiles.
(Princess, name us shepherd of your smiles.)

Debussy

Trois Poèmes de Stéphane Mallarmé

Three Poems of Stéphane Mallarmé

Eventail

Fan

O rêveuse, pour que je plonge Au pur délice sans chemin,
Oh dreamer, for that I plunge To-the pure delight without path,
(Oh dreamer, so that I may plunge into a pure directionless path,)

Sache, par un subtil mensonge, Garder mon aile dans ta main.
Know, by a subtle lie, To-keep my wing in your hand.
(Know, by a subtle illusion, How to keep my wing in your hand.)

Une fraîcheur de crépuscule Te vient à chaque battement
A freshness of twilight To-you comes at each beating
(A twilight freshness comes To you at each flutter)

Dont le coup prisonnier recule L'horizon délicatement.
Whose the blow prisoner recoils The-horizon delicately.
(Whose prisoner blow pushes back delicately The horizon.)

Vertige! voici que frissonne L'espace comme un grand baiser Qui,
Vertige! here-is that shivers The-space like a large kiss Which,
(Dizziness! here The space shivers like a big kiss Which,)

fou de naître pour personne, Ne peut jaillir
mad from to-be-born for no-one, Not can to-burst-out
(crazy from being born for no one, Can neither burst out)

ni s'apaiser. Sens-tu le paradis farouche Ainsi
nor itself-to-appease. Feel-you the paradise fierce Thus
(nor calm itself. Do you feel the fierce paradise Which,)

qu'un rire enseveli Se couler du coin
that-a smile enshrouded Itself to-pour from-the corner
(like an enshrouded smile, pours from the corner)

de ta bouche Au fond de l'unanime pli!
of your mouth At-the base of the-unanimous fold!
(of your mouth At the base of the unanimous fold!)

Le sceptre des rivages roses Stagnants
The scepter of-the shores pink Stagnating
(The fan of the pink shores, Stagnating)

sur les soirs d'or, ce l'est, Ce blanc
on the evenings of-gold, which it-is, This white
(on golden evenings, which this is, This white)

vol fermé que tu poses Contre
flight closed that you place Against
(flight that you place Against

le feu d'un bracelet.
the fire of-a bracelet.
(the fire of a bracelet.)

Voici que le Printemps
Here that the Spring
(Here is Spring)

Voici que le printemps, ce fils léger d'Avril,
Here-is that the spring, that son light of-April,
(Here is spring, the nimble son of April,)

Beau page en pourpoint vert brodé de roses blanches
Handsome page in doublet green embroidered with roses white
(Handsome page in a green doublet embroidered with white roses)

Paraît leste, fringant et les poings sur les hanches,
Appears agile, smart and the fists on the hips,
(Appearing agile, smart and his fists on his hips,)

Comme un prince acclamé revient d'un long exil.
As a prince acclaimed returns from-a long exile.
(Like an acclaimed prince returning from a long exile.)

Les branches des buissons verdis rendent étroite
The branches of-the bushes green render narrow
(The branches of the green bushes make narrow)

La route qu'il poursuit en dansant comme un fol;
The route which-he follows in dancing like a fool;
(The path which he follows, dancing like a fool;)

Sur son épaule gauche il porte un rossignol,
On his shoulder left he carries a nightingale,
(On his left shoulder he carries a nightingale,)

Un merle s'est posé sur son épaule droite.
A blackbird itself-is placed on his shoulder right.
(A blackbird is perched on his right shoulder.)

Et les fleurs qui dormaient
And the flowers which were-sleeping
(And the flowers which were sleeping)

sous les mousses des bois
under the mosses of-the woods
(under the moss of the woods)

Ouvrent leurs yeux où flotte une ombre vague et tendre;
Open their eyes where floats a shadow faint and tender;
(Open their eyes where a faint and tender shadow floats;)

Et sur leurs petits pieds se dressent, pour entendre
And on their little feet themselves stand, for to-hear
(And stand on their little feet, to hear)

Les deux oiseaux siffler et chanter à la fois.
The two birds to-whistle and to-sing at the time.
(The two birds whistle and sing at the same time.)

Car le merle sifflote et le rossignol chante;
For the blackbird whistles and the nightingale sings;
(For the blackbird whistles and the nightingale sings;)

Le merle siffle ceux qui ne sont pas aimés,
The blackbird whistles those who not are not loved,
(The blackbird whistles for those who are unloved,)

Et pour les amoureux languissants et charmés,
And for the lovers languishing and charmed,
(And for the languishing and charmed lovers,)

Le rossignol prolonge une chanson touchante.
The nightingale prolongs a song touching.
(The nightingale prolongs a touching song.)

Au pays où se fait la guerre

To-the country where itself makes the war

(To the country where war is waging)

Au pays où se fait la guerre
To-the country where itself makes the war
(To the country where war is waging)

Mon bel ami s'en est allé
My beautiful friend himself-from-here is gone
(My beautiful love has gone)

Il semble à mon coeur désolé
It seems to my heart desolated
(It seems to my desolate heart)

Qu'il ne reste que moi sur terre.
That-it not remains but me on earth.
(That I alone am left on earth.)

En partant, au baiser d'adieu,
In parting, to-the kiss of-farewell,
(In parting, at the farewell kiss,)

Il m'a pris mon âme à ma bouche...
He me-has taken my soul to my mouth...
(He took my soul from my mouth...)

Qui le tient si longtemps, mon Dieu?
Who him holds so long-time, my God?
(What keeps him so long, my God?)

Voici le soleil qui se couche,
Here-is the sun that itself sets,
(Here the sun is setting,)

Et moi toute seule en ma tour,
And me, all alone in my tower,
(And I, all alone in my tower,)

J'attends encore son retour.
I-await still his return.
(I still await his return.)

Les pigeons sur le toit roucoulent,
The pigeons on the roof coo,
(The pigeons on the roof coo,)

Roucoulent amoureusement,
Coo amourously,
(Coo amourously,)

Avec un son triste et charmant;
With a sound sad and charming;
(With a sad and charming sound;)

Les eaux sous les grands saules coulent.
The waters under the large willows flow.
(The waters under the large willows flow.)

Je me sens tout près de pleurer,
I myself feel all close of to-cry,
(I feel close to crying,)

Mon coeur comme un lys plein s'épanche,
My heart like a lily full itself-opens,
(My heart like a full lily opens,)

Et je n'ose plus espérer,
And I not-dare more to-hope,
(And I dare not hope any longer,)

Voici briller la lune blanche.
Here-is to-shine the moon white.
(Here the white moon shines.)

Quelqu'un monte à grands pas la rampe...
Someone climbs at large steps the stairs...
(Someone quickly climbs the stairs...)

Serait-ce lui, mon doux amant?
Might-it-be he, my sweet lover?
(Might it be he, my sweet lover?)

Ce n'est pas lui, mais seulement
It not-is not he, but only
(It is not he, but only)

Mon petit page avec ma lampe...
My little page with my lamp...
(My little page with my lamp...)

Vents du soir, volez, dites-lui
Winds of-the evening, fly, tell-him
(Winds of evening, fly, tell him)

Qu'il est ma pensée et mon rêve
That-he is my thought and my dream
(That he is my thought and my dream)

Toute ma joie et mon ennui.
All my joy and my weariness.
(All my joy and my weariness.)

Voici que l'aurore se lève.
Here-is that the-dawn itself rises.
(Here the dawn rises.)

Duparc
Chanson Triste
Song Sad
(Sad Song)

Dans ton coeur dort un clair de lune,
In your heart sleeps a light of moon,
(In your heart a moonlight sleeps,)

Un doux clair de lune d'été,
(A gentle light of moon of-summer,
(A gentle moonlight of summer,)

Et pour fuir la vie importune
(And for to-flee the life importune
(And in order to flee the importune life)

Je me noierai dans ta clarté.
I myself will-drown in your radiance.
(I will drown myself in your radiance.)

J'oublierai les douleurs passées,
I-will-forget the sorrows past,
(I will forget past sorrows,)

Mon amour, quand tu berceras
My love, when you shall-cradle
(My love, when you cradle)

Mon triste coeur et mes pensées,
My sad heart and my thoughts,
(My sad heart and my thoughts,)

Dans le calme aimant de tes bras.
In the calm loving of your arms.
(In the loving calm of your arms.)

Tu prendras ma tête malade
You shall-take my head sick
(You shall take my sick head)

Oh! quelquefois sur tes genoux,
Oh! sometimes on your knees,
(Oh! sometimes on your knee,)

Et lui diras une ballade
And to-it will-tell a ballad
(And will tell it a ballad)

Qui semblera parler de nous.
That will-seem to-speak of us.
(That will seem to speak of us.)

Et dans tes yeux pleins de tristesses,
And in your eyes full of sadnesses,
(And in your eyes full of sadness,)

Dans tes yeux alors je boirai
In your eyes then I will-drink
(In your eyes then I will drink)

Tant de baisers et de tendresses
So-many of kisses and of tenderness
(So many kisses and so much tenderness)

Que, peut-être, je guérirai....
That, perhaps, I will-heal....
(That, perhaps, I will heal....)

Duparc

Elégie

Elegy

Oh! ne murmurez pas son nom! qu'il dorme dans l'ombre,
Oh! not murmur not his name! that-it sleep in the-shadow,
(Oh! murmur not his name! let it sleep in the shade,)

Où froide et sans honneur repose sa dépouille.
Where cold and without honor rest his remains.
(Where cold and without honor lay his remains.)

Muettes, tristes, glacées, tombent nos larmes,
Silent, sad, frozen, fall our tears,
(Our tears fall, silent, sad, frozen,)

Comme la rosée de la nuit qui sur sa tête humecte le gazon.
Like the dew of the night that on his head moistens the grass.
(Like the dew of the night that, over his head, moistens the grass.)

Mais la rosée de la nuit, bien qu'elle pleure en silence,
But the dew of the night, well that-it weeps in silence,
(But the dew of the night, although it weeps in silence,)

Fera briller la verdure sur sa couche,
Will-make to-shine the verdure on his bed,
(Will make the greenery shine on his bed,)

Et nos larmes, en secret répandues,
And our tears, in secret poured-out,
(And our tears, poured out in secret,)

Conserveront sa mémoire fraîche et verte dans nos coeurs.
Will-conserve his memory fresh and green in our hearts.
(Will keep his memory fresh and green in our hearts.)

Duparc
Extase
Ecstasy

Sur un lys pâle mon coeur dort
On a lily pale my heart sleeps
(On a pale lily my heart sleeps)

D'un sommeil doux comme la mort...
Of-a slumber sweet like the death...
(a slumber sweet as death...)

Mort exquise, mort parfumée
Death exquisite, death perfumed
(Exquisite death, death perfumed)

Du souffle de la bien-aimée...
Of-the breath of the well-loved...
(By the breath of my beloved...)

Sur un lys pâle mon coeur dort
On a lily pale my heart sleeps
(On a paly lily my heart sleeps)

D'un sommeil doux comme la mort....
Of-a slumber sweet like the death....
(a slumber sweet as death....)

Duparc

Le Galop

The Gallop

Agite, bon cheval, ta crinière fuyante,
Agitate, good horse, your mane flying,
(Shake, good horse, your flying mane,)

Que l'air autour de nous se remplisse de voix,
That the-air around of us itself fills with voices,
(Let the air around us fill with voices,)

Que j'entende craquer sous ta corne bruyante
That I-hear to-crack under your hoof noisy
(May I hear cracking under your noisy hooves)

Le gravier des ruisseaux et les débris des bois.
The gravel of-the brooks and the debris of-the woods.
(The gravel of the brooks and the debris of the woods.)

Aux vapeurs de tes flancs mêle ta chaude haleine,
With-the vapors of your flanks mixes your hot breath,
(Mix your hot breath with the vapors of your flanks,)

Aux éclairs de tes pieds, ton écume et ton sang.
With-the flashes of your feet, your foam and your blood.
(With the flashes of your feet, your foam and your blood.)

Cours, comme on voit un aigle, en effleurant,
Run, as one sees an eagle, in flying-low,
(Run, as one sees an eagle, skimming the plain,)

Fouetter l'herbe d'un vol sonore et frémissant. Allons!
To-whip the-grass of-a flight sonorous and shivering. Let's-go!
(Whipping the grass in a sonorous and shivering flight. "Let's go!)

Les jeunes gens, à la nage, à la nage, Crie à ses
The young men, to the swim, to the swim. Cries to his
(Young men, to swim, to swim," The old tribal chief)

cavaliers le vieux chef de tribu, Et les fils du désert respirent
horsemen the old chief of tribe, And the sons of-the desert respire
(cries to the horsemen, And the sons of the desert breathe)

le pillage, Et les chevaux sont fous
the pillage, And the horses are crazy
(the pillage, And the horses are mad)

du grand air qu'ils ont bu.
from-the large air which-they have drunk.
(with the open air they have drunk.)

Nage ainsi dans l'espace, ô mon cheval rapide.
Swim thus in the-space, o my horse rapid.
(Swim thus into space, o my rapid horse.)

Abreuve-moi d'air pur, baigne-moi dans le vent,
Water-me with-air pure, bathe-me in the wind,
(Wash me with pure air, bathe me in the wind,)

L'étrier bat ton ventre, et j'ai lâché la bride.
The-stirrup beats your stomach, and I-have let-go the bridle.
(The stirrup beats your stomach, and I have let go of the bridle.)

Mon corps te touche à peine il vole en te suivant.
My body you touches to pain it flies in you following.
(My body hardly touches you it flies in following you.)

Brise tout, le buisson, la barrière ou la branche.
Break everything, the thicket, the gate or the branch.
(Break everything, the thicket, the gate or the branches.)

Torrents, fossés, talus, Franchis tout d'un seul bond.
Torrents, ditches, slopes, Leap-over all of-a single bound.
(Torrents, ditches, slopes, Clear everything in a single bound.)

Cours, cours, je rêve et sur toi, les yeux clos, je me penche,
Run, run, I dream and on you, the eyes closed, I myself lean,
(Run, run, I dream of you, my eyes closed, I lean,)

Emporte, emporte-moi dans l'inconnu profond!
Carry, carry-me into the-unknown deep!
(Carry, carry me away into the deep unknown!)

Duparc

Lamento

Lament

Connaissez-vous la blanche tombe
Know-you the white tomb
(Do you know the white tomb)

Où flotte avec un son plaintif
Where floats with a sound plaintive
(Where the shadow of a yew tree)

L'ombre d'un if?
The-shadow of-a yew-tree?
(waves with a plaintive sound?)

Sur l'if une pâle colombe,
On the-yew-tree a pale dove,
(On the yew tree a pale dove,)

Triste et seule au soleil couchant,
Sad and alone to-the sun setting,
(Sad and alone in the setting sun,)

Chante son chant.
Sings its song.
(Sings its song.)

On dirait que l'âme éveillée
One would-say that the-soul awakened
(It is as if the awakened soul)

Pleure sous terre à l'unisson
Cries under earth to the-unison
(Cries under the earth in unison)

De la chanson,
With the song,
(With the song,)

Et du malheur d'être oubliée
And of-the unhappiness of-to-be forgotten
(And of the unhappiness of being forgotten)

Se plaint dans un roucoulement
Itself complains in a cooing
(Complains in a cooing)

Bien doucement.
Well softly.
(Very softly.)

Ah! jamais plus près de la tombe
Ah! never more near of the tomb
(Ah! never again near the tomb)

Je n'irai, quand descend le soir
I not-will-go, when descends the evening
(will I go, when evening descends)

Au manteau noir,
To-the cloak black,
(in its black cloak,)

Ecouter la pâle colombe
To-listen the pale dove
(To listen to the pale dove)

Chanter sur la branche de l'if
To-sing on the branch of the-yew-tree
(Singing on the branch of the yew tree)

Son chant plaintif!
Its song plaintive!
(Its plaintive song!)

Duparc
L'invitation au Voyage
The-invitation to-the Journey

Mon enfant, ma soeur, Songe à la douceur
My infant, my sister, Dream of the sweetness
(My child, my sister, Dream of the sweetness)

D'aller là-bas vivre ensemble!
Of-to-go there-down to-live together!
(Of going over there to live together!)

Aimer à loisir, Aimer et mourir
To-love at leisure, To-love and to-die
(To love at leisure, To love and to die)

Au pays qui te ressemble!
To-the country that you resembles!
(In a country that resembles you!)

Les soleils mouillés De ces ciels brouillés
The suns humid Of these skies hazy
(The humid suns Of these hazy skies)

Pour mon esprit ont les charmes
For my spirit have the charms
(Have, for my spirit, the charm)

Si mystérieux De tes traîtres yeux
So mysterious Of your traitorous eyes
(So mysterious, Of your traitorous eyes)

Brillant à travers leurs larmes.
Shining to traverse their tears.
(Shining through their tears.)

Là, tout n'est qu'ordre et beauté,
There, all not-is but-order and beauty,
(There, all is order and beauty,)

Luxe, calme et volupté.
Luxury, calm and voluptuousness.
(Luxury, calm and voluptuousness.)

Vois sur ces canaux Dormir ces vaisseaux
See on those canals To-Sleep these ships
(See on these canals these sleeping ships)

Dont l'humeur est vagabonde;
Whose the-mood is vagabond;)
(Whose nature is vagabond;)

C'est pour assouvir Ton moindre désir
It-is to satiate Your least desire
(It is to fulfil Your least desire)

Qu'ils viennent du bout du monde.
That-they come from-the end of-the world.
(That they come from the ends of the earth.)

Les soleils couchants Revêtent les champs,
The suns setting Reclothe the fields,
(The setting suns Reclothe the fields,)

Les canaux, la ville entière,
The canals, the town entire,
(The canals, the entire town,)

D'hyacinthe et d'or;
Of-hyacinth and of-gold;
(With hyacinth and gold;)

Le monde s'endort
The world itself-falls-asleep
(The world falls asleep)

Dans une chaude lumière!
In a warm light!
(In a warm light!)

La Vague et la Cloche
The Wave and the Bell

Une fois, terrassé par un puissant breuvage
One time, earthed by a powerful potion
(Once, knocked down by a powerful drink)

J'ai rêvé que parmi les vagues et le bruit
I-have dreamed that among the waves and the noise
(I dreamed that amid the waves and the noise)

De la mer, je voguais sans fanal dans la nuit,
Of the sea, I sailed without ships-lantern in the night,
(Of the sea, I sailed without a ship's lantern in the night,)

Morne rameur, n'ayant plus l'espoir du rivage.
Mournful rower, not-having more the-hope of-the shore.
(Mournful rower, with no more hope of reaching the shore.)

L'océan me crachait ses baves sur le front,
The-ocean me spat its spittle on the forehead,
(The ocean spat its spittle on my forehead,)

Et le vent me glaçait d'horreur jusqu'aux entrailles.
And the wind me froze of-horror until-to-the entrails.
(And the wind froze me to my entrails with horror.)

Les vagues s'écroulaient ainsi que des murailles
The waves themselves-crushed-down thus that some walls
(The waves crushed down like great walls)

Avec ce rythme lent qu'un silence interrompt.
With that rhythm slow that-a silence interrupts.
(With that slow rhythm interrupted by silence.)

Puis tout changea. La mer et sa noire mêlée
Then all changed. The sea and its black melee
(Than everything changed. The sea and its black melee)

Sombrèrent. Sous mes pieds s'effrondra le plancher
Quieted. Under my feet itself-collapsed the floor)
(Quieted. Under my feet the floor of the boat)

De la barque. Et j'étais seul dans un vieux clocher,
Of the boat. And I-was alone in an old belfry,
(collapsed. And I was alone in an old belfry,)

Chevauchant avec rage une cloche ébranlée.
Riding with rage a bell shaking.
(Riding with fury a ringing bell.)

J'étreignais la criarde opiniâtrement,
I-grasped the clamourous-thing stubbornly,
(I grasped the clamourous thing stubbornly,)

Convulsif et fermant dans l'effort mes paupières.
Convulsive and closing in the-effort my eyelids.
(Convulsive and in the effort, closed my eyes.)

Le grondement faisait trembler les vieilles pierres,
The booming made to-tremble the old stones,
(The booming made the old stones tremble,)

Tant j'activais sans fin le lourd balancement.
So-much I-activated without end the heavy rocking.
(So much did I unceasingly accelerate the swinging.)

Pourquoi n'as-tu pas dit, o rêve où Dieu nous mène?
Why not-have-you not said, o dream where God us guides?
Why didn't you say, o dream, where God guides us?)

Pourquoi n'as-tu pas dit s'ils ne finiraient pas
Why not-have-you not said if-they not would-end not
(Why didn't you say if there is to be no end to)

L'inutile travail et l'éternel fracas
The-useless toil and the-eternal fracas
(The useless toil and the eternal strife)

Dont est faite la vie, hélas, la vie humaine!
Of-which is made the life, alas, the life human!
(Of which life is made, alas, human life!)

Duparc

La Vie Antérieure
The Life Former
(The Former Life)

J'ai longtemps habité sous de vastes portiques
I-have long-time lived under some vast porticos
(I have lived for a long time under vast porticos)

Que les soleils marins teignaient de mille feux,
That the suns marine tinted with of thousand fires,
(That the marine suns tinted with a thousand fires,)

Et que leurs grands piliers, droits et majestueux,
And that their great pillars, straight and majestic,
(And whose great pillars, straight and majestic,)

Rendaient pareils, le soir, aux grottes basaltiques.
Rendered like, the evening, to-the grottos basaltic.
(Made them look, at evening, like basaltic grottos.)

Les houles, en roulant les images des cieux,
The surges, in rolling the images of-the skies,
(The surging waves, in mirroring the images of the skies,)

Mêlaient d'une façon solennelle et mystique
Mixed in-a way solemn and mystical
(Mixed in a solemn and mystical way)

Les tout-puissants accords de leur riche musique
The all-powerful chords of their rich music
(The all powerful chords of their rich music)

Aux couleurs du couchant reflété par mes yeux.
With-the colors of-the sunset reflected by my eyes.
(With the colors of the sunset reflected in my eyes.)

C'est là que j'ai vécu dans les voluptés calmes,
It-is there that I-have lived in the voluptous calm,
(It is there that I lived in the voluptous calm,)

Au milieu de l'azur, des vagues, des splendeurs
In-the midst of the-azure, of-the waves, of-the splendors
(In the midst of the azure skies, the waves, the splendors)

Et des esclaves nus, tout imprégnés d'odeurs,
And some slaves nude, all impregnated with-odors,
(And the naked slaves, all imbued with fragrance,)

Qui me rafraîchissaient le front avec des palmes,
Who me refreshed the forehead with some palms,
(Who refreshed my forehead with palms,)

Et dont l'unique soin était d'approfondir
And whose the-only care was of-to-deepen
(And whose only care was to deepen)

Le secret douloureux qui me faisait languir.
The secret dolorous that me made to-languish.
(The painful secret that made me languish.)

Duparc
Le Manoir de Rosemonde
The Manor of Rosamund

De sa dent soudaine et vorace,
With its tooth sudden and voracious,
(With its sudden and voracious tooth,)

Comme un chien, l'amour m'a mordu.
Like a dog, the-love me-has bitten.
(Like a dog, love has bitten me.)

En suivant mon sang répandu,
In following my blood spilled,
(By following my spilled blood,)

Va, tu pourras suivre ma trace.
Go, you will-be-able to-follow my trace.
(Go, you will be able to follow my trail.)

Prends un cheval de bonne race,
Take a horse of good stock,
(Take a thoroughbred horse,)

Pars, et suis mon chemin ardu,
Part, and follow my path arduous,
(Leave, and follow my arduous path,)

Fondrière ou sentier perdu,
Bog or path lost,
(Bog or lost path,)

Si la course ne te harasse!
If the course not you harass!
(If the course does not harass you!)

En passant par où j'ai passé,
In passing by where I-have passed,)
(In passing where I have passed,)

Tu verras que seul et blessé,
You will-see that alone and wounded,
(You will see that alone and wounded,)

J'ai parcouru ce triste monde,
I-have traversed this sad world,
(I have traveled this sad world,)

Et qu'ainsi je m'en fus mourir
And that-thus I meself from-it went to-die
(And that thus I went to die)

Bien loin, bien loin, sans découvrir
Well far-away, well far-away, without to-discover
(Far away, far away, without discovering)

Le bleu manoir de Rosemonde.
The blue manor of Rosamund.
(The blue manor of Rosamund.)

Duparc
Phidylé
Phidylé

L'herbe est molle au sommeil sous les frais peupliers,
The-grass is soft to-the slumber under the fresh poplars,
(The grass is soft for slumber under the fresh poplars,)

Aux pentes des sources moussues,
To-the slopes of-the springs mossy,
(On the slopes of the mossy springs,)

Qui dans les prés en fleurs germant
Which in the meadows in flower sprouting
(Which in the flowering meadows sprouting)

par mille issues,
by thousand issues,
(with a thousand shoots,)

Se perdent sous les noirs halliers.
Themselves lose under the black thickets.
(Lose themselves under the black thickets.)

Repose, ô Phidylé! Midi sur les feuillages
Rest, o Phidylé! Midday on the leaves
(Rest, o Phydilé! Midday shines on the leaves)

Rayonne et t'invite au sommeil!
Shines and you-invites to-the slumber!
(and invites you to slumber!)

Par le trèfle et le thym, seules, en plein soleil
By the clover and the thyme, alone, in full sun
(Near the clover and the thyme, alone in full sunlight)

Chantent les abeilles volages;
Sing the bees fickle;
(the fickle bees hum;)

Un chaud parfum circule au détour des sentiers,
A warm perfume circulates to-the turning of-the paths,
(A warm perfume hovers in the winding paths,)

La rouge fleur des blés s'incline,
The red flower of-the wheat itself-inclines,
(The red flower of the wheat bends,)

Et les oiseaux, rasant de l'aile la colline,
And the birds, shaving of the-wing the hill,)
(And the birds, grazing the hill with their wings,)

Cherchent l'ombre des églantiers.
Search the-shade of-the briars.
(Search for the shade of the briars.)

Mais quand l'Astre incliné sur sa courbe éclatante,
But when the-Star inclined on its curve brilliant,
(But when the Sun, bent on its brilliant course,)

Verra ses ardeurs s'apaiser,
Will-see its ardors themselves-to-appease,
(Sees its ardors appeased,)

Que ton plus beau sourire et ton meilleur baiser
That your most beautiful smile and your best kiss
(Let your most beautiful smile and your best kiss)

Me récompensent de l'attente!
Me recompensate for the-wait!
(Compensate me for waiting!)

Duparc

Romance de Mignon

Romance of Mignon

Le connais-tu, ce radieux pays
It know-you, this radiant country
(Do you know it, this radiant country)

Où brillent dans les branches d'or des fruits?
Where shines in the branches of-gold some fruits?
(Where fruit shines in the golden branches?)

Un doux zéphir Embaume l'air et le laurier s'unit
A gentle zephyr Embalms the-air and the laurel itself-unites
(A gentle breeze Perfumes the air and the laurel and the)

au myrte vert. Le connais-tu?
to-the myrtle green. It know-you?
(green myrtle unite. Do you know it?)

Courons porter nos pas.
Let's-run to-carry our steps.
(Let's hurry our steps.)

Le connais-tu, ce merveilleux séjour
It know-you, this marvellous abode
(Do you know it, this marvellous abode)

Où tout me parle encore de notre amour?
Where all to-me speaks still of our love?
(Where everything still speaks to me of our love?)

Où chaque objet me dit avec douleur:
Where each object to-me says with sorrow:
(Where every object says to me with sorrow:)

Qui t'a ravi ta joie et ton bonheur?
Who you-has ravished your joy and your happiness?
(Who has stolen your joy and your happiness?)

Le connais-tu?
It know-you?
(Do you know it?)

Duparc

Sérénade

Serenade

Si j'étais, ô mon amoureuse, La brise au souffle parfumé.
If I-were, o my loving-one, The breeze to-the breath perfumed.
(If I were, o my lover, The breeze with perfumed breath,)

Pour frôler ta bouche rieuse,
For to-touch your mouth laughing,
(To touch your laughing mouth,)

Je viendrais craintif et charmé.
I would-come fearful and charmed.
(I would come, fearful and charmed.)

Si j'étais l'abeille qui vole, Ou le papillon séducteur,
If I-were the-bee who flies, Or the butterfly seductive,
(If I were the bee who flies, Or the seductive butterfly,)

Tu ne me verrais pas, frivole,
You not me would-see not, frivolous,
(You would not see me, frivolous,)

Te quitter pour une autre fleur
You to-leave for an other flower
(Leaving you for another flower)

Si j'étais la rose charmante
If I-were the rose charming
(If I were the charming rose)

Que ta main place sur ton coeur
Which your hand places on your heart
(Which your hand places on your heart)

Si près de toi toute tremblante
So close to you all trembling
(So close to you all trembling,)

Je me fanerais de bonheur.
I myself would-wither of happiness.
(I would wither with happiness.)

Duparc
Sérénade Florentine
Serenade Florentine

Etoile dont la beauté luit Comme un diamant dans la nuit,
Star of-which the beauty shines Like a diamond in the night,
(Star whose beauty shines Like a diamond in the night,)

Regarde vers ma bien-aimée Dont la paupière s'est fermée,
Look toward my well-loved Of-Whom the eyelid itself-is closed,
(Look on my beloved Whose eyelids have closed,)

Et fais descendre sur ses yeux La bénédiction des cieux.
And make to-descend on her eyes The benediction of-the heavens.
(And bring down on her eyes The blessing of the heavens.)

Elle s'endort...Par la fenêtre
She herself-falls-asleep...By the window
(She is falling asleep...By the window)

En sa chambre heureuse pénètre:
In her room happy penetrate:
(Of her happy room enters)

Sur sa blancheur, comme un baiser,
On her whiteness, like a kiss,
(On her whiteness, like a kiss,)

Viens jusqu'à l'aube te poser,
Come until-to the-dawn yourself to-place,
(Come and sit until dawn,)

Et que sa pensée, alors, rêve
And that her thought, then, dream
(And let her, then, dream)

D'un astre d'amour qui se lève!
Of-a star of-love which itself rises!
(Of a star of love which rises!)

Duparc
Soupir
Sigh

Ne jamais la voir ni l'entendre,
Not ever her to-see nor her-to-hear
(Never see her nor hear her,)

Ne jamais tout haut la nommer,
Not ever all high her to-name,)
(Never say her name aloud,)

Mais, fidèle, toujours l'attendre, Toujours l'aimer.
But, faithful, always her-to-await, Always her-to-love.
(But, faithful, always await her, Always love her.)

Ouvrir les bras, et, las d'attendre,
To-open the arms, and, tired to-await,
(Open my arms, and tired of waiting,)

Sur le néant les refermer!
On the void them to-close!
(Close them on a void!)

Mais encore, toujours les lui tendre, Toujours l'aimer.
But still, always them to-her to-stretch, Always her-to-love.
(But still, always to stretch them to her, Always to love her.)

Ah! ne pouvoir que les lui tendre
Ah! not to-be-able but them to-her to-stretch-out
(Ah! to be able only to stretch them out to her)

Et dans les pleurs se consumer,
And in the tears oneself to-consume,
(And to be consumed in tears,)

Mais ces pleurs toujours les répandre,
But these tears always them to-pour-out,
(But always pour out these tears,)

Toujours l'aimer.
Always her-to-love.
(Always love her.)

Duparc
Testament
Testament

Pour que le vent te les apporte
For that the wind to-you them carry
(So that the wind may carry them to you)

Sur l'aile noire d'un remord,
On the-wing black of-a remorse,
(On the black wing of remorse,)

J'écrirai sur la feuille morte
I-will-write on the leaf dead
(I will write on the dead leaf)

Les tortures de mon coeur mort!
The tortures of my heart dead!
(The tortures of my dead heart!)

Toute ma sève s'est tarie
All my sap itself-has dried-up
(All my sap has dried up)

Aux clairs midis de ta beauté,
At-the clear middays of your beauty,
(In the clear midday of your beauty,)

Et, comme à la feuille flétrie,
And, like to the leaf dried,
(And, like the dried leaf,)

Rien de vivant ne m'est resté.
Nothing of living not to-me-is left.
(Nothing living is left to me.)

Tes yeux m'ont brûlé jusqu'à l'âme
Your eyes me-have burned until the-soul
(Your eyes have burned me to the soul)

Comme des soleils sans merci!
Like some suns without mercy!
(Like merciless suns!)

Feuille que le gouffre réclame,
Leaf that the gulf reclaims,
(Leaf that the abyss reclaims,)

L'autan va m'emporter aussi...
The-south-wind is-going me-to-carry-away also...
(The south wind will carry me away also...)

Mais avant, pour qu'il te les porte
But before, for that it to-you them carry
(But before that, so that it may carry them to you)

Sur l'aile noire d'un remord,
On the-wing black of-a-remorse,
(On the black wing of remorse,)

J'écrirai sur la feuille morte
I-will-write on the leaf dead
(I will write on the dead leaf)

Les tortures de mon coeur mort!
The tortures of my heart dead!
(The tortures of my dead heart!)

Fauré

A Clymene

To Clymene

Mystiques barcarolles, Romances sans paroles,
Mystical barcarolles, Romances without words,
(Mystical barcarolles, Romances without words,)

Chère, puisque tes yeux, Couleur des cieux,
Dear, since your eyes, Color of-the skies,
(Dear, since your eyes, the color of the skies,)

Puisque ta voix, étrange Vision qui dérange
Since your voice, strange Vision that deranges
(Since your voice, strange Vision that disturbs)

Et trouble l'horizon De ma raison,
And troubles the-horizon Of my reason,
(And troubles the horizon Of my sanity,)

Puisque l'arome insigne De ta pâleur de cygne,
Since the-aroma distinguished Of your pallor of swan,
(Since the distinguished aroma of your pale skin,)

Et puisque la candeur De ton odeur,
And since the candor Of your odor,
(And since the candor of your scent,)

Ah! puisque tout ton être, Musique qui pénètre,
Ah! since all your being, Music that penetrates,
(Ah! since all your being, Music that penetrates,)

Nimbes d'anges défunts, Tons et parfums,
Haloes of-angels defunct, Tones and perfumes,
(Haloes of deceased angels, Sounds and perfumes,)

A, sur d'almes cadences, En ces correspondances
Has, on some-beneficent cadences, In these correspondences
(Has, on beneficent cadences, Though such correspondences)

Induit mon coeur subtil, Ainsi soit-il!
Induced my heart subtle, Thus be-it!
(Induced my subtle heart, So be it!)

Accompagnement
Accompaniment

Tremble argenté, tilleul, bouleau ...
Aspen silvered, linden, birch...
(Silvery aspen, linden, birch...)

La lune s'effeuille sur l'eau ...
The moon itself-un-leafs on the-water...
(The moon sheds its leaves on the water...)

Comme de longs cheveux peignés au vent du soir,
Like some long hairs combed to-the wind of-the evening,
(Like long hair combed by the evening wind,)

L'odeur des nuits d'été parfume le lac noir.
The-odor of-the nights of-summer perfumes the lake black.
(The smell of summer nights perfumes the black lake.)

Le grand lac parfumé brille comme un miroir.
The large lake perfumed shines like a mirror.
(The large scented lake shines like a mirror.)

Ma rame tombe et se relève, ma barque glisse dans le rêve.
My oar falls and itself raises, my bark glides in the dream.
(My oar rises and falls, my boat glides in a dream.)

Ma barque glisse dans le ciel sur le lac immatériel ...
My bark glides in the sky on the lake immaterial...
(My boat glides in the sky on the intangible lake...)

En cadence, les yeux fermés, Rame, ô mon coeur,
In cadence, the eyes closed, Row, o my heart,
(Rhythmically, eyes closed, Row, o my heart,)

ton indolence à larges coups lents et pamés.
your indolence to large blows slow and swooning.
(your indolence in large, slow and swooning strokes.)

Là-bas la lune écoute, accoudée au coteau,
There-down the moon listens, on-elbow to-the hill,
(Over there the moon listens, leaning on the hill,)

(cont.)

Le silence qu'exhale en glissant le bateau ...
The silence that-exhales in gliding the boat...
(To the silence that the gliding boat exhales...)

Trois grands lys frais-coupées meurent sur mon manteau.
Three large lilies fresh-cut die on my mantle.
(Three newly cut lilies die on my cloak.)

Vers tes lèvres, ô Nuit voluptueuse et pâle, est-ce leur âme,
Toward your lips, o Night voluptuous and pale, is-this their soul,
(Toward your lips, voluptuous and pale night, is it their soul,)

est-ce mon âme qui s'exhale?
is-this my soul which itself-exhales?
(Is it my soul which exhales?)

Cheveux des nuits d'argent peignés aux longs roseaux ...
Hairs of-the nights of-silver combed to-the long reeds...
(Hair of silver nights combed by long reeds...)

Comme la lune sur les eaux, Comme la rame sur les flots,
Like the moon on the waters, Like the oar on the waves,
(Like the moon on the waters, Like the oar on the waves,)

Mon âme s'effeuille en sanglots!
My soul itself-un-leafs in sobs!
(My soul sheds its leaves in sobs!)

Fauré

Après un Rêve

After a Dream

Dans un sommeil que charmait ton image
In a sleep that charmed your image
(In a sleep charmed by your image)

Je rêvais le bonheur, ardent mirage.
I dreamed the happiness, ardent mirage.
(I dreamed of happiness, ardent mirage.)

Tes yeux étaient plus doux, ta voix pure et sonore,
Your eyes were more sweet, your voice pure and sonorous,
(Your eyes were sweeter, your voice pure and sonorous,)

Tu rayonnais comme un ciel éclairé par l'aurore;
You shone like a heaven lit by the-dawn;
(You shone like a sky lit-up by dawn;)

Tu m'appelais, et je quittais la terre
You me-called, and I left the earth
(You called me, and I left the earth)

pour m'enfuir avec toi vers la lumière.
for myself-to-flee with you toward the light.
(to flee with you toward the light.)

Les cieux pour nous entr'ouvraient leurs nues,
The heavens for us between-opened their clouds,
(The heavens opened their clouds to us,)

Splendeurs inconnues, lueurs divines entrevues.
Splendors unknown, flashes divine glimpsed.
(Unknown splendors, glimpses of divine light.)

Hélas! hélas! triste réveil des songes.
Alas! alas! sad awakening from-the dreams.
(Alas! alas! sad awakening from dreams.)

Je t'appelle, ô nuit, rends-moi tes mensonges.
I you-call, o night, render-me your lies.
(I call you, o night, return me your lies.)

Reviens, reviens radieuse!
Come-back, come-back radiant-one!
(Return, return radiant!)

Reviens, ô nuit mystérieuse!
Return, o night mysterious!
(Return, o mysterious night!)

Arpège
Arpeggio

L'âme d'une flûte soupire au fond du parc mélodieux.
The-soul of-a flute sighs at-the depth of-the park melodious.
(A flute's soul sighs in the depth of the melodious park.)

Limpide est l'ombre où l'on respire ton poème silencieux,
Limpid is the-shadow where the-one breathes your poem silent,
(The shadow is limpid where one breathes your silent poem,)

Nuit de langueur, nuit de mensonge, qui pose,
Night of languor, night of lie, which places,
(Night of languor, night of lie, which places,)

d'un geste ondoyant, dans ta chevelure de songe la lune
of-a gesture undulating, in your hair of dream the moon
(with an undulating gesture, in your dreamy hair, the jewel)

bijou d'Orient. Sylva, Sylvie, et Sylvanire,
jewel of-Orient. Sylva, Sylvia, and Sylvanire,
(of the Orient. Sylva, Sylvia, and Sylvanire,)

Belles au regard bleu changeant,
Beauties to-the look blue changing,
(Beauties with a changing blue look,)

L'étoile aux fontaines se mire, allez par les sentiers d'argent;
The-star of-the fountains itself mirrors, go by the paths of-silver;
(The star admires itself in the fountains, go by the silvery paths;)

Allez vite, l'heure est si brêve,
Go quickly, the-hour is so brief,
(Go quickly, the time is so short,)

Cueillir au jardin des aveux les coeurs
to-Gather at-the garden of-the vows the hearts
(Gather from the garden of vows hearts)

qui se meurent du rêve, de mourir parmi vos cheveux!
which themselves die from-the dream, to die among your hairs!
(which die from the dream, of dying in your hair!)

Au Bord de l'Eau
On-the Bank of the-Water

S'asseoir tous deux au bord du flot
Oneself-to-sit all two on-the bank of-the float
(To sit together on the bank of the)

qui passe le voir passer; Tous deux,
that passes, it to-see to-pass; All two,
(passing water, to see it passing; Together,)

s'il glisse un nuage en l'espace le voir glisser;
if-it glides a cloud in the-space, it to-see to-glide;
(if a cloud glides by in space, to see it gliding;)

A l'horizon s'il fume un toit de chaume, le voir fumer:
At the-horizon if-it smokes a roof of thatch, it to-see to-smoke:
(On the horizon if a thatch roof is smoking, to see it smoking:)

Aux alentours, si quelque fleur embaume:
To-the surrounding, if some flower gives-of-a-scent:
(All around, if some flower is scented:)

s'en embaumer; entendre,
itself-to-fragrance; to-listen,
(to drink its fragrance; to listen,)

au pied du saule où l'eau murmure,
to-the foot of-the willow where the-water murmurs,
(at the foot of the willow where the water murmurs,)

l'eau murmurer; ne pas sentir, tant que ce rêve dure,
the-water to-murmur; not not to-feel, while that this dream lasts,
(to the murmuring water, not to feel, while this dream lasts,)

le temps durer; mais, n'apportant de passion profonde
the time to-last; but, not-bringing of passion profound
(time passing; but, bringing only the deep passion)

qu'à s'adorer, sans nul souci
but-to ourselves-to-adore, without any care
(of adoring each other, without any care)

des querelles du monde les ignorer;
of-the quarrels of-the world them to-ignore;
(of the world's strife, ignoring them;)

et seuls, tous deux devant tout ce qui lasse
and alone, all two before all this that wearies
(and alone, together facing all that wearies)

sans se lasser, sentir l'amour,
without ourselves to-weary, to-feel the-love,
(without wearying, feeling love,)

devant tout ce qui passe; ne point passer.
before all this that passes; not never to-pass.
(before all that passes; to never pass!)

Au Cimetière
At-the Cemetery

Heureux qui meurt ici Ainsi Que les oiseaux des champs!
Happy who dies here Thus That the birds of-the fields!
(Happy whoever dies here Like the birds of the fields!)

Son corps près des amis Est mis Dans l'herbe
His body near of-the friends Is put In the-grass
(His body near his friends Is laid In the grass)

et dans les chants. Il dort d'un bon sommeil Vermeil
and in the songs. He sleeps of-a good sleep Vermillion
(amid songs. He sleeps a good Crimson sleep)

Sous le ciel radieux. Tous ceux qu'il a connus, Venus,
Under the sky radiant. All those whom-he has known, Came,
(Under the radiant sky. All those whom he knew, Have come,)

Lui font de longs adieux. A sa croix les parents
Him make some long adieus. At his cross the relatives
(To bid him long farewells. At his cross his relatives,)

Pleurants Restent agenouillés; Et ses os, sous les fleurs,
Weeping, Rest kneeled; And his bones, under the flowers,
(Weeping, Remain kneeling; And his bones, under the flowers,)

De pleurs Sont doucement mouillés. Chacun sur le bois noir
Of tears Are sweetly moistened. Each-one on the wood black
(Are sweetly moistened with tears. Everyone on the black wood)

Peut voir S'il était jeune ou non, Et peut avec de vrais
Can see If-he was young or not, And can with some true
(Can see if he were young or not, And can with true)

Regrets L'appeler par son nom. Combien plus malchanceux
Regrets Him-to-call by his name. How-much more unfortunate
(Regret call him by his name. How much more unfortunate)

Sont ceux Qui meurent à la mer, Et sous le flot profond
Are those Who die at the sea, And under the float deep
(Are those who die at sea, And under the deep wave)

S'en vont Loin du pays aimé!
Themselves-from-there go Far from-the country loved!
(Go Far from their beloved country!)

Ah! pauvres, qui pour seuls
Ah! poor-ones, who for only
(Ah! poor ones, whose only)

Linceuls Ont les goëmons verts Où l'on roule inconnu,
Shrouds Have the seaweed green Where the-one rolls unknown,
(Shroud is the green seaweed Where one rolls unknown,)

Tout nu, Et les yeux grands ouverts.
All nude, And the eyes wide open.
(Naked, And with wide-open eyes.)

Fauré

Aubade

Song-at-Dawn

L'oiseau dans le buisson a salué l'aurore,
The-bird in the bush has saluted the-dawn,
(The bird in the bushes has hailed the dawn,)

et d'un pâle rayon l'horizon se colore,
and of-a pale ray the-horizon itself colors,
(and with a pale ray the horizon is colored,)

Voici le frais matin! Pour voir les fleurs
Here-is the fresh morning! For to-see the flowers
(The fresh morning is here! To see the flowers)

à la lumière s'ouvrir de toute part, entr'ouvre ta paupière,
to the light itself-to-open of all side, open your eyelid,
(open all over to the light, open your eyes,)

ô vierge au doux regard!
o virgin to-the sweet regard!
(o virgin with the sweet gaze!)

La voix de ton amant a dissipé ton rêve.
The voice of your lover has dissipated your dream.
(The voice of your lover has dispelled your dream.)

Je vois ton rideau blanc qui tremble et se soulève,
I see your curtain white which trembles and itself raises,
(I see your white curtain which trembles and rises,)

d'amour signal charmant! Descends sur ce tapis de mousse
of-love signal charming! Descend on this tapestry of moss
(charming sign of love! Descend on this mossy carpet,)

la brise est tiède encore, et la lumière est douce.
the breeze is tepid still, and the light is sweet.
(the breeze is still warm, and the light is sweet.)

Accours, ô mon trésor!
Run, o my treasure!
(Run to me, o my treasure!)

Fauré
Aurore
Dawn

Des jardins de la nuit s'envolent les étoiles,
From-the gardens of the night themselves-flee the stars,
(From the gardens of night the stars flee,)

abeilles d'or qu'attire un invisible miel.
bees of-gold that-attracts an invisible honey.
(golden bees that an invisible honey attracts.)

Et l'aube, au loin, tendant la candeur de ses toiles,
And the-dawn, to-the distance, stretching the candor of its cloths,
(And the dawn, far away, stretching the candor of its cloths,)

trame de fils d'argent le manteau bleu du ciel.
weaves of threads of-silver the cloak blue of-the sky.
(weaves with silver thread the blue cloak of the sky.)

Du jardin de mon coeur qu'un rêve lent enivre,
From-the garden of my heart that-a dream slow intoxicates,
(From the garden of my heart, intoxicated by a slow dream,)

s'envolent mes désirs sur les pas du matin.
themselves-flee my desires on the steps of-the morning.
(my desires flee on the steps of morning.)

Comme un essaim troublé qu'à l'horizon de cuivre,
Like a swarm troubled that-to the-horizon of copper,
(Like a troubled swarm called by a plaintive song,)

appelle un chant plaintif éternel et lointain.
calls a song plaintive eternal and distant.
(toward the copper horizon, eternal and far away.)

Ils volent à tes pieds, astres chassés des nues.
They flee to your feet, stars chased from-the clouds.
(They flee to your feet, stars chased from the clouds.)

Exilés du ciel d'or où fleurit ta beauté,
Exiled from-the heaven of-gold where flowers your beauty,
(Exiled from the golden sky where your beauty unfolds,)

Aurore
(cont.)

Et, cherchant jusqu'à toi des routes inconnues,
And, searching until-to you some routes unknown,
(And, searching unknown routes toward you,)

mêlent au jour naissant leur mourante clarté.
mix to-the day new-born their dying light.
(They-mix their dying light with the new-born day.)

Automne
Autumn

Automne au ciel brumeux, aux horizons navrants,
Autumn to-the sky foggy, of-the horizons distressing,
(Autumn of foggy sky, of distressing horizons,)

Aux rapides couchants, aux aurores pâlies;
To-the rapid sunsets, to-the dawns pale;
(Of rapid sunsets, of pale dawns;)

je regarde couler, comme l'eau du torrent,
I watch to-flow, like the-water of-the torrent,
(I watch flowing like torrential waters,)

tes jours faits de mélancolie. Sur l'aile des regrets
your days made of melancholy. On the-wing of-the regrets
(your melancholy days. My thoughts carried away)

mes esprits emportés, comme s'il se pouvait
my spirits carried-away, like if-it itself could-be
(On the wing of regrets, as if our past age)

que notre âge renaisse! Parcourent en rêvant
that our age be-reborn! Wander in dreaming
(could be reborn! Wander, dreaming)

les coteaux enchantés, où jadis, sourit ma jeunesse!
the hillsides enchanted, where once, smiled my youth!
(on the enchanted hillsides, where once, my youth smiled!)

Je sens, au clair soleil du souvenir vainqueur,
I feel, to-the clear sun of-the memory victorious,
(I feel, in the clear sun of victorious memory,)

Refleurir en bouquet les roses déliées, et monter à mes yeux,
To-Reflower in bouquet the roses untied, and to-mount to my eyes,
(Flowing roses, reflowering in bouquets, and tears welling-up,)

des larmes, qu'en mon coeur mes vingt ans avaient oubliées!
some tears, that-in my heart my twenty years had forgotten!
(in my eyes, Which in my heart my twenty years had forgotten!)

Fauré

Barcarolle

Barcarolle

Gondolier du Rialto, mon château c'est la lagune,
Gondolier of-the Rialto, my chateau it-is the lagoon,
(Gondolier of the Rialto, my chateau is the lagoon,)

mon jardin c'est le Lido, mon rideau le clair de lune,
my garden it-is the Lido, my curtain the light of moon,
(my garden is the Lido, my curtain is the moonlight,)

gondolier du grand canal.
gondolier of-the grand canal.
(gondolier of the grand canal.)

Pour fanal j'ai la croisée où s'allument
For signal I-have the window where themselves-illuminate
(As a beacon, I have the window illuminated)

tous les soirs, tes yeux noirs, mon épousée.
all the evenings, your eyes black, my spouse.
(every evening, by your black eyes, my wife.)

Ma gondole est aux heureux, deux à deux je les promène,
My gondola is to-the happy, two by two I them promenade,
(My gondola is for happy people, two by two I carry them,)

et les vents légers et frais sont discrets sur mon domaine.
and the winds light and fresh are discreet on my domain.
(and the light and fresh winds are discreet in my domain.)

J'ai passé dans les amours, plus de jours et de nuits folles,
I-have passed in the loves, more of days and of nights crazy,
(I have spent in love, more crazy days and nights,)

que Venise n'a d'ilots que ses flots n'ont de gondoles.
than Venice not-has of-islets than its floats not-have of gondolas.
(Than Venice has islets, than its waves have gondolas.)

C'est l'Extase
It-is the-Ecstasy

C'est l'extase langoureuse, C'est la fatigue amoureuse,
It-is the-ecstasy languorous, It-is the fatigue amorous,
(It is languorous ecstasy, It is amorous fatigue,)

C'est tous les frissons des bois Parmi l'étreinte des brises,
It-is all the shivers of-the woods Among the-embrace of-the breezes,
(It is all the shivers of the wood Among the breeze's embrace,)

C'est, vers les ramures grises, Le choeur des petites voix.
It-is, toward the branches grey, The choir of-the little voices.
(It is, near the grey branches, The choir of little voices.)

O le frêle et frais murmure! Cela gazouille et susurre,
O the frail and fresh murmur! That chirps and whispers,
(O frail and fresh murmur! It chirps and whispers,)

Cela ressemble au cri doux Que l'herbe agitée expire...
That resembles to-the cry sweet That the-grass agitated breathes...
(It resembles the sweet cry Breathed by the agitated grass...)

Tu dirais, sous l'eau qui vire,
You would-say, under the-water that swirls,
(You might say, beneath the swirling water,)

Le roulis sourd des cailloux.
The rolling deaf of-the pebbles.
(The quiet rolling of the pebbles.)

Cette âme qui se lamente En cette plainte dormante
This soul which itself laments In this complaint sleeping
(This soul which laments In this sleeping complaint)

C'est la nôtre, n'est-ce pas? La mienne, dis, et la tienne,
It-is the ours, not-is-it not? The mine, say, and the yours,
(Is ours, is it not? Mine, say, and yours,)

Dont s'exhale l'humble antienne Par ce tiède soir, tout bas?
From-which itself-exhales the-humble hymn By this tepid evening, all low?
(Breathing its humble hymn In the warm evening, very softly?)

Fauré

C'est la Paix

It-is the Peace

Pendant qu'ils étaient partis pour la guerre,
While that-they were left for the war,
(While they were away at war,)

on ne dansait plus, on ne parlait guère,
one not danced more, one not spoke hardly,
(we didn't dance, we hardly spoke,)

on ne chantait pas. Mes soeurs, c'est la paix!
one not sang not. My sisters, it-is the peace!
(we didn't sing. My sisters, it's peace time!)

La guerre est finie dans la paix bénie;
The was is finished in the peace blessed;
(The war is over in blessed peace;)

courons au devant de nos chers soldats,
let-us-run to-the before of our dear soldiers,
(let us run to our dear soldiers,)

et joyeusement, toutes en cadence,
and joyously, all in rhythm,
(and joyously, all in rhythm,)

nous irons vers eux en dansant la danse
we will-go toward them while dancing the dance
(we will go toward them dancing the dance)

qu'on danse chez nous. Nous les aimerons!
that-one dances at-the-home-of us. We them will-love!
(that we dance at home. We will love them!)

la guerre est finie, ils seront aimés,
the war is finished, they will-be loved,
(the war is over, they will be loved,)

dans la paix bénie, sitôt leur retour.
in the peace blessed, as-soon their return.
(in blessed peace, upon their return.)

Pour avoir chassé la horde germaine ils auront
For to-have chased the horde German they will-have
(For chasing the German horde they will have)

nos coeurs, au lieu de la haine ils auront l'amour.
our hearts, in-the place of the hate they will-have the-love
(our hearts, in place of hate they will have love.)

Fauré
Chanson
Song

Que me fait toute la terre inutile où tu n'as pas,
What me makes all the earth useless where you not-have not,
(All the earth is useless where you have not,)

en marchant, marqué ton pas dans le sable ou la poussière!
in walking, marked your step in the sand or the dust!
(Walking, marked your step in the dust or the sand!)

Il n'est de fleuve attendu par ma soif
It not-is of river awaited by my thirst
(There is no river awaited by my thirst)

qui s'y étanche que l'eau
that itself-there quenches but the-water
(that could be assuaged but the water)

qui sourd et s'épenche,
that rises-up and itself-overflows,
(that rises and flows,)

de la source où tu as bu.
from the source where you have drunk.
(from the spring where you have drunk.)

La seule fleur qui m'attire est celle où
The only flower that me-attracts is that-one where
(The only flower that attracts me is the one in which)

je trouverai le souvenir empourpré de ta bouche
I will-find the remembrance made-purple of your mouth
(I will find crimson memory of your mouth)

et de ton rire;
and of your laughter;
(and of your laughter;)

et, sous la courbe des cieux
and, under the curve of-the skies
(and, under the curve of the skies)

la mer pour moi n'est immense que parce
the sea for me not-is immense but because
(the sea is immense to me only because)

qu'elle commence à la couleur de tes yeux.
that-it commences at the color of your eyes.
(it begins in the color of your eyes.)

Fauré

Chanson d'Amour

Song of-Love

J'aime tes yeux, j'aime ton front, ô ma rebelle,
I-love your eyes, I-love your face, o my rebel,
(I love your eyes, I love your face, o my rebellious one,)

ô ma farouche. J'aime tes yeux, j'aime ta bouche
o my fierce-one. I-love your eyes, I-love your mouth
(o my fierce one. I love your eyes, I love your mouth)

où mes baisers s'épuiseront. J'aime ta voix,
where my kissses themselves-will-exhaust. I-love your voice,
(where my kisses will exhaust themselves. I love your voice,)

j'aime l'étrange grâce de tout ce que tu dis,
I-love the-strange grace of all that which you say,
(I love the strange grace of all that you say,)

ô ma rebelle, ô mon cher ange, mon enfer et mon paradis!
o my rebellious-one, o my dear angel, my hell and my paradise!
(o my rebellious one, o my dear angel, my hell and my paradise!)

J'aime tout ce qui te fait belle,
I-love all that which you makes beautiful,
(I love all that makes you beautiful,)

de tes pieds jusqu'à tes cheveux,
from your feet until-to your hairs,
(from your feet to your hair,)

ô toi vers qui montent mes voeux, ô ma farouche,
o you toward whom mount my vows, o my fierce-one,
(o you toward whom my vows ascend, o my fierce one,)

ô ma rebelle.
o my rebel.
(o my rebellious one.)

Fauré
Chanson de Shylock
Song of Shylock

Oh, les filles! Venez, les filles aux voix douces!
Oh, the girls! Come, the girls to-the voices sweet!
(Oh, girls! Come, girls with sweet voices!)

C'est l'heure d'oublier l'orgueil et les vertus,
It-is the-hour of-to-forget the-pride and the virtues,
(It is time to forget pride and virtues,)

Et nous regarderons éclore dans les mousses
And we will-watch to-blossom in the mosses
(And we will watch blossom in the moss)

La fleur des baisers défendus. Les baisers défendus,
The flower of-the kisses forbidden. The kisses forbidden,
(The flower of forbidden kisses. Forbidden kisses,)

c'est Dieu qui les ordonne. Oh, les filles!
it-is God who them ordains. Oh, the girls!
(it is God who ordains them. Oh, girls!)

Il fait le printemps pour les nids, Il fait votre beauté
He makes the spring for the nests, He makes your beauty
(He makes spring for nests, He makes your beauty)

pour qu'elle nous soit bonne, Nos désirs
for that-it to-us be good, Our desires
(to be good for us, Our desires)

pour qu'ils soient unis. Oh, filles!
for that-they be united. Oh, girls!
(to be united. Oh, girls!)

Hors l'amour, rien n'est bon sur la terre
Out-of the-love, nothing not-is good on the earth
(Outside of love, nothing is good on earth)

Et depuis les soirs d'or jusqu'aux matins rosés
And since the evenings of-gold until-to-the mornings rosy
(And from golden evenings to rosy mornings)

Les morts ne sont jaloux, dans leur paix solitaire,
The dead not are jealous, in their peace solitary,
(The dead are only jealous, in their solitary peace,)

Que du murmure des baisers.
But of-the murmur of-the kisses.
(Of the murmur of kisses.)

Chant d'Automne
Song of-Autumn

Bientôt nous plongerons dans les froides ténèbres;
Soon we will-plunge in the cold darknesses;
(Soon we will plunge into cold darkness;)

adieu, vive clarté de nos étés trop courts!
farewell, living clarity of our summers too short!
(farewell, living brightness of our too short summers!)

J'entends déjà tomber avec un choc funèbre,
I-hear already to-fall with a shock funereal,
(Already I hear with a funereal thump,)

le bois retentissant sur le pavé des cours.
the wood resounding on the pavement of-the courtyards.
(the resounding wood fall on the courtyards' pavement.)

J'écoute en frémissant chaque bûche qui tombe;
I-listen in trembling each log that falls;
(Trembling, I listen to each tree that falls;)

l'échafaud qu'on bâtit n'a pas d'écho plus sourd.
the-scaffold that-one builds not-has not of-echo more deaf.
(The gallows being built has no duller echo.)

Mon esprit est pareil à la tour qui succombe
My spirit is like to the tower that succumbs
(My spirit is like the tower that falls)

sous les coups du bélier infatigable et lourd.
under the blows of-the ram unfatigable and heavy.
(under the blows of an untiring and heavy ram.)

Il me semble, bercé par ce choc monotone,
It to-me seems, cradled by this shock monotonous,
(It seems to me, cradled by this monotonous thump,)

qu'on cloue en grande hâte un cercueil quelque part ...
that-one nails in great haste a coffin some part...
(that someone, in great haste, nails a coffin somewhere...)

Chant d'Automne
(cont.)

Pour qui? -- C'était hier l'été; voici l'automne!
For whom?-- It-was yesterday the-summer; here-is the-autumn!
(For whom? Summer was yesterday; this is autumn!)

Ce bruit mystérieux sonne comme un départ!
This noise mysterious rings like a departure!
(This mysterious noise rings like a departure!)

J'aime de vos longs yeux la lumière verdâtre,
I-love of your long eyes the light greenish,
(I love the greenish light of your long eyes,)

douce beauté! Mais aujourd'hui tout m'est amer.
sweet beauty! But today all to-me-is bitter.
(sweet beauty! But today everything is bitter to me.)

Et rien, ni votre amour, ni le boudoir, ni l'âtre,
And nothing, neither your love, nor the boudoir, nor the-hearth,
(And nothing, neither your love, nor boudoir, nor hearth,)

ne me vaut le soleil rayonnant sur la mer!
not to-me values the sun shining on the sea!
(is worth the sun shining on the sea!)

Clair de Lune
Light of Moon
(Moonlight)

Votre âme est un paysage choisi que vont charmants masques
Your soul is a landscape chosen where go charming masks
(Your soul is a select landscape where go masks and bergamasks)

et bergamasques, jouant du luth; et dansant, et quasi tristes
and bergamasks, playing of-the lute; and dansing, and almost sad
(charm, playing the lute; and dansing, and almost sad)

sous leurs déguisements fantasques. Tout en chantant sur le mode
under their disguises fantastical. All in singing in the mode
(under their fantastical disguises. All the while singing in the minor)

minuer l'amour vainqueur et la vie opportune,
minor the-love victorious and the life opportune,
(mode of victorious love and the opportune life,)

ils n'ont pas l'air de croire à leur bonheur
they not-have not the-air of to-believe to their happiness
(they do not seem to believe in their happiness)

et leur chanson se mêle au clair de lune,
and their song itself mixes with-the light of moon,
(and their song mixes with the moonlight,)

au calme clair de lune triste et beau,
with-the calm light of moon sad and beautiful,
(with the calm moonlight sad and beautiful,)

qui fait rêver les oiseaux dans les arbres
which makes to-dream the birds in the trees
(which makes the birds in the trees dream)

et sangloter d'extase les jets d'eau,
and to-sob from-ecstasy the jets of-water,
(and fountains sob from ecstasy,)

les grands jets d'eau sveltes parmi les marbres.
the great jets of-waters slender among the marbles.
(the great slender fountains among the marbles.)

Dans la Forêt de Septembre
In the Forest of September
(In the September Forest)

Ramure aux rumeurs amollies,
Branch to-the murmurings softened,
(Branch with softened murmurings,)

troncs sonores que l'âge creuse.
trunks resonant that the-age hollows.
(resonant trunks hollowed by age.)

L'antique forêt douloureuse s'accorde à nos mélancolies.
The-aged forest sorrowful itself-agrees to our melancholies.
(The sorrowful aged forest suits our melancholies.)

O sapins agriffés au gouffre, nids déserts aux branches brisées.
Oh firs gripped to-the gulf, nests deserted to-the branches broken.
(Oh firs gripping the edge of the abyss, deserted nests in broken branches.)

Halliers brûlés, fleurs sans rosées, vous savez bien comme l'on
Thickets burnt, flowers without dew, you know well like the-one
(Burnt thickets, flowers without dew, you know well how one)

souffre! Et lorsque l'homme, passant blême, pleure dans le bois
suffers! And when the-man, passing pale, weeps in the woods
(suffers! And when man, passing, pale, weeps in the solitary)

solitaire, des plaintes d'ombre et de mystère l'accueillent
solitary, some complaints of-darkness and of mystery him-welcome
(woods, cries of darkness and mystery welcome him)

en pleurant de même. Bonne forêt! promesse ouverte de l'exil que
in crying of same. Good forest! promise open of the-exile that
(by crying like him. Good forest! open promise of the exile that)

la vie implore, je viens d'un pas alerte encore dans ta profondeur
the life implores, I come of-a step alert still in your profundity
(life implores. I come with a step still alert into your still green)

encor verte. Mais d'un fin bouleau de la sente, une feuille,
still green. But of-a thin birch of the footpath, a leaf,
(profundity. But from a thin birch on the footpath, a leaf,)

un peu rousse, frôle ma tête et tremble à mon épaule;
a little reddish, grazes my head and trembles at my shoulder;
(a little reddish, grazes my head and trembles on my shoulder;)

c'est que la forêt vieillissante, sachant l'hiver,
it-is that the forest aging, knowing the-winter,
(it is the aging forest, knowing winter,)

où tout avorte, déjà proche en moi comme en elle,
where all aborts, already near in me as in it,
(when all comes to an end, already near in me as in it,)

me fait l'aumône fraternelle de sa première feuille morte!
me makes the-alms fraternal of its first leaf dead!
(gives me the fraternal alm of its first dead leaf!)

Dans les Ruines d'une Abbaye

In the Ruins of-an Abbey

Seuls, tous deux, ravis, chantants, comme on s'aime;
Alone, all two, ravished, singing, like one each-other-loves;
(Alone, together, delighted, singing, how we love each other;)

Comme on cueille le printemps que Dieu sème.
How one gathers the spring that God sows.
(How we gather the spring that God sows.)

Quels rires étincelants dans ces ombres jadis
What laughs sparkling in these shadows formerly
(What sparkling laughs in the shadows of yore)

pleines de fronts blancs de coeurs sombres.
full of faces white with hearts somber.
(Full of white faces with somber hearts.)

On est tout frais mariés; on s'envoie,
One is all fresh married; one to-each-other-sends,
(We are newly married; we send out,)

les charmants cris variés de la joie--
the charming cries varied of the joy--
(the charming varied cries of joy--)

frais échos mêlés au vent qui frissonne,
fresh echoes mixed to-the wind that shivers,
(fresh echoes mixed with the shivering wind,)

gaité que le noir couvent assaisonne.
gaity that the black convent seasons.
(cheerfulness that the black convent spices.)

On effeuille des jasmins sur la pierre où l'abbesse
One picks some jasmine on the stone where the-abbess
(We pick the jasmine on the stone where the abbess)

joint les mains en prière.
joins the hands in prayer.
(joins her hands in prayer.)

On se cherche, on se poursuit,
One each-other searches, one each-other pursues,
(We seek, chase each other,)

on sent croître ton aube, amour, dans la nuit du vieux cloître.
one feels to-grow your dawn, love, in the night of-the old cloister.
(we feel your dawn rising, love, in the night of the old cloister.)

On s'en va se becquetant, on s'adore;
One from-there goes each-other pecking, one each-other-adores;
(We go away, pecking at each other, adoring each other;)

on s'embrasse à chaque instant, puis encore.
one each-other-embraces at every instant, then again.
(we embrace each other at every instant, then again.)

Sous les piliers, les arceaux, et les marbres:
Under the pillars, the arches, and the marbles:
(Under the pillars, the arches, and the marbles:)

C'est l'histoire des oiseaux dans les arbres.
It-is the-story of-the birds in the trees.
(It is the story of birds in the trees.)

Fauré

En Prière

In Prayer

Si la voix d'un enfant peut monter jusqu'à vous,
If the voice of-a child can to-raise until-to you,
(If the voice of a child can rise to you,)

ô mon Père, écoutez de Jésus, devant Vous à genoux,
oh my Father, listen-to of Jesus, before You on knees,
(on my Father, listen to the prayer of Jesus, who kneels before you!)

la prière! Si Vous m'avez choisi pour enseigner
the prayer! If you me-have chosen for to-teach
(If you have chosen me to teach)

vos lois sur la terre, je saurai Vous servir,
your laws on the earth, I will-know You to-serve,
(your laws on earth, I will know how to serve you,)

auguste Roi des rois, ô lumière! Sur mes lèvres,
august King of-the kings, oh light! On my lips,
(august King of kings, oh light! On my lips,)

Seigneur, mettez la vérité Salutaire, pour que celui qui doute,
Lord, place the truth Salutary, so that he who doubts,
(Lord, place the wholesome truth, so that he who doubts,)

avec humilité Vous révère! Ne m'abondonnez pas,
with humility You reveres! Not me-abandon not,
(may honor you with humility! Do not abandon me,)

donnez-moi la douceur nécessaire, pour apaiser les maux,
give-me the mildness necessary, For to-appease the evils,
(give me the necessary mildness, to appease evil,)

soulager la douleur, la misère! Révelez-Vous à moi,
to-sooth the pain, the misery! Reveal You to me,
(to sooth pain, misery! Reveal yourself to me,)

Seigneur en qui je crois et j'espère:
Lord in whom I believe and I-hope:
(Lord in whom I believe and hope:)

Pour Vous je veux souffrir
For You I want to-suffer
(For you I want to suffer)

et mourir sur la croix, au calvaire!
and to-die on the cross, at-the Calvary!
(and die on the cross, at Calvary!)

Fauré

En Sourdine

Muted

Calmes dans le demi-jour Que les branches hautes font,
Calm in the half-day That the branches high make,
(Calm in the twilight That the high branches make,)

Pénétrons bien notre amour De ce silence profond.
Let-us-penetrate well our love Of this silence profound.
(Let us penetrate our love deeply With this profound silence.)

Fondons nos âmes, nos coeurs Et nos sens extasiés,
Let-us-melt our souls, our hearts And our senses ecstatic,
(Let us melt our souls, our hearts And our ecstatic senses,)

Parmi les vagues langueurs Des pins et des arbousiers.
Among the vague languors Of-the pines and of-the arbutus.
(Among the vague languors Of the pines and the arbutus.)

Ferme tes yeux à demi, Croise tes bras sur ton sein,
Close your eyes to half, Cross your arms on your breast,
(Half close your eyes, Cross your arms on your breast,)

Et de ton coeur endormi Chasse à jamais tout dessein.
And from your heart sleeping Chase to never all design.
(And from your sleeping heart Chase away all plans forever.)

Laissons-nous persuader Au souffle berceur et doux
Let-us-ourselves to-persuade To-the breeze cradling and soft
(Let us be persuaded by the cradling and soft breeze)

Qui vient à tes pieds rider Les ondes de gazon roux.
That comes to your feet to-ripple The waves of grass reddish.
(That comes to your feet to ripple The waves of reddish grass.)

Et quand, solennel, le soir Des chênes noirs tombera
And when, solemn, the evening Of-the oaks black will-fall
(And when, solemnly, the evening Of the black oaks falls)

Voix de notre désespoir, Le rossignol chantera.
Voice of our despair, The nightingale will-sing.
(Voice of our despair, The nightingale will sing.)

Fleur Jetée
Flower Thrown
(Thrown Flower)

Emporte ma folie au gré du vent,
Carry-away my folly to-the will of-the wind,
(Carry-away my folly at the will of the wind,)

fleur en chantant cueillie, et, jetée en rêvant,
flower in singing gathered, and, thrown in dreaming,
(flower gathered while singing, and, thrown away while dreaming,)

Comme la fleur fauchée, périt l'amour.
Like the flower cut, perishes the-love.
(Love perishes like the cut flower.)

La main qui t'a touchée fuit ma main sans retour.
The hand that you-has touched flees my hand without return.
(The hand that touched you flees from my hand forever.)

Que le vent qui te sèche, ô pauvre fleur,
That the wind that you dries, oh poor flower,
(Let the wind that dries you, oh poor flower,)

tout à l'heure si fraîche et demain sans couleur;
all at the-hour so fresh and tomorrow without color;
(recently so fresh and tomorrow without color;)

que le vent qui te sèche, ô pauvre fleur,
that the wind that you dries, o poor flower,
(let the wind that dries you, o poor flower,)

sèche mon coeur.
dry my heart.
(dry my heart.)

Fauré

Green

Green

Voici des fruits, des fleurs,
Here-are some fruits, some flowers,
(Here are fruits, flowers,)

des feuilles et des branches
some leaves and some branches
(leaves and branches)

Et puis voici mon coeur qui ne bat que pour vous.
And then here-is my heart, which not beats but for you.
(And then here is my heart, which beats only for you.)

Ne le déchirez pas avec vos deux mains blanches
Not it destroy not with your two hands white
(Do not destroy it with your two white hands)

Et qu'à vos yeux si beaux l'humble présent soit doux.
And that-to your eyes so beautiful the-humble gift be sweet.
(And to your eyes so beautiful may the humble gift be sweet.)

J'arrive tout couvert encore de rosée
I-arrive all covered still with dew
(I come still all covered with dew)

Que le vent du matin vient glacer à mon front.
Which the wind of-the morning comes to-chill at my brow.
(Which the morning wind has chilled on my brow.)

Souffrez que ma fatigue à vos pieds reposée
Suffer that my fatigue at your feet rested
(Allow my fatigue to rest at your feet)

Rêve des chers instants qui la délasseront.
Dream of-the dear instants which it will-repose.
(Dream of the precious moments which will bring it repose.)

Sur votre jeune sein laissez rouler ma tête
On your young breast let to-roll my head
(On your young breast let my head rest)

Toute sonore encor de vos derniers baisers;
All sonorous still from your last kisses;
(Still all sonorous from your last kisses;)

Laissez-la s'apaiser de la bonne tempête,
Let-it itself-calm from the good tempest,
(Let it rest from the good tempest,)

Et que je dorme un peu puisque vous reposez.
And may I sleep a little as you rest.
(And may I sleep a little as you rest.)

Fauré

Hymne

Hymn

A la très chère, à la très belle,
To the very dear, to the very beautiful.
(To the very dear and beautiful one,)

qui remplit mon coeur de clarté, à l'ange,
who refills my heart with clarity, to the-angel,
(who fills my heart with clarity, to the angel,)

à l'idole immortelle, salut en l'immortalité!
to the-idol immortal, hail in the-immortality!
(to the immortal idol, hail in immortality!)

Elle se répand dans ma vie comme un air imprégné de sel,
She herself spreads in my life like an air impregnated with salt,
(She fills my life like a salty wind,)

et dans mon âme inassouvie verse le goût de l'éternel.
and in my soul unsatisfied pours the taste of the-eternal.
(and in my unsatisfied soul pours the taste of the eternal.)

Comment, amour incorruptible, t'exprimer avec vérité?
How, love incorruptible, you-to-express with truth?
(How, incorruptible love, to express you truly?)

Grain de musc, qui gis, invisible au fond de mon éternité!
Grain of musk, which lies, invisible at-the depth of my eternity!
(Grain of fragrance, which lies, invisible at the depth of my eternity!)

Hymne à Apollon
Hymn to Apollo

O Muses de l'Hélicon aux bois profonds,
Oh Muses of the-Bombardon to-the woods deep,
(Oh Muses of the deep woods of the Bombardon,)

filles de Zeus retentissant, vierges aux bras glorieux:
daughters of Zeus resounding, virgins of-the arms glorious:
(daughters of resounding Zeus, virgins with glorious arms:)

venez par vos accents charmer le dieu Phébus,
come by your accents to-charm the god Phoebus,
(come to charm the god Phoebus with your expressions,)

votre frère à la chevelure d'or, le dieu
your brother to the hair of-gold, the god
(your brother with golden hair, the god)

qui sur les flancs de Parnasse, parmi les belles Delphines,
who on the flanks of Parnassus, among the beautiful Delphians,
(who on the sides of Parnassus, among the beautiful Delphians,)

sur la roche à double cime, monte vers le cristal pur
on the rock to two peaks, rises toward the crystal pure
(on the two-peaked rock, rises toward the pure crystal)

des eaux de Castalle, maître étincelant du mont
of-the water of Castalle, master sparkling of-the mountain
(of the water of Castalle, sparkling master of the mountain)

l'antre prophétique. Venez à nous, enfants d'Athènes,
the-lair prophetic. Come to us, children of-Athens,
(the prophetic lair. Come to us, children of Athens,)

dont la grande cité, grâce à Pallas, la déesse
whose the great city, grace to Pallas, the goddess
(whose great city, thanks to Pallas, the goddess)

au bras vainqueur, reçut un sol ferme, inviolable.
at-the arms victorious, received a ground firm, inviolable.
(with victorious arms, received firm ground, impregnable.)

Sur les autels brille la flamme,
On the altars burns the flame,
(On the altars burns the flame,)

qui des jeunes taureaux consume les chairs; vers
which of-the young bulls consumes the flesh; toward
(which consumes the flesh of young bulls; toward)

le ciel monte l'encens d'Arabie ... Le doux murmure
the heavens rises the-incense of-Arabia... The sweet murmur
heaven rises the incense of Arabia... The sweet murmur)

des flûtes sonne en chants modulés,
of-the flutes sounds in songs modulated,
of flutes sounds in pleasant songs,)

et la cithare d'or, la cithare aux doux sons,
and the zither of-gold, the zither to-the sweet sounds,
(and the golden zither, the sweet sounds of the zither)

répond aux voix qui chantent les hymnes ...
responds to-the voices that sing the hymns...
(answers the voices that sing the hymns....)

O pèlerins de l'Attique, chantez tous le dieu vainqueur!
Oh pilgrims from the-Attica, sing all the god victorious!
(Oh pilgrims from Attica, all sing the victorous god!)

Dieu dont la lyre est d'or, ô fils du grand Zeus!
God whose the lyre is of-gold, oh son of-the great Zeus!
(God whose lyre is golden, oh son of great Zeus!)

sur le sommet de ces monts neigeux.
on the summit of these mountains snowy.
(on the summit of those snowy mountains.)

Toi qui répands sur tous les mortels d'infaillibles,
You who spreads on all the mortals some-infallible,
(You who spreads on all mortals infallible,)

d'éternels oracles, je dirai comment tu conquis
some-eternals oracles, I will-tell how you conquered
(eternal oracles, I will tell how you conquered)

le trépied fatidique, gardé par le dragon.
the trivet fatidic, guarded by the dragon.
(the prophetic tripod, guarded by the dragon.)

Quand de tes traits tu mis en fuite l'affreux
When from your arrows you put in flight the-frightful
(When you put the frightful reptile with the monstrous coils)

reptile aux replis monstrueux. O muses,
reptile with-the coils monstrous. Oh muses,
(to flight with your arrows. Oh muses,)

formez le choeur autour du dieu prophète.
form the choir around of-the god prophet.
(form the choir around the prophetic god.)

Fauré

Ici-Bas

Here-Below

Ici-bas tous les lilas meurent,
Here-below all the lilacs die,
(Here below all the lilacs die,)

tous les chants des oiseaux sont courts.
all the songs of-the birds are short.
(all the songs of the birds are short.)

Je rêve aux étés qui demeurent toujours ...
I dream to-the summers which live always...
(I dream of the summers which always live...)

Ici-bas les lèvres effleurent
Here-below the lips lightly-touch
(Here below lips lightly touch)

sans rien laisser de leur velours;
without nothing to-leave of their velvets;
(without leaving any of their velvet;)

je rêve aux baisers qui demeurent Toujours ...
I dream to-the kisses which live Always...
(I dream of kisses which always live...)

Ici-bas tous les hommes pleurent leurs amitiés
Here-below all the men cry their friendships
(Here below all the people mourn their friendships

ou leurs amours; je rêve aux couples qui demeurent
or their loves; I dream to-the couples who live
(or their loves; I dream of couples who live)

Toujours...
Always...
(Always...)

Fauré
L'Absent
The-Absent-One

Sentiers où l'herbe se balance, vallons, côteaux,
Paths where the-grass itself sways, valleys, hills,
(Paths where the grass sways, valleys, hills,)

bois chevelus, pourquoi ce deuil et ce silence?
woods hairy, why this grieving and this silence?
(tufted woods, why this sorrow and this silence?)

"Celui qui venait ne vient plus!"
"The-one who came not comes more!"
("The one who came comes no more!")

Pourquoi personne à ta fenêtre?
Why no-one at your window?
(Why the empty window?)

Et pourquoi ton jardin sans fleurs?
And why your garden without flowers?
(And why this garden with no flowers?)

O maison, où donc est ton maître? "Je ne sais pas!
O house, where then is your master? "I not know not!
(O house, where then is your master? "I do not know!)

Il est ailleurs" Chien, veille au logis! "Pourquoi faire?
He is elsewhere" Dog, watch to-the house! "Why to-do?
(He is elsewhere" Dog, watch the house! "Why?)

La maison est vide à présent!" Enfant, qui pleures-tu?
The house is empty at present!" Child, who cry-you?
(The house is empty now!" Child, whom do you mourn?)

"Mon père!" Femme, qui pleures-tu? "L'absent!"
"My father!" Woman, who cry-you? "The-absent-one!"
("My father!" Woman, whom do you mourn? "The absent one!")

Où donc est-il allé? "Dans l'ombre!"
Where then is-he gone? "In the-shadows!"
(Where then has he gone? "Into the shadows!")

Flots qui gémissez sur l'écueil, d'où venez-vous?
Waves which groan on the-reef, from-where come-you?
(Waves which moan on the reef, where do you come from?)

"Du bagne sombre!" Et qu'apportez-vous? "Un cercueil!"
"From-the prison dark!" And what-bring-you? "A coffin"
("From the dark prison!" And what do you bring? "A coffin")

Larmes
Tears

Pleurons nos chagrins, chacun le nôtre.
Let-us-cry our sorrows, each the ours.
(Let us mourn our sorrows, each our own.)

Une larme tombe, puis une autre. Toi, que pleures-tu?
A tear falls, then an other. You, what cry-you?
(A tear falls, then another. You, what do you mourn?)

Ton doux pays, Tes parents lointains, ta fiancée.
Your sweet country, Your relatives far-away, your fiancée.
(Your gentle land, Your far-away relatives, your fiancée.)

Moi, mon existence dépensée En voeux trahis.
Me, my existence spent In vows betrayed.
(Me, my existence spent In vows betrayed.)

Semons dans la mer ces pâles fleurs.
Let-us-sow in the sea these pale flowers.
(Let us sow these pale flowers on the sea.)

A notre sanglot qui se lamente
To our sob who itself laments
(To our sob which laments)

Elle répondra par la tourmente Des flots hurleurs.
She will-answer by the tempest Of-the waves howling.
(She will answer with the storm Of the howling waves.)

Peut-être toi-même, ô triste mer,
Maybe yourself, o sad sea,
(Perhaps you yourself, o sad sea,)

Mer au goût de larme âcre et salée,
Sea to-the taste of tear acrid and salty,
(Sea with taste of bitter and salty tears,)

Es-tu de la terre inconsolée Le pleur amer?
Are-you of the earth unconsoled The tear bitter?
(Are you the bitter lament of the unconsoled earth?)

Fauré

L'Aurore

The-Dawn

L'aurore s'allume, L'ombre épaisse fuit;
The-dawn itself-lights, The-shadow thick flees;
(The dawn lights up, The thick shadows flee;)

Le rêve et la brume Vont où va la nuit;
The dream and the haze Go where goes the night;
(The dream and the haze Go where the night goes;)

Paupières et roses S'ouvrent demi-closes;
Eyelids and roses Themselves-open half-closed;
(Eyelids and roses open half-closed;)

Du réveil des choses On entend le bruit.
Of-the waking of-the things One hears the noise.
(One hears the noise of things waking.)

Tout chante et murmure, Tout parle à la fois,
All sings and murmurs, All speaks to the time,
(Everything sings and murmurs, Everything speaks together,)

Fumée et verdure, Les nids et les toits;
Smoke and verdure, The nests and the roofs;
(Smoke and verdure, The nests and roofs;)

Le vent parle aux chênes, L'eau parle aux fontaines;
The wind speaks to-the oaks, The-water speaks to-the fountains;
(The wind speaks to the oaks, The water speaks to the fountains;)

Toutes les haleines Deviennent des voix!
All the breaths Become some voices!
(All the breath Becomes voices!)

Tout reprend son âme, L'enfant son hochet,
All retakes its soul, The-child its rattle,
(Everything recovers its soul, The child its rattle,)

Le foyer sa flamme, Le luth son archet;
The fire its flame, The lute its bow;
(The fire its flame, The lute its bow;)

Folie ou démence, Dans le monde immense,
Folly or insanity, In the world immense,
(Folly or insanity, In the immense world,)

Chacun recommence Ce qu'il ébauchait.
Everyone rebegins That which-he sketched.
(Everyone begins again That which he had sketched.)

Fauré

L'Horizon Chimerique
The-Horizon Chimerical
(The Fantastic Horizon)

La Mer est Infinie
The sea is Infinite

La mer est infinie et mes rêves sont fous.
The sea is infinite and my dreams are insane.
(The sea is infinite and my dreams are insane.)

La mer chante au soleil en battant les falaises,
The sea sings to-the sun in beating the cliffs,
(The sea sings to the sun, beating the cliffs,)

et mes rêves légers ne se sentent plus d'aise
and my dreams light not themselves feel more of-ease
(and my light dreams no longer feel at ease)

de danser sur la mer comme des oiseaux soûls.
of to-dance on the sea like some birds drunk.
(dancing on the sea like drunken birds.)

Le vaste mouvement des vagues les emporte,
The vast movement of-the waves them carries-away,
(The vast movement of the waves carries them away.)

la brise les agite et les roule en ses plis;
the breeze them agitates and them rolls in its folds;
(the breeze agitates them and rolls them in its folds;)

jouant dans le sillage,
playing in the wake,
(playing in the wake,)

ils feront une escorte aux vaisseaux
they will-make an escort to-the ships
(they will escort the ships)

que mon coeur dans leur fuite a suivis.
that my heart in their flight has followed.
(that my heart has followed in their flight.)

Ivres d'air et de sel et brûlés par l'écume,
Drunk from-air and from salt and burned by the-foam,
(Drunk from air and from salt and burned by the foam,)

de la mer qui console et qui lave des pleurs,
of the sea which consoles and which washes some tears,
(of the sea which consoles and which washes away tears,)

ils connaîtront le large et sa bonne amertume;
they will-know the large and its good bitterness;
(they will know its vastness and its sweet bitterness;)

les goélands perdus les prendront pour des leurs.
the gulls lost them will-take for of-the theirs.
(the lost gulls will take them for their own.)

Fauré

L'Horizon Chimerique
The-Horizon Chimerical
(The Fantastic Horizon)

Je Me Suis Embarqué
I Myself Am Embarked
(I Have Embarked)

Je me suis embarqué sur un vaisseau qui danse
I myself am embarked on a ship that dances
(I have embarked on a ship that dances)

et roule bord sur bord et tangue et se balance.
and rolls side on side and pitches and itself balances.
(and rolls side to side and pitches and rocks.)

Mes pieds ont oublié la terre et ses chemins;
My feet have forgotten the earth and its paths;
(My feet have forgotten the earth and its paths;)

les vagues souples m'ont appris d'autres cadences
the waves supple me-have taught some-other cadences
(the supple waves have taught me other rhythms)

plus belles que le rythme las des chants humains.
more beautiful than the rhythm tired of-the songs human.
(more beautiful than the tired rhythm of human songs.)

A vivre parmi vous, hélas! avais-je une âme?
To to-live among you, alas! had-I a soul?
(Living among you, alas! did I have a soul?)

Mes frères, j'ai souffert sur tous vos continents.
My brothers, I-have suffered on all your continents.
(My brothers, I have suffered on all of your continents.)

Je ne veux que la mer,
I not wish but the sea,
(I wish nothing but the sea,)

je ne veux que le vent pour me bercer,
I not wich but the wind for me to-rock,
(I wish for nothing but the wind to rock me,)

comme un enfant, au creux des lames. Hors du port
like an infant, to-the hollow of-the waves. Beyond of-the port
(like a child, in the hollow of the waves. Beyond the port)

qui n'est plus qu'une image effacée, les larmes
which not-is more than-an image effaced, the tears
(which is no more than an blurred image, the tears)

du départ ne brûlent plus mes yeux. Je ne me souviens
of-the departure not burn more my eyes. I not myself remember
(of departure no longer burn my eyes. I do not remember)

pas de mes derniers adieux ... O ma peine, ma peine,
not of my last goodbyes ... Oh my pain, my pain,
(my last goodbyes ... Oh my pain, my pain)

où vous ai-je laissée?
where you have-I left?
(where did I leave you?)

Fauré

L'Horizon Chimerique
The-Horizon Chimerical
(The Fantastic Horizon)

Diane, Séléné
Diane, Séléné

Diane, Séléné, lune de beau métal, qui reflètes
Diane, Selene, moon of beautiful metal, who reflects
(Diane, Selene, moon of beautiful metal, who reflects)

vers nous, par ta face déserte,
toward us, by your face deserted,
(upon us, in your deserted face,)

dans l'immortel ennui du calme sidéral,
in the-immortal boredom of-the calm sidereal,
(in the immortal boredom of a sidereal calm,)

le regret d'un soleil dont nous pleurons la perte.
the regret of-a sun of-whom we cry the loss.
(regret for a sun whose loss we weep.)

O lune, je t'en veux de ta limpidité injurieuse
O moon, I you-of-it wish of your limpidity injurious
(O moon, I am angry at your limpidity injurious to the)

au trouble vain des pauvres âmes, et mon coeur,
to-the trouble vain of-the poor souls, and my heart,
(vain trouble of poor souls, and my heart,)

toujours las et toujours agité, aspire vers la paix
always tired and always agitated, aspires toward the peace
(always tired and always agitated, aspires toward the peace)

de ta nocturne flamme.
of your nocturnal flame.
(of your nocturnal flame.)

Fauré

L'Horizon Chimerique

The-Horizon Chimerical

(The Fantastic Horizon)

Vaisseaux, nous vous aurons aimés

Ships, we you will-have loved

(Ships, we will have loved you)

Vaisseaux, nous vous aurons aimés en pure perte;
Ships, we you will-have loved in pure loss;
(Ships, we will have loved you in vain;)

le dernier de vous tous est parti sur la mer.
the last of you all is left on the sea.
(the last of you has left for the sea.)

Le couchant emporta tant de voiles ouvertes
The setting-sun carried-away so-many of sails open
(The setting sun carried away so many open sails)

que ce port et mon coeur sont à jamais déserts.
that this port and my heart are to ever deserted.
(that this port and my heart are forever deserted.)

La mer vous a rendus à votre destinée,
The sea you has returned to your destiny,
(The sea has returned you to your destiny,)

au delà du rivage où s'arrêtent nos pas.
to-the beyond of-the bank where themselves arrest our steps.
(beyond the banks where our steps must stop.)

Nous ne pouvions garder vos âmes enchaînées;
We not could to-keep our souls enchained;
(We could not keep your souls enchained;)

Il vous faut des lointains que je ne connais pas.
It to-you is-necessary some far-aways that I not know not.
(You need far away places I do not know.)

Je suis de ceux dont les désirs sont sur la terre.
I am of those of-which the desires are on the earth.
(I am one of those whose desires are on earth.)

Le souffle qui vous grise emplit mon coeur d'effroi,
The wind that you intoxicates fills my heart of-fear,
(The wind that intoxicates you fills my heart with fear,)

mais votre appel, au fond des soirs, me désespère,
but your call, to-the deep of-the evenings, me despairs,
(but your call, in the deep of night, makes me despair,)

car j'ai de grands départs inassouvis en moi.
for I-have some great departures, unsatisfied in me.
(for I have great unsatisfied departures within me.)

Fauré
Lydia
Lydia

Lydia, sur tes roses joues,
Lydia, on your rosy cheeks,
(Lydia, on your rosy cheeks,)

et sur ton col frais et si blanc, roule,
and on your neck cool and so white, rolls,
(and on your neck cool and so white, rolls,)

étincelant l'or fluide que tu dénoues.
sparkling the-gold fluid that you untie.
(Sparkling the golden fluid that you untie.)

Le jour qui luit est le meilleur:
The day that shines is the best:
(The day that shines is the best:)

oublions l'éternelle tombe.
let-us-forget the-eternal tomb.
(let us forget the eternal tomb.)

Laisse tes baisers, tes baisers de colombe,
Let your kisses, your kisses of dove,
(Let your kisses, your dove-like kisses,)

chanter sur ta lèvre en fleur.
to-sing on your lip in flower.
(sing on your flowering lips.)

Un lys caché répand sans cesse
A lily hidden pours-out without cease
(A hidden lily unceasingly pours out)

une odeur divine en ton sein:
a scent divine in your breast:
(a divine scent on your breast:)

les délices, comme un essaim, sortent de toi, jeune déesse!
the delights, like a swarm, go-out from you, young goddess!
(delights, like a crowd, emerge from you, young goddess!)

Lydia
(cont.)

Je t'aime et meurs, ô mes amours!
I you-love and die, o my loves!
(I love you and die, o my love!)

Mon âme en baisers m'est ravie.
My soul in kisses me-is ravished.
(My soul is ravised from me by kisses.)

O Lydia, rends-moi la vie, que je puisse mourir toujours!
O Lydia, return-me the life, that I may to-die always!
(O Lydia, give back my life, that I may always die!)

Fauré

La Bonne Chanson

The Good Song

Une Sainte En Son Auréole

A Saint in her Aureole

(A Saint in her Halo)

Une Sainte en son auréole, Une Châtelaine en sa tour,
A Saint in her aureole, A Lady in her tower,
(A Saint in her halo, A Lady in her tower,)

tout ce que contient la parole humaine de grâce et d'amour;
all this that contains the word human of grace and of-love;
(all the grace and love that the human language contains;)

la note d'or que fait entendre le cor dans le lointain
the note of-gold that makes to-hear the horn in the distance
(the golden note made by the distant horn in the wood,)

des bois, mariée à la fierté tendre des nobles dames
of-the wood, married to the pride tender of-the noble ladies
(complied with the tender pride of noble ladies)

d'autrefois; avec cela le charme insigne d'un frais
of-othertimes; with that the charm distinguished of-a fresh
(of yesteryear; along with the distinguished charm of a fresh)

sourire triomphant éclos dans des candeurs de cygne
smile triumphant un-closed in some candors of swan
(triumphant smile opened in swan-like candor)

et des rougeurs de femme enfant; des aspects nacrés,
and some blushes of wife child; some aspects pearly,
(and the blushes of a child-bride; pearly,)

blancs et roses, un doux accord patricien: Je vois,
white and rose, a sweet accord patrician: I see,
(white and pink aspects, a sweet patrician accord: I see,)

j'entends toutes ces choses dans son nom Carlovingien.
I-hear all these things in her name Carlovingian.
(I hear all these things in her Carlovingian name.)

Fauré

La Bonne Chanson

The Good Song

Puisque L'Aube Grandit

Since the-dawn grows

Puisque l'aube grandit, puisque voici l'aurore,
Since the-dawn grows, since here-is the-dawn,
(Since the dawn is growing, since sunrise is here,)

puisque après m'avoir fui longtemps,
since after me-to-have fled longtime,
(since having fled me for so long,)

l'espoir veut bien revoler devers moi qui
the-hope wishes well to-re-fly toward me who
(hope will has flown back to me who)

l'appelle et l'implore, puisque tout ce bonheur
it-calls and it-implores, since all this happiness
(calls and implores it, since all this happiness)

veut bien être le mien, je veux, guidé par vous,
wants well to-be the mine, I wish, guided by you,
(wishes to be mine, I wish, guided by you,)

beaux yeux aux flammes douces, par toi conduit,
beautiful eyes to-the flames sweet, by you conducted,
(beautiful eyes with sweet flames, led by you)

ô main où tremblera ma main, marcher droit,
oh hand where will-tremble my hand, to-walk straight,
(oh hand in which my hand will tremble, to walk straight,)

que ce soit par des sentiers de mousse
that this be by some paths of moss
(be it on mossy paths)

ou que rocs et cailloux encombrent le chemin:
or that rocks and pebbles encumber the way:
(or where rocks and pebbles encumber the way:)

et comme, pour bercer les lenteurs de la route,
and as, for to-rock the slowness of the route,
(and since, to rock the slowness of the route,)

je chanterai des airs ingénus, je me dis qu'elle
I will-sing some songs ingenuous, I to-me say that-she
(I will sing some ingenuous songs, I tell myself that she)

m'écoutera san déplaisir sans doute:
me-will-listen without displeasure without doubt:
(will undoubtedly listen to me without displeasure:)

et vraiment je ne veux pas d'autre Paradis.
and truly I not wish not of-other Paradise.
(and truly I wish for no other Paradise.)

Fauré

La Bonne Chanson
The Good Song

La Lune Blanche
The Moon White
(The White Moon)

La lune blanche luit dans les bois;
The moon white shines in the woods;
(The white moon shines in the woods;)

de chaque branche part une voix sous la ramée ...
from every branch leaves a voice under the bough...
(from every branch sings a voice under the bough...)

ô bien aimée. L'étang reflète, profond miroir,
oh well loved. The-pond reflects, deep mirror,
(oh beloved. The pond reflects, deep mirror,)

la silhouette du saule noir où le vent pleure ...
the silhouette of-the willow black where the wind cries...
(the silhouette of the black willow where the wind weeps...)

Rêvons; c'est l'heure.
Let-us-dream; it-is the-hour.
(Let us dream; it is the hour.)

Un vaste et tendre apaisement semble descendre
A vast and tender appeasement seems to-descend
(A vast and tender appeasement seems to descend)

du firmament que l'astre irise ...
from-the firmament that the-star illuminates...
(from the firmament that the star colors...)

C'est l'heure exquise.
It-is the-hour exquisite.
(It is the exquisite hour.)

La Bonne Chanson
The Good Song

J'Allais Par Des Chemins Perfides
I-was-going On Some Paths Perfidious
(I went on some Treacherous Paths)

J'allais par des chemins perfides, douloureusement incertain.
I-was-going on some paths perfidious sorrowfully uncertain.
(I was following some treacherous paths, sorrowfully uncertain.)

Vos chères mains furent mes guides.
Your dear hands were my guides.
(Your dear hands were my guides.)

Si pâle à l'horizon lointain luisait
So pale to the-horizon distant shone
(So pale on the distant horizon shone)

un faible espoir d'aurore:
a feeble hope of-dawn:
(a weak hope of dawn:)

votre regard fut le matin.
your glance was the morning.
(your glance was the morning.)

Nul bruit, sinon son pas sonore,
Not-a noise, if-not his step resonant,
(No noise, except his resonant step,)

n'encourageait le voyageur.
not-encouraged the voyager.
(encouraged the traveler.)

Votre voix me dit:
Your voice me said:
(Your voice told me:)

"Marche encore!" Mon coeur craintif,
"Walk still!" My heart fearful,
("Keep walking!" My fearful heart,)

mon sombre coeur pleurait, seul,
my dark heart cried, alone,
(my gloomy heart wept, alone.)

sur la triste voie;
on the sad way;
(on the sad way;)

l'amour, délicieux vainqueur,
the-love, delicious victor,
(love, delicious victor,)

nous a réunis dans la joie.
us has reunited in the joy.
(has reunited us in joy.)

Fauré
La Bonne Chanson
The Good Song

J'ai presque peur en vérité
I-have almost fear, in truth
(I am almost scared, truthfully)

J'ai presque peur, en vérité,
I-have almost fear, in truth,
(I am almost scared, truthfully,)

tant je sens ma vie enlacée à la
so-much I sense my life enlaced to the
(so much I feel my life entwined with the)

radieuse pensée qui m'a pris l'âme l'autre été,
radiant thought that me-has taken the-soul the-other summer,
(radiant thought that seized my soul the other summer,)

tant votre image, à jamais chère habite
so-much your image, to never dear lives
(so much your image, forever dear lives)

en ce coeur tout à vous,
in this heart all to you,
(in this heart which is all yours,)

ce coeur uniquement jaloux de vous aimer
this heart uniquely jealous of you to-love
(this heart desirous only of loving you)

et de vous plaire; et je tremble,
and of you to-please; and I tremble,
(and pleasing you; and I tremble,)

pardonnez-moi d'aussi franchement vous le dire,
pardon-me of-also frankly you it to-say,
(pardon me for so frankly telling you,)

à penser qu'un mot, qu'un sourire
to to-think that-a word, that-a smile
(to think that a word, a smile)

de vous est désormais ma loi,
from you is henceforth my law,
(from you is henceforth my law)

et qu'il vous suffirait d'un geste,
and that-it you would-suffice of-a gesture,
(and that a gesture from you would suffice,)

d'une parole ou d'un clin d'oeil
of-a word or of-a wink of-eye
(a word or a wink would suffice)

pour mettre tout mon être en deuil
for to-put all my being in mourning
(to throw all my being in grief)

de son illusion céleste.
from its illusion celestial.
(from its heavenly illusion.)

Mais plutôt je ne veux vous voir,
But rather I not want you to-see,
(But rather I want to see you,)

l'avenir dût-il m'être sombre et fécond
the-future should-it me-to-be somber and abundant
(even though the future be somber and abundant)

en peines sans nombre,
in pains without number,
(in numberless pains,)

qu'à travers un immense espoir,
only-to traverse an immense hope,
(only through my immense hope,)

plongé dans ce bonheur suprême
plunged in this happiness supreme
(plunged in this supreme happiness)

de me dire encore et toujours en dépit
of myself to-say still and always in spite
(of telling myself again and always, in spite)

des mornes retours que je vous aime,
of-the mournful returns that I thee love,
(of mournful returns, that I love thee,)

que je t'aime!
that I you-love!
(that I love you!)

Fauré

La Bonne Chanson

The Good Song

Avant que tu ne t'en ailles

Before that you not you-from-it go

(Before you go)

Avant que tu ne t'en ailles, pâle étoile du matin,
Before that you not you-from-here go, pale star of-the morning,
(Before you go away, pale morning star,)

Mille cailles chantent dans le thym.
A-thousand quails sing in the thyme.
(A thousand quails sing in the thyme.)

Tourne devers le poète, dont les yeux sont pleins d'amour,
Turn toward the poet, whose the eyes are full of-love,
(Turn toward the poet, whose eyes are full of love,)

L'alouette monte au ciel avec le jour.
The-lark mounts to-the sky with the day.
(The lark ascends to the sky with the day.)

Tourne ton regard que noie l'aurore dans son azur;
Turn your glance that drowns the-dawn in its azure;
(Turn your glance drowned by the dawn in its azure;)

Quelle joie parmi les champs de blé mûr!
What joy among the fields of wheat ripe!
(What joy among the fields of ripe wheat!)

Et fais luire ma pensée là-bas:
And make to-shine my thought down-there:
(And make my thought shine over there:)

bien loin; oh, bien loin,
well far; oh, well far,
(far away; oh, far away,)

La rosée, gaîment brille sur le foin.
The dew, gayly shines on the hay.
(The dew, cheerfully shines on the hay.)

Dans le doux rêve où s'agite ma mie endormie encor
In the sweet dream where herself-agitates my love sleeping still
(In the sweet dream where my still-sleeping love stirs)

Vite, vite, car voici le soleil d'or!
Quickly, quickly, for here-is the sun of-gold!
(Quickly, quickly, because the golden sun is here!)

Fauré

La Bonne Chanson

The Good Song

Donc, ce sera par un clair jour d'été

Thus, this will-be by a bright day of-summer

Donc, ce sera par un clair jour d'été:
Thus, this will-be by a clear day of-summer:
(Thus it will be on a clear summer day:)

Le grand soleil, complice de ma joie, fera,
The great sun, accomplice of my joy, will-make,
(The great sun, accessory to my joy, will cause,)

parmi le satin et la soie, plus belle
among the satin and the silk, more beautiful
(amidst the silk and satin, your beauty)

encor votre chère beauté; le ciel tout bleu,
still your dear beauty; the heaven all blue,
(to become even more beautiful; the blue sky,)

comme une haute tente frissonnera somptueux à longs plis
like a high tent will-shiver sumptuous to long folds
(like a high tent will shiver sumptuously in long folds)

sur nos deux fronts heureux
on our two faces happy
(on our two happy faces)

qu'auront pâlis l'émotion du bonheur et l'attente;
that-will-have paled the-emotion of-the happiness and the-waiting;
(that the emotion of happiness and waiting will have paled;)

et quand le soir viendra,
and when the evening will-come,
(and when the evening comes,)

l'air sera doux qui se jouera,
the-air will-be gentle that itself will-play,
(the air will be gentle as it plays,)

caressant, dans vos voiles,
caressing, in your veils,
(caressing, in your veils,)

et les regards paisibles des étoiles
and the glances peaceful of-the stars
(and the peaceful glances of the stars)

bienveillamment souriront aux epoux.
benevolently will-smile to-the spouses.
(will smile benevolently on the couple.)

Fauré

La Bonne Chanson

The Good Song

N'est-ce Pas?

Not-is-it Not?

(Isn't It?)

N'est-ce pas? nous irons, gais et lents,
Not-is-it not? we shall-go, gay and slow,
(Isn't it so? we will go, happy and slow,)

dans la voie modeste que nous montre en souriant
in the path modest that to-us shows in smiling
(along the modest path smilingly shown to us by)

l'Espoir, peu soucieux qu'on nous ignore
the-Hope, little anxious that-one us ignores
(Hope, not caring whether anyone knows us)

ou qu'on nous voie. Isolés dans l'amour ainsi
or that-one us sees. Isolated in the-love like
(or sees us. As isolated in love)

qu'en un bois noir, nos deux coeurs, exhalant
that-in a wood black, our two hearts, exhaling
(as in a black wood, our two hearts, breathing)

leur tendresse paisible, seront deux rossignols
their tenderness peaceful, will-be two nightingales
(their peaceful tenderness, will be two nightingales)

qui chantent dans le soir. Sans nous préoccuper
who sing in the evening. Without ourselves to-preoccupy
(who sing in the evening. Without worrying about)

de ce que nous destine le Sort, nous marcherons
of that which us destines the Fate, we will-walk
(what Fate destines for us, we will walk)

pourtant du même pas, et la main dans la main,
nevertheless of-the same step, and the hand in the hand,
(nevertheless in step, and hand in hand,)

avec l'âme enfantine de ceux
with the-soul child-like of those
with the child-like soul of those)

qui s'aiment sans mélange,
who each-other-love without mix,
(who love each other purely,)

n'est-ce pas?
not-is-it-not?
(isn't it so?)

Fauré

La Bonne Chanson

The Good Song

L'Hiver a cessé

The-Winter has ceased

(Winter has ended)

L'hiver a cessé: la lumière est tiède,
The-winter has ceased: the light is tepid,
(Winter has ended: the light is warm,)

et danse, du sol au firmament clair.
and dances, from-the ground to-the firmament bright.
(and dances, from the ground to the bright firmament.)

Il faut que le coeur le plus triste
It is-necessary that the heart the most sad
(The saddest heart must)

cède à l'immense joie éparse dans l'air.
cede to the-immense joy sparse in the-air.
(yield to the immense joy scattered in the air.)

J'ai depuis un an le printemps dans l'âme
I-have since a year the spring in the-soul
(For a year I have had spring in my soul)

et le vert retour du doux floréal;
and the green return of-the sweet floreal;
(and the green return of the sweet floreal;)

ainsi qu'une flamme entoure une flamme,
thus that-a flame surrounds a flame,
(as a flame surrounds a flame,)

met de l'idéal sur mon idéal. Le ciel bleu prolonge,
place of the-ideal on my ideal. The heaven blue prolongs,
(place ideal on my ideal. The blue heaven lengthens,)

exhausse et couronne l'immuable azur où rit mon amour.
raises and crowns the-immutable azure where laughs my love.
(raises and crowns the unchangeable azure where my love laughs.)

L'Hiver a cessé
(cont.)

La saison est belle et ma part est bonne
The season is beautiful and my part is good
(The season is beautiful and my part is good)

et tous mes espoirs ont enfin leur tour.
and all my hopes have at-last their turn.
(and all my hopes have their turn at last.)

Que vienne l'été! que viennent encore l'automne
That come the-summer! that come still the-autumn
(Let summer come! let come again autumn)

et l'hiver! Et chaque saison me sera charmante,
and the-winter! And each season to-me will-be charming,
(and winter! And each season will be charming to me,)

ô toi qui décore cette fantasie et cette raison!
oh you who decorates this fantasy and this reason!
(oh you who this fantasy and reason decorates!)

Fauré
La Chanson d'Eve
The Song of-Eve

Paradis
Paradise

C'est le premier matin du monde.
It-is the first morning of-the world.
(It's the first morning of the world.)

Comme une fleur confuse exhalée de la nuit,
Like a flower confused exhaled from the night,
(Like a confused flower exhaled from the night,)

Au souffle nouveau qui se lève des ondes,
To-the breath new that itself rises from-the waves,
(With the new breath that rises from the waves,)

Un jardin bleu s'épanouit.
A garden blue itself-blooms.
(A blue garden blooms.)

Tout s'y confond encore et tout s'y mêle,
All itself-there mingles still and all itself-there blends,
(All still mingles and all blends there,)

Frissons de feuilles, chants d'oiseaux, Glissements d'ailes,
Shivers of leaves, songs of-birds, Glidings of-wings,
(Shivers of leaves, bird songs, Glidings of wings,)

Sources qui sourdent, voix des airs, voix des eaux,
Springs that rumble, voices of-the airs, voices of-the waters,
(Springs that rumble, voices of the air, voices of the water,)

Murmure immense; Et qui pourtant est du silence.
Murmur immense; And which nevertheless is of-the silence.
(Immense murmur; And which is nevertheless silent.)

Ouvrant à la clarté ses doux et vagues yeux,
Opening to the light his sweet and vague eyes,
(Opening to the light its sweet and faint eyes,)

La jeune et divine Eve S'est éveillée de Dieu.
The young and divine Eve Herself-is awakened by God.
(The young and divine Eve is awakened by God.)

Et le monde à ses pieds s'étend comme un beau rêve.
And the world at her feet itself-extends like a beautiful dream.
(And the world at her feet stretches out like a beautiful dream)

Or Dieu lui dit: Va, fille humaine,
Now God to-her said: Go, daughter human,
(Now God said to her: Go, human daughter,)

Et donne à tous les êtres
And give to all the beings
(And give to all the beings)

Que j'ai créés, une parole de tes lèvres, Un son
That I-have created, a word from your lips, A sound
(That I have created, a word from your lips, A sound)

pour les connaître.
for them to-know.
(by which to know them.)

Et Eve s'en alla, docile à son seigneur,
And Eve herself-from-there went, docile to her Lord,
(And Eve went, docile to her Lord,)

En son bosquet de roses,
In her grove of roses,
Into her grove of roses,)

Donnant à toutes choses Une parole, un son
Giving to all things A word, a sound
(Giving to all things A word, a sound)

de ses lèvres de fleur:
of her lips of flower:
(from her flowering lips:)

(cont.)

Chose qui fuit, chose qui souffle, chose qui vole...
Thing that runs, thing that breathes, thing that flies...
(Things that run, thing that breathe, things that fly...)

Cependant le jour passe, et vague, comme à l'aube,
Meanwhile the day passes, and vague, like at the-dawn,
(Meanwhile the day passes, and faint, as at dawn,)

Au crépuscule, peu à peu, L'Eden s'endort et se dérobe
At-the twilight, little by little, The-Eden itself-sleeps and itself steals
(At twilight, little by little, Eden falls asleep and steals)

Dans le silence d'un songe bleu.
In the silence of-a dream blue.
(Into the silence of a blue dream.)

La voix s'est tue, mais tout l'écoute encore,
The voice itself-is silenced, but all it-listen-for still,
(The voice is silent, but all listen for it still,)

Tout demeure en attente;
Everything lies in waiting;
(Everything lies in expectation;)

Lorsque avec le lever de l'étoile du soir, Eve chante.
When with the rising of the-star of-the evening, Eve sings.
(When with the rising of the evening star, Eve sings.)

Fauré

La Chanson d'Eve
The Song of-Eve

Prima Verba
First Word

Comme elle chante Dans ma voix, L'âme longtemps murmurante
How she sings In my voice, The-soul long-time murmuring
(How it sings in my voice, The long-murmuring soul)

Des fontaines et des bois! Air limpide du paradis,
Of-the fountains and of-the woods! Air limpid of-the paradise,
(Of the fountains and woods! Limpid air of paradise,)

Avec tes grappes de rubis, Avec tes gerbes de lumière,
With your clusters of ruby, With your sheaves of light,
(With your ruby clusters, With your sheaves of light,)

Avec tes roses et tes fruits;
With your roses and your fruits;
(With your roses and your fruits;)

Quelle merveille en nous à cette heure!
What marvel in us at this hour!
(What a marvel within us at this hour!)

Des paroles depuis des âges endormies
Some words since some ages asleep
(Words asleep for ages)

En des sons, en des fleurs,
In some sounds, in some flowers,
(In sounds, in flowers,)

Sur mes lèvres enfin prennent vie.
On my lips at-last take life.
(On my lips at last come to life.)

Depuis que mon souffle a dit leur chanson,
Since that my breath has said their song,
(Since my breath sang their song,)

Depuis que ma voix les a créees,
Since that my voice them has created,
(Since my voice created them,)

Quel silence heureux et profond
What silence happy and profound
(What happy and profound silence,)

Naît de leurs âmes allégées!
Is-born of their souls made-light!
(Is born in their relieved souls!)

Fauré

La Chanson d'Eve
The Song of-Eve

Roses Ardentes
Roses Ardent
(Ardent Roses)

Roses ardentes Dans l'immobile nuit,
Roses ardent In the-immoble night,
(Ardent roses In the motionless night,)

C'est en vous que je chante, Et que je suis.
It-is in you that I sing, And that I am.
(It is through you that I sing, And that I exist.)

En vous, étincelles, A la cime des bois,
In you, sparkles, at the peak of-the wood,
(Through you, sparkles, at the top of the woods,)

Que je suis éternelle, Et que je vois.
That I am eternal, And that I see.
(That I am eternal, And that I see.)

O mer profonde, C'est en toi que mon sang Renaît vague blonde,
O sea deep, It-is in you that my blood is-reborn wave blond,
(O deep sea, it is through you that my blood is reborn, blond wave,)

Et flot dansant. Et c'est en toi, force suprême,
And float dancing. And it-is in you, force supreme,
(And dancing billow. And it is in you, supreme force,)

Soleil radieux, Que mon âme elle-même Atteint son dieu!
Sun radiant, That my soul itself Attains its god!
(Radiant sun, That my soul itself Attains its god!)

Fauré

La Chanson d'Eve

The Song of-Eve

Comme Dieu Rayonne

How God Shines

Comme Dieu rayonne aujourd'hui, Comme il exulte,
How God shines today, How he exults,
(How God shines today, How he exults,)

comme il fleurit. Parmi ces roses et ces fruits!
how he flowers. Among these roses and these fruits!
(how he flowers. Among these roses and fruits!)

Comme il murmure en cette fontaine!
How he murmurs in this fountain!
(How he murmurs in this fountain!)

Ah! comme il chante en ces oiseaux...
Ah! how he sings in these birds...
(Ah! how he sings in these birds...)

Qu'elle est suave son haleine
How-it is sweet his breath
(How sweet his breath is)

Dans l'odorant printemps nouveau!
In the-odorous spring new!
(In the scented new spring!)

Comme il se baigne dans la lumière Avec amour, mon jeune dieu!
How he himself bathes in the light With love, my young god!
(How he bathes himself in the light With love, my young god!)

Toutes les choses de la terre
All the things of the earth
(All the things of the earth)

Sont ses vêtements radieux.
Are his garments radiant.
(Are his radiant garments.)

La Chanson d'Eve
The Song of-Eve

L'Aube Blanche
The-Dawn White

L'aube blanche dit à mon rêve:
The-dawn white says to my dream:
(The white dawn says to my dream:)

Éveille-toi, le soleil luit.
Awake-yourself, the sun shines.
(Wake up, the sun is shining.)

Mon âme écoute, et je soulève
My soul listens, and I lift-up
(My soul hears, and I open)

Un peu mes paupières vers lui. Un rayon de lumière touche
A little my eyelids toward him. A ray of light touches
(My eyes a little toward him. A ray of light touches)

La pâle fleur de mes yeux bleus;
The pale flower of my eyes blue;
(The pale flower of my blue eyes;)

Une flamme éveille ma bouche, Un souffle éveille mes cheveux.
A flame awakens my mouth, A breath awakens my hairs.
(A flame awakens my mouth, A breath awakens my hair.)

Et mon âme, comme une rose
And my soul, like a rose
(And my soul, like a rose)

Tremblante, lente, tout le jour,
Trembling, slow, all the day,
(Trembling, slowly, all day long,)

S'éveille à la beauté des choses, Comme mon coeur à leur amour.
Itself-awakens to the beauty of things, Like my heart to their love.
(Awakens to the beauty of things, Like my heart to their love.)

La Chanson d'Eve
The Song of-Eve

Eau Vivante
Water Living
(Lively Water)

Que tu es simple et claire, Eau vivante, Qui,
How you are simple and bright, Water living, Which,
(How simple and bright you are, Lively water, Which,)

du sein de la terre, Jaillis en ces bassins et chantes!
from-the breast of the earth, Gushes in these basins and sings!
(from the heart of the earth, Gushes in these ponds and sings!)

O fontaine divine et pure, Les plantes aspirent
O fountain divine and pure, The plants inhale
(O fountains divine and pure, The plants inhale)

Ta liquide clarté; La biche et la colombe en toi se désaltèrent.
Your liquid clarity; The doe and the dove in you themselves quench.
(Your liquid clarity; In you doe and dove quench their thirst.)

Et tu descends par des pentes douces
And you descend by the slopes gentle
(And you flow down from the gentle slopes)

De fleurs et de mousses, Vers l'océan originel,
Of flowers and of mosses, Toward the-ocean original,
(Of flowers and mosses, Toward the ocean of your origin,)

Toi qui passes et vas, sans cesse, et jamais lasse
You who passes and goes, without cease, and never weary
(You who passes and goes, ceaselessly, never weary)

De la terre à la mer et de la mer au ciel.
From the earth to the sea and from the sea to-the heaven.
(From earth to sea and from sea to heavens.)

La Chanson d'Eve
The Song of-Eve

Veilles-Tu, Ma Senteur de Soleil
Watch-you, My Smell of Sun
(Are you keeping watch, my sunny smell)

Veilles-tu, ma senteur de soleil,
Watch-you, my smell of sun,
(Are you keeping watch, my sunny smell,)

Mon arôme d'abeilles blondes,
My aroma of-bees blond,
(My aroma of blond bees,)

Flottes-tu sur le monde,
Float-you on the world,
(Do you float in the world,)

Mon doux parfum de miel?
My sweet perfume of honey?
(My sweet honeyed perfume?)

La nuit, lorsque mes pas Dans le silence rôdent,
The night, when my steps In the silence prowl,
(At night, when my steps prowl about the silence,)

M'annonces-tu, senteur de mes lilas,
Me-announce-you, smell of my lilacs,
(Do you announce me, lilac smell,)

Et de mes roses chaudes?
And of my roses warm?
(And smell of roses?)

Suis-je comme une grappe de fruits Cachés dans les feuilles,
Am-I like a cluster of fruits Hidden in the leaves,
(Am I like a cluster of fruits hidden in the leaves,)

Et que rien ne décèle, Mais qu'on odore dans la nuit?
And that nothing not reveals, But that-one smells in the night?
(Which nothing reveals, but is smelled in the night?)

Sait-il, à cette heure, Que j'entr'ouvre ma chevelure,
Knows-he, at this hour, that I-half-open my tresses,
(Does he know, at this hour, that I let down my tresses,)

Et qu'elle respire; Le sent-il sur la terre?
And that-she breathes; It feels-he on the earth?
(And that it breathes; Does he smell it on earth?)

Sent-il que j'étends les bras,
Feel-he that I-stretch-out the arms,
(Does he feel that I stretch out my arms,)

Et que des lys de mes vallées
And that of-the lilies of my valleys
(And that the lilies of my valleys--)

Ma voix qu'il n'entend pas Est embaumée?
My voice that-he not-hears not Is perfurmed?
(Perfume my voice that he does not hear?)

Fauré

La Chanson d'Eve

The Song of-Eve

Dans un Parfum de Roses Blanches

In a Perfume of Roses White

Dans un parfum de roses blanches
In a perfume of roses white
(In the perfume of white roses)

Elle est assise et songe;
She is sitting and dreams;
(She sits and dreams;)

Et l'ombre est belle
And the-shade is beautiful
(And the shade is beautiful)

comme s'il s'y mirait un ange.
like if-it itself-there mirrored an angel.
(as if it reflected an angel.)

Le soir descend, le bosquet dort;
The evening descends, the grove sleeps;
(Evening falls, the grove sleeps;)

Entre ses feuilles et ses branches,
Between its leaves and its branches,
(Between its leaves and its branches,)

Sur le paradis bleu s'ouvre un paradis d'or.
On the paradise blue itself-opens a paradise of-gold.
(A golden paradise opens onto the blue paradise.)

Sur le rivage expire un dernier flot lointain.
On the shore expires a last wave far-away.
(A final, faraway wave expires on the shore.)

Une voix qui chantait, tout à l'heure, murmure.
A voice that sang, all to the-hour, murmurs.
(A voice that sang, just now, murmurs.)

Un murmure s'exhale en haleine, et s'éteint.
A murmur itself-exhales in breath, and itself-extiguishes.
(A murmur exhales in a breath, and dies.)

Dans le silence il tombe des pétales....
In the silence it falls some petals....
(In the silence there fall some petals....)

La Chanson d'Eve
The Song of-Eve

Le Crépuscule
The Twilight

Ce soir, à travers le bonheur, Qui donc soupire,
This evening, to across the goodness, Who then sighs,
(This evening, amidst the happiness, Who then sighs,)

qu'est-ce qui pleure? Qu'est-ce qui vient palpiter
what-is-this that weeps? What-is-this which comes to-palpitate
(what is this that weeps? What is this which comes beating?)

sur mon coeur, Comme un oiseau blessé?
on my heart, Like a bird wounded?
(on my heart, Like a wounded bird?)

Est-ce une plainte de la terre, Est-ce une voix future,
Is-this a complaint from the earth, Is-this a voice future,
(Is it a complaint from the earth, Is it a voice from the future,)

Une voix du passé? J'écoute, jusqu'à la souffrance,
A voice from-the past? I-listen, until the suffering,
(A voice from the past? I listen, to the point of suffering,)

Ce son dans le silence. Ile d'oubli, ô Paradis!
This sound in the silence. Isle of-oblivion, O Paradise!
(To the sound of silence. Isle of forgetfulness, O Paradise!)

Quel cri déchire, cette nuit, Ta voix qui me berce?
What cry tears, this night, Your voice which me cradles?
(What cry rips, tonight, Your voice which cradles me?)

Quel cri traverse Ta ceinture de fleurs,
What cry traverses Your sash of flowers,
(What cry cuts through Your sash of flowers,)

Et ton beau voile d'allégresse?
And your beautiful veil of-cheerfulness?
(And your beautiful veil of brightness?)

Fauré
La Chanson d'Eve
The Song of-Eve

O Mort, Poussiere d'Etoiles
O Death, Dust of-Stars
(O Death, Stardust)

O mort, poussière d'étoiles, Lève-toi sous mes pas!
O death, dust of-stars, Rise-you under my steps!
(O death, stardust, rise up under my steps!)

Viens, ô douce vague qui brille Dans les ténèbres;
Come, o sweet wave that shines In the darknesses;
(Come, o sweet wave that shines in the darkness;)

Emporte-moi dans ton néant! Viens, souffle sombre où je vacille,
Carry-me in your nothingness! Come, sigh sombre where I vacillate,
(Carry me into your emptiness! Come sombre breath in which I wavver,)

Comme une flamme ivre de vent! C'est en toi
Like a flame drunk from wind! It-is in you
(Like a flame drunk on the wind! In you)

que je veux m'étendre,
that I wish myself-to-stretch-out,
(I wish to lie down,)

M'éteindre et me dissoudre,
Myself-to-extinguish and myself to-dissolve,
(To extend myself and to dissolve,)

Mort, où mon âme aspire!
Death, where my soul aspires!
(Death, to which my soul aspires!)

Viens, brise-moi comme une fleur d'écume,
Come, break-me like a flower of-foam,
(Come, break me like a blossom of foam,)

Une fleur de soleil à la cime Des eaux,
A flower of sun at the top Of-the waters,
(A burst of sun on the crest of the water,)

Et comme d'une amphore d'or Un vin de flamme
And like of-an Amphora of-gold A wine of flame
(And as if from an Amphora of gold A wine of flame)

et d'arome divin,
and of-aroma divine,
(and divine aroma,)

Epanche mon âme En ton abîme, pour qu'elle embaume
Pour-out my soul In your abyss, for that-it perfumes
(Pour out my soul into your abyss, so that it may perfume)

La terre sombre et le souffle des morts.
The earth sombre and the breath of-the dead.
(The sombre earth and the breath of the dead.)

Fauré

La Chanson du Pêcheur

The Song of-the Fisherman

Ma belle amie est morte: je pleurerai toujours;
My beautiful love is dead: I will-cry always;
(My beautiful love is dead: I will always cry;)

sous la tombe elle emporte mon âme et mes amours.
under the tomb she carries-away my soul and my loves.
(into the tomb she carries away my soul and my love.)

Dans le ciel, sans m'attendre, elle s'en retourna;
In the heaven, without me-to-wait-for, she herself-of-there returned;
(To heaven, without waiting for me, she returned;)

l'ange qui l'emmena ne voulut pas me prendre.
the-angel who her-took-away not wanted not me to-take.
(the angel who took her away did not want to take me.)

Que mon sort est amer!
How my fate is bitter!
(How bitter is my fate!)

Ah! sans amour, s'en aller sur la mer!
Ah! without love, one's-self-from-there to-go on the sea!
(Ah! without love, to go away to the sea!)

La blanche créature est couchée au cercueil.
The white creature is laid to-the coffin.
(The white creature is laid out in the coffin.)

Comme dans la nature tout me paraît en deuil!
How in the nature all me seems in mourning!
(How everything in nature seems to mourn!)

La colombe oubliée pleure et songe à l'absent;
The dove forgotten weeps and dreams of the-absent-one;
(The forgotten dove weeps and dreams of the absent one;)

mon âme pleure et sent qu'elle est dépareillée.
my soul weeps and feels that-it is incomplete.
(my soul weeps and feels that it is incomplete.)

Sur moi la nuit immense plane comme un lincueil;
On me the night immense hovers like a shroud;
(The immense night hovers over me like a shroud;)

je chante ma romance que le ciel entend seul.
I sing my romance that the heaven hears alone.
(I sing my romance, heard by heaven alone.)

Ah! comme elle était belle et combien je l'aimais!
Ah! how she was beautiful and how-much I her-loved!
(Ah! how beautiful she was and how much I loved her!)

Je n'aimerai jamais une femme autant qu'elle.
I not-will-love ever a woman as-much as-her.
(Never will I love a woman as much as her.)

La Fée aux Chansons
The Fairy of-the Songs
(The Songs of the Fairy)

Il était une Fée d'herbe folle coiffée,
It was a Fairy of-grass wild coiffed,
(There once was a Fairy with hair of wild grass,)

qui courait les buissons sans s'y laisser surprendre,
who ran the bushes without herself-there to-allow to-surprise,
(who ran through the bushes without letting herself be surprised,)

en Avril, pour apprendre aux oiseaux leurs chansons.
in April, for to-teach to-the birds their songs.
(in April, to teach the birds their songs.)

Lorsque geais et linottes faisaient des fausses notes en récitant
When jays and linnets made some false notes in reciting
(When jays and linnets sang wrong notes in singing)

leur chants, la Fée, avec constance,
their songs, the Fairy, with constancy,
(their songs, the Fairy, with constancy,)

gourmandait d'importance ces élèves méchants.
reprimanded of-importance these students wicked.
(with pompously reprimanded these wicked students.)

Sa petite main nue, d'un brin d'herbe menue
Her petite hand nude, of-a blade of-grass slender
(Her small bare hand, with a slender blade of grass)

cueilli dans les halliers, pour stimuler leurs zèles,
gathered in the thickets, for to-stimulate their zeal,
(gathered in the thickets, to stimulate their zeal,)

fouettait sur leurs ailes ces mauvais écoliers.
whipped on their wings these bad pupils.
(whipped these bad pupils on their wings.)

Par un matin d'automne,
By one morning of-autumn,
(One autumn morning,)

elle vient et s'étonne de voir les bois déserts:
she comes and herself-amazes to to-see the woods deserted:
(she came and was amazed to see the woods deserted:)

Avec les hirondelles ses amis infidèles avaient fui dans les airs.
With the swallows her friends unfaithful had fled in the airs.
(Her faithful friends had fled with the swallows in the air.)

Et tout l'hiver la Fée, d'herbe morte coiffée,
And all the-winter the Fairy, of-grass dead coiffed,
(And all winter the Fairy, with hair of dead grass,)

et comptant les instants sous les forêts immenses,
and counting the instants under the forests immense,
(and counting the moments under the immense forest,)

compose des romances pour le prochain Printemps!
composes some romances for the following Spring!
(composes romances for the following Spring!)

La fleur qui va sur l'eau
The flower that goes on the-water
(The flower that floats on the water)

Sur la mer voilée d'un brouillard amer,
On the sea veiled from-a fog harsh,
(On the sea veiled by a harsh fog,)

la belle est allée, la nuit, sur la mer!
the beauty is gone, the night, on the sea!
(the beauty went, at night, to the sea!)

Elle avait aux lèvres d'un air irrité,
She had to-the lips of-an air irritated,
(She had on her lips an irritated air,)

La Rose des Fièvres, La Rose Beauté!
The Rose of-the Fevers, The Rose Beauty!
(The Rose of Fevers, The Beauty Rose!)

D'un souffle farouche l'ouragan hurleur
Of-a breath fierce the-hurricane howling
(With a fierce breath the howling hurricane)

lui baisa la bouche et lui prit la fleur!
her kissed the mouth and her took the flower!
(kissed her mouth and took her flower away!)

Dans l'océan sombre, moins sombre déjà,
In the-ocean dark, less dark already,
(On the dark ocean, already less dark,)

où le trois-mâts sombre, la fleur surnagea,
where the three-mast sinks, the flower floated,
(where the three-masted ship sinks, the flower floated,)

l'eau s'en est jouée, dans ses noirs sillons:
the-water itself-with-it is played, in its black furrows:
(the water played with it, in its black furrows:)

c'est une bouée pour les papillons et l'embrun,
it-is a buoy for the butterflies and the-spray,
(it is a buoy for the butterflies and the spray,)

la houle depuis cette nuit, les brisants
the swell since that night, the breakers
(since that night the swell, the breakers)

où croule un sauvage bruit, l'alcyon, la voile,
where collapses a savage noise, the-halcyon, the sail,
(where a savage noise collapses, the halcyon, the sail,)

l'hirondelle autour, et l'ombre
the-swallow around, and the-shadow
(the circling swallow, the darkness,)

et l'étoile se meurent d'amour,
and the-star themselves die of-love,
(and the star die of love,)

et l'aurore éclose sur le gouffre clair,
and the-dawn un-closes on the abyss clear,
(and the dawn opens on the clear gulf,)

pour la seule rose de toute la mer!
for the only rose of all the sea!
(for the only rose on all the sea!)

La Rançon
The Ransom

L'homme a, pour payer sa rançon,
The-man has, for to-pay his ransom,
(Man has, to pay his ransom,)

deux champs au tuf profond et riche,
two fields to-the bedrock profound and rich,
(two solid fields, deep and rich,)

qu'il faut qu'il remue et défriche
that-it is-necessary that-he move and clear
(that he must move and clear)

avec le fer de la raison.
with the iron of the reason.
(with the strength of reason.)

Pour obtenir la moindre rose,
For to-obtain the least rose,
(To obtain the smallest rose,)

pour extorquer quelques épis,
for to-extort some stalks-of-wheat,
(to extort some grain,)

des pleurs salés de son front gris,
of-the tears salted from his brow grey,
(with the salted tears of his gray brow)

sans cesse il faut qu'il les arrose!
without cease it is-necessary that-he them water!
(unceasingly he must water them!)

L'un est l'Art et l'autre, l'Amour:
The-one is the-Art and the-other, the-Love:
(One is Art and the other, Love:)

Pour rendre le juge propice,
For to-render the judge propitious,
(To render the judge favorable,)

lorsque de la stricte justice paraitra le terrible jour,
when of the strict justice will-appear the terrible day,
(when the terrible day of strict justice appears,)

il faudra lui montrer des granges pleines de moissons
it will-be-necessary him to-show the granges full of harvests
(it will be necessary to show him great barns full of harvests)

et de fleurs, dont les formes et les couleurs
and of flowers, whose the forms and the colors
(and of flowers, whose forms and colors)

gagnent le suffrage des Anges.
gain the suffrage of-the Angels.
(gain the vote of the Angels.)

Fauré

La Rose

The Rose

Je dirai la rose aux plis gracieux.
I will-tell the rose to-the folds gracious.
(I will tell of the rose, with its gracious folds.)

La rose est le souffle embaumé des dieux,
The rose is the breath fragrant of-the gods,
(The rose is the scented breath of the gods,)

Le plus cher souci des Muses divines.
The most dear care of-the Muses divine.
(The dearest care of the divine Muses.)

Je dirai ta gloire, ô charme des yeux,
I will-tell your glory, o charm of-the eyes,
(I will tell of your glory, o charm of the eyes,)

O fleur de Kypris, reine des collines!
O flower of Kypris, queen of-the hills!
(O flower of Kypris, queen of the hills!)

Tu t'épanouis entre les beaux doigts
You yourself-bloom between the beautiful fingers
(You bloom between the beautiful fingers)

De l'Aube, écartant les ombres moroses;
Of the-Dawn, scattering the shadows morose;
(Of Dawn, scattering the morose shadows;)

L'air bleu devient rose et roses les bois;
The-air blue becomes pink and pink the woods;
(The blue air and the woods become pink;)

La bouche et le sein des vierges sont roses!
The mouth and the breast of-the virgins are pink!
(The mouth and the breast of the virgins are pink!)

Heureuse la vierge aux bras arrondis
Happy the virgin to-the arms extended
(Happy the virgin with extended arms)

Qui dans les halliers humides te cueille!
Who in the thickets humid you gathers!
(Who in the humid thickets gathers you!)

Heureux le front jeune où tu resplendis!
Happy the face young where you shine!
(Happy the young face upon which you shine!)

Heureuse la coupe où nage ta feuille!
Happy the cup where swims your leaf!
(Happy the cup where floats your leaf!)

Ruisselante encor du flot paternel,
Dripping still of-the wave paternal,
(When blossoming Aphrodite, Still dripping)

Quand de la mer bleue Aphrodite éclose
When from the sea blue Aphrodite opens
(from the paternal wave of the blue sea)

Étincela nue aux clartés du ciel,
Sparkled naked to-the clarity of-the heaven,
(Sparkled naked in the brightness of heaven,)

La Terre jalouse enfanta la rose;
The Earth jealous birthed the rose;
(The jealous Earth gave birth to the rose;)

Et l'Olympe entier, d'amour transporté,
And the-Olympus entire, of-love transported,
(And all of Olympus, transported with love,)

Salua la fleur avec la Beauté!
Saluted the flower with the Beauty!
(Hailed the flower with Beauty!)

Fauré
Le Don Silencieux
The Gift Silent
(The Silent Gift)

Je mettrai mes deux mains sur ma bouche,
I will-put my two hands on my mouth,
(I will place my two hands on my mouth,)

pour taire ce que je voudrais tant vous dire,
for to-silence that which I would-like so-much you to-tell,
(to silence that which I would like so much to tell you,)

âme bien chère! Je mettrai mes deux mains sur mes yeux,
soul well dear! I will-put my two hands on my eyes,
(precious soul! I will place my two hands over my eyes,)

pour cacher ce que je voudrais tant
for to-hide that which I would-like so-much
(to hide that which I wish, nevertheless,)

que pourtant vous cherchiez.
that nevertheless you would-seek.
(that you would seek out.)

Je mettrai mes deux mains sur mon coeur, chère vie,
I will-place my two hands on my heart, dear life,
(I will place my two hands on my heart, dear life,)

pour que vous ignoriez de quel coeur je vous prie!
for that you will-ignore of what heart I you pray!
(so that you will not know with what heart I beg you!)

Et puis je les mettrai doucement dans vos mains,
And then I them will-put softly in your hands,
(And then I will place them softly in your hands,)

Ces deux mains-ci qui meurent d'un fatigant chagrin ...
These two hands-here which die of-a fatiguing sorrow...
(These two hands which die of a wearisome sorrow...)

Elles iront, à vous, pleines de leur faiblesse,
They will-go, to you, full of their feebleness,
(They will go, to you, full of their weakness,)

toutes silencieuses, et même sans caresse,
all silent, and even without caress,
(All silent, and even without caresses,)

lasses d'avoir porté tout le poids
tired from-to-have carried all the weight
(tired from having carried all the weight)

d'un secret dont ma bouche et mes yeux
of-a secret of-which my mouth and my eyes
(of a secret of which my mouth and my eyes)

et mon front parleraient. Elles iront à vous,
and my face would-speak. They will-go to you,
(and my face would speak. They will go to you,)

légères d'être vides, et lourdes d'être tristes,
light from-to-be empty, and heavy from-to-be sad,
(light from being empty, and heavy from being sad,)

tristes d'être timides; Malheureuses et douces,
sad from-to-be timid; Unhappy and sweet,
(sad from being timid; Unhappy and sweet,)

et si découragées que peut-être, mon Dieu,
and so discouraged that may-to-be, my God,
(and so discouraged that perhaps, My God,)

vous les recueillerez.
you them will-gather.
(you will recieve then.)

Fauré

Le Jardin Clos

The Garden Enclosed
(The Enclosed Garden)

Exaucement

Fulfillment

Alors qu'en tes mains de lumière tu poses ton front défaillant
Then that-in your hands of light you place your face faltering
(When you place your faltering face in your hands of light)

que mon amour en ta prière vienne comme un exaucement.
that my love in your prayer come like a fulfillment.
(may my love come like a fulfillment to your prayer.)

Alors que la parole expire sur ta lèvre qui tremble encore,
Then that the word expires on your lip which trembles still,
(Then the word expires on your still-trembling lips,)

et s'adoucit en un sourire de roses en des rayons d'or;
and itself-softens in a smile of roses in some rays of-gold;
(and softens in a smile of roses in golden rays;)

que ton âme calme et muette,
that your soul calm and mute,
(may your calm and mute soul,)

fée endormie au jardin clos,
fairy asleep to-the garden enclosed,
(a sleeping fairy in the enclosed garden,)

en sa douce volonté faite trouve la joie et le repos.
in its sweet wish done find the joy and the repose.
(in its sweet accomplished wish find joy and repose.)

Fauré

Le Jardin Clos

The Garden Enclosed

(The Enclosed Garden)

Quand tu plonges tes yeux dans mes yeux

When you plunge your eyes into my eyes

Quand tu plonges tes yeux dans mes yeux,
When you plunge your eyes in my eyes,
(When you plunge your eyes into my eyes,)

je suis toute dans mes yeux. Quand ta bouche
I am all in my eyes. When your mouth
(I am all in my eyes. When your mouth)

dénoue ma bouche, mon amour n'est que ma bouche.
unties my mouth, my love not-is but my mouth.
(loosens my mouth, my love is but my mouth.)

Si tu frôles mes cheveux, je n'existe
If you caress my hairs, I not-exist
(If you caress my hair, I exist no more)

plus qu'en eux, si ta main effleure mes seins,
more but-in them, if your hand grazes my breasts,
(but in them, if your hand grazes my breasts,)

j'y monte comme un feu soudain. Est-ce moi
I-there mount like a fire sudden. Is-it me
(I rise there like a sudden fire. Is it I)

que tu as choisie? Là est mon âme, là est ma vie.
whom you have chosen? There is my soul, there is my life.
(whom you have chosen? There is my soul, there is my life.)

Fauré

Le Jardin Clos
The Garden Enclosed
(The Enclosed Garden)

La Messagère
The Messenger

Avril, et c'est le point du jour.
April, and it-is the point of-the day.
(April, and it is the break of the day.)

Tes blondes soeurs qui te ressemblent en ce moment,
Your blond sisters who you resemble in this moment,
(Your blond sisters who resemble you at this moment,)

toutes ensemble s'avancent vers toi, cher amour.
all together themselves-advance toward you, dear love.
(all together advance toward you, dear love.)

Tu te tiens dans un clos ombreux
You yourself hold in an enclosure shadowy
(You keep yourself in a dark enclosure)

de myrte et d'aubépine blanche:
of mytle and of-hawthorn white:
(of myrtle and white hawthorn:)

La porte s'ouvre sous les branches: le chemin est mystérieux.
The door itself-opens under the branches: the path is mysterious.
(The door opens under the branches: the path is mysterious.)

Elles, lentes, en longues robes, une à une, main dans la main,
They, slow, in long gowns, one by one, hand in the hand,
(They, slowly, in long gowns, one by one, hand in hand,)

franchissant le seuil indistinct
crossing-over the threshold indistinct
(crossing the indistinct threshold)

où de la nuit devient de l'aube.
where from the night becomes of the dawn.
(where night becomes dawn.)

Celle qui s'avance d'abord, regarde l'ombre,
The-one who herself-advances at-first, looks-at the-shadow,
(The one who advances first, sees the darkness,)

te découvre, crie, et la fleur de ses yeux
you discovers, shouts, and the flower of her eyes
(discovers you, shouts, and the flower of her eyes)

s'ouvre splendide, dans un rire d'or.
itself-opens splendid, in a laughter of-gold.
(opens, with splendor in golden laughter.)

Et jusqu'à la dernière soeur, toutes tremblent,
And until the last sister, all tremble,
(And all to the last sister, tremble,)

tes lèvres touchent leurs lèvres,
your lips touch their lips,
(your lips touch their lips,)

l'éclair de ta bouche éclate jusque dans leur coeur.
the-flash of your mouth bursts even-to in their heart.
(the flash of your mouth bursts into their hearts.)

Fauré

Le Jardin Clos
The Garden Enclosed
(The Enclosed Garden)

Je me poserai sur ton coeur
I myself will-place on your heart
(I will lie on your heart)

Je me poserai sur ton coeur
I myself will-place on your heart
(I will lie on your heart)

comme le printemps sur la mer,
like the spring on the sea,
(like the spring on the sea,)

sur les plaines de la mer stérile,
on the plains of the sea sterile,
(on the plains of the sterile sea,)

où nulle fleur ne put croître à ses souffles agile,
where no flower not could grow to its breaths agile,
(where no flower could grow in its agile breath,)

que des fleurs de lumière. Je me poserai sur ton coeur comme
but of-the flowers of light. I myself will-place on you heart like
(except flowers of light. I will lie on your heart like)

l'oiseau sur la mer, dans le repos de ses ailes lasses,
the-bird on the sea, in the repose of its wings weary,
(the bird on the sea, while resting its weary wings,)

et que berce le rythme éternel des flots et de l'espace.
and that rocks the ryhthm eternal of-the waves and of the-space.
(and that the eternal rhythm of the waves and of space rocks.)

Fauré

Le Jardin Clos
The Garden Enclosed
(The Enclosed Garden)

Dans la Nymphée
In the Nymph-Place
(In the Grotto)

Quoique tes yeux ne la voient pas,
Although your eyes not her see not,
(Although your eyes do not see her,)

pense en ton âme qu'elle est là, comme autrefois,
think in your soul that-she is there, like other-time,
(believe in your soul that she is there, as before,)

divine et blanche. Sur ce bord reposent ses mains.
divine and white. On this border repose her hands.
(divine and pure. On this bank lay her hands.)

Sa tête est entre ces jasmins, là ses pieds effleurent
Her head is between these jasmines, there her feet graze
(Her head is between these jasmines, there her feet skim)

les branches. Elle sommeille en ces rameaux,
the branches. She sleeps in these boughs,
(the branches. She sleeps in these boughs,)

ses lèvres et ses yeux sont clos,
her lips and her eyes are closed,
(her lips and her eyes are closed,)

et sa bouche à peine respire. Parfois, la nuit,
and her mouth to hardly breathes. Sometimes, the night,
(and her mouth hardly breathes. Sometimes, at night,)

dans un éclair, elle apparaît, les yeux ouverts,
in a flash, she appears, the eyes open,
(in a flash, she appears, eyes open,)

et l'eclair dans ses yeux se mire.
and the-flash in her eyes itself is-mirrored.
(and the flash is reflected in her eyes.)

Un bref éblouissement bleu la découvre en ses
A brief dazzlement blue her discovers in her
(A brief blinding blue flash spotlights her in her)

longs cheveux, elle s'éveille, elle se lève,
long hair, she herself-awakens, she herself rises,
(long hair, she awakens, she rises,)

et tout un jardin ébloui s'illumine au fond de la nuit,
and all a garden dazzled itself-illuminates in-the depth of the night,
(and she illuminates all the dazzled garden in the depth of the night,)

dans le rapide éclair d'un rêve.
in the rapid flash of-a dream.
(in the rapid flash of a dream.)

Le Jardin Clos
The Garden Enclosed
(The Enclosed Garden)

Dans la Pénombre
In the Half-Light

A quoi, dans ce matin d'avril, si douce,
At what, in this morning of-April, so gentle,
(By what, on this April morning, so gentle,)

et d'ombre enveloppée, la chère enfant au coeur subtil,
and of-shadow enveloped, the dear child to-the heart subtle,
(and enveloped in shadow, is the dear child with subtle heart,)

est-elle ainsi toute occupée? Pensivement, d'un geste lent,
is-she thus all occupied? Pensively, of-a gesture slow,
(so completely occupied? Pensively, with a slow gesture,)

en longue robe, en robe à queue,
in long dress, in gown with train,
(in long dress, in gown with train,)

sur le soleil au rouet blanc à filer de la laine bleue,
on the sun at-the spinning-wheel white to to-spin of the wool blue,
(on the sun's white spinning wheel spinning blue wool,)

à sourire à son rêve encor avec ses yeux de fiancée,
to to-smile at her dream still with her eyes of fiancée,
(still smiling at her dream with the eyes of a fiancée,)

à tresser les feuillages d'or, parmi les lys de sa pensée.
to to-plait the foliages of-gold, among the lilies of her thought.
(braiding the golden foliage, among the liles of her thought.)

Fauré

Le Jardin Clos
The Garden Enclosed
(The Enclosed Garden)

Il m'est cher, Amour, le Bandeau
It to-me-is dear, Love, the Bandage
(It is dear to me, Love, the Ribbon)

Il m'est cher, Amour, le bandeau
It to-me-is dear, Love, the bandage
(It is dear to me, Love, the blindfold)

qui me tient les paupières closes;
which me holds the eyelids closed;
(which holds my eyes closed;)

Il pèse comme un doux fardeau de soleil sur de faibles roses.
It weighs like a sweet burden of sun on some feeble roses.
(It weighs like the sweet burden of sun on feeble roses.)

Si j'avance, l'étrange chose! je parais marcher sur les eaux;
If I-advance, the-strange thing! I appear to-walk on the waters;
(If I go forward, a strange thing! I appear to walk on water;)

mes pieds plus lourds où je les pose,
my feet more heavy where I them place,
(my feet heavier where I place them,)

s'enfoncent comme en des anneaux.
themselves-sink as in some rings.
(sink as if they were enchained.)

Qui donc a délié dans l'ombre
Who then has untied in the-shadow
(Who then, in the shadows, has untied)

le faix d'or de mes longs cheveux?
the weight of-gold from my long hairs?
(the weight of gold from my long hair?)

Toute ceinte d'étreinte sombre,
All encircled of-embrace somber,
(Encircled by a dark embrace,)

je plonge en des vagues de feu.
I plunge in some waves of fire.
(I plunge into waves of fire.)

Mes lèvres où mon âme chante,
My lips where my soul sings,
(My lips, where my soul sings,)

toute d'extase et de baisers,
all of-ecstassy and of kisses,
(full of ecstasy and kisses,)

s'ouvrent comme une fleur ardente
themselves-open like a flower ardent
(open like an ardent flower)

au-dessus d'un fleuve embrasé!
above of-a river afire!
(on a river all aflame!)

Fauré

Le Jardin Clos
The Garden Enclosed
(The Enclosed Garden)

Inscription sur le Sable
Inscription in the Sand

Toute, avec sa robe et ses fleurs,
All, with her gown and her flowers,
(All, with her gown and her flowers,)

elle, ici, redevint poussière,
she, here, returned dust,
(she, here, returned to dust,)

et son âme emportée ailleurs renaquit
and her soul carried-away elsewhere was-reborn
(and her soul, carried elsewhere, was reborn)

en chant et lumière. Mais un léger lien fragile
in song and light. But a loose bond fragile
(in song and light. But a fragile bond)

dans la mort brisé doucement, encerclait ses tempes débiles
in the death broken lightly, encircled her temples debilitated
(gently broken in death, encircled her weak temples)

d'impérissables diamants. En signe d'elle,
of-imperishable diamonds. In sign of-her,
(with imperishable diamonds. As a sign of her,)

à cette place, seule, parmi le sable blond,
at this place, alone, among the sand blond,
(in this place, alone, among the blond sand,)

les pierres éternelles tracent encore l'image de son front.
the stones eternal trace still the-image of her face.
(the eternal stones still trace the image of her face.)

Fauré

Le Papillon et la Fleur

The Butterfly and the Flower

La pauvre fleur disait au papillon céleste: Ne fuis pas!
The poor flower said to-the butterfly celestial: Not flee not!
(The poor flower said to the heavenly butterfly: Don't Flee!)

Vois comme nos destins sont différents.
See how our destinies are different.
(See how different our destinies are.)

Je reste, tu t'en vas! Pourtant nous nous aimons,
I stay, you yourself-from-here go! Nevertheless we each-other love,
(I stay, you go! Nonetheless we love each other,)

nous vivons sans les hommes et loin d'eux,
we live without the men and far from-them,
(we live without people and far from them,)

et nous nous ressemblons, et l'on dit
and we each-other resemble, and the-one says
(and we are like one another, and they say)

que nous sommes fleurs tous deux! Mais, hélas!
that we are flowers all two! But, alas!
(that we are both flowers! But, Alas!)

l'air t'emporte et la terre m'enchaine. Sort cruel!
the-air you-carries-off and the earth me-enchains. Fate cruel!
(the air carries you off and the earth enchains me. Cruel Fate!)

je voudrais embaumer ton vol de mon haleine dans le ciel!
I would-like to-perfume your flight of my breath in the sky!
(I would like to perfume your flight with my breath in the sky!)

Mais non, tu vas trop loin! Parmi des fleurs sans nombre
But no, you go too far! Among some flowers without number
(But no, you go too far! Among the innumerable flowers)

vous fuyez, et moi je reste seule à voir tourner
you flee, and me I stay alone to to-watch to-turn
(you flee, and I stay alone to watch my shadow)

mon ombre à mes pieds! Tu fuis, puis tu reviens,
my shadow at my feet! You flee, then you come-back,
(turning at my feet! You flee, then you return,)

puis tu t'en vas encore luire ailleurs.
then you yourself-from-here go again to-shine elsewhere.
(then you go away again to shine elsewhere.)

Aussi me trouves-tu toujours à chaque aurore toute en pleurs!
Also me find-you always at each dawn all in tears!
(Thus you always find me at each dawn in tears!)

Ah! pour que notre amour coule des jours fidèles, ô mon roi,
Ah! for that our love flows of-the days faithful, o my king,
(Ah! so that our love may flow faithful for days, o my king,)

Prends comme moi racine, ou donne-moi des ailes
Take like me root, or give-me some wings
(Take root like me, or give me wings)

comme à toi!
like to you!
(like you!)

Fauré

Le Parfum Imperissable

The Perfume Imperishable

(The Imperishable Perfume)

Quand la fleur du soleil, la rose de Lahor,
When the flower of-the sun, the rose of Lahor,
(When the flower of the sun, the rose of Lahor,)

De son âme odorante a rempli goutte à goutte
Of its soul fragrant has filled drop to drop
(With its fragrant soul has filled drop by drop)

la fiole d'argile ou de cristal ou d'or,
the flask of-clay or of crystal or of-gold,
(the flask of clay or crystal or gold,)

sur le sable qui brûle on peut l'épandre toute.
on the sand that burns one can it-to-scatter all.
(one can scatter it all on the burning sand.)

Les fleuves et la mer inonderaient en vain
The rivers and the sea would-inundate in vain
(The rivers and the sea would flood in vain)

ce sanctuaire étroit qui la tint enfermée:
this sanctuary narrow that it held enclosed:
(this narrow sanctuary that it held enclosed:)

Il garde en se brisant son arôme divin,
It guards while itself breaking its aroma divine,
(Even as it breaks it keeps its divine aroma,)

et sa poussière heureuse en reste parfumée.
and its dust happy of-it remains perfumed.
(and its fortunate dust remains perfumed by it.)

Puisque par la blessure ouverte de mon coeur
Since by the wound open of my heart
(Since through the open wound of my heart)

tu t'écoules de même, ô céleste liqueur,
you yourself-flow-away of same, oh celestial liqueur,
(you likewise flow away, oh heavenly liqueur,)

inexprimable amour, qui m'enflammais pour elle!
inexpressible love, that me-enflamed for her!
(inexpressible love, that enflamed me for her!)

Qu'il lui soit pardonné, que mon mal soit béni!
That-it her be pardonned, that my pain be blessed!
(May she be pardoned, may my pain be blessed!)

Par delà l'heure humaine et le temps infini mon coeur
By beyond the-hour human and the time infinite my heart
(Beyond the human hour and infinite time my heart)

est embaumé d'une odeur immortelle!
is perfumed of-a fragrance immortal!
(is perfumed by an immortal fragrance!)

Fauré

Le Pays des Rêves

The Land of-the Dreams

Veux-tu qu'au beau pays des rêves nous allions
Want-you that-to-the beautiful land of-the dreams we go
(Would you like to go, hand in hand, to the beautiful)

la main dans la main? Plus loin que l'odeur des jasmins,
the hand in the hand? More far than the-smell of-the jasmines,
(land of dreams? Farther than the smell of the jasmines,)

plus haut que la plainte des grèves? Veux-tu du
more high than the complaint of-the beaches? Want-you of-the
(higher than the sighing of the beaches? Would you like)

beau pays des rêves, tous les deux chercher le chemin?
beautiful land of-the dreams, all the two to-search the path?
(to search for the path to the beautiful land of dreams, together?)

J'ai taillé dans l'azur les toiles du vaisseau
I-have tailored from the-blue the sails of-the ship
(From the blue skies I have cut the sails of the ship)

qui nous portera, et doucement nous conduira jusqu'au
that us will-carry, and softly us will-lead until-to-the
(that will carry us, and will softly lead us to the)

verger d'or des étoiles. Mais combien la terre est
orchard of-gold of-the stars. But how the land is
(golden orchard of the stars. But how far is the land,)

lointaine, que poursuivent ses blancs sillons;
far, that follow its white furrows;
(that its white furrows follow;)

au caprice des papillons demandons la route incertaine.
at-the caprice of-the butterflies let-us-ask the route uncertain.
(at the caprice of the butterflies let us ask the uncertain route.)

Ah, combien la terre est lointaine où fleurissent nos visions.
Ah, how the land is far where flourish our visions.
(Ah, how far is the land where our visions flourish.)

Vois-tu: le beau pays des rêves est trop haut
See-you: the beautiful land of-the dreams is too high
(You see: the beautiful land of dreams is too high)

pour les pas humains. Respirons à deux les jasmins,
for the steps human. Let-us-breathe at two the jasmines,
(for human steps. Together let us breathe the jasmines,)

et chantons encor sur les grèves. Vois-tu:
and sing again on the beaches. See-you:
(and again sing on the beaches. You see:)

du beau pays des rêves l'amour
of-the beautiful land of-the dreams the-love
(to the beautiful land of dreams, only love)

seul en sait les chemins.
only of-it knows the paths.
(knows the paths.)

Le Plus Doux Chemin
The Most Sweet Path
(The Sweetest Path)

A mes pas le plus doux chemin mène à la porte
To my steps the most sweet path leads to the door
(To my steps the sweetest path leads to the door)

de ma belle, et, bien qu'elle me soit rebelle,
of my beauty, and, well that-she to-me be rebel,
(of my beauty, and although she may refuse me,)

j'y veux encor passer demain.
I-there wish again to-pass tomorrow.
(I want to pass there again tomorrow.)

Il est tout fleuri de jasmin au temps
It is all flowered of jasmin at-the time
(It is all flowered with jasmin at the time)

de la saison nouvelle, et, bien qu'elle me soit
of the season new, and, well that-she to-me be
(of the new season, and although she may be)

cruelle j'y passe, des fleurs à la main.
cruel I-there pass, some flowers in the hand.
(cruel to me I pass there, flowers in hand.)

Pour toucher son coeur inhumain je chante ma peine cruelle,
For to-touch her heart inhuman I sing my pain cruel,
(To touch her inhuman heart I sing of my cruel pain,)

et, bien qu'elle me soit rebelle,
and, well that-she to-me be rebel,
(and, although she may refuse me,)

c'est pour moi le plus doux chemin.
it-is for me the most sweet path.
(it is for me the sweetest path.)

Fauré

Le Ramier

The Dove

Avec son chant doux et plaintif, ce ramier blanc
With its song sweet and plaintive, this dove white
(With its sweet and plaintive song, this white dove)

te fait envie: S'il te plaît l'avoir pour captif,
to-you makes envy: If-it you pleases it-to-have for captive,
(makes you envious: If it pleases you to have him captive,)

j'irai te le chercher, Sylvie. Mais là,
I-will-go you it to-search-for, Sylvie. But there,
(I will go catch him for you, Sylvie. But there,)

près de toi dans mon sein, comme ce ramier
close to you in my breast, like this dove
(close to you in my breast, like this dove)

mon coeur chante: S'il t'en plaît faire le larcin,
my heart sings: If-it you-of-it pleases to-make the spoils,
(my heart sings: If it pleases you to make it yours,)

il sera mieux à toi, méchante.
it will-be better to you, wicked-one.
(it will be better to you, wicked one.)

Pour qu'il soit tel qu'un ramier blanc,
For that-it be such that-a dove white,
(So that it may be like a white dove,)

le prisonnier que tu recèles, sur mon coeur,
the prisoner that you conceal, on my heart,
(the prisoner that you conceal, on my heart,)

oiselet tremblant, Pose tes mains comme deux ailes.
little-bird trembling, Place your hands like two wings.
(trembling little bird, Place your hands like two wings.)

Fauré

Le Secret

The Secret

Je veux que le matin l'ignore le nom que
I want that the morning it-not know the name that
(I want the morning not to know the name that)

j'ai dit à la nuit, et qu'au vent de l'aube,
I-have said to the night, and that-at-the wind of the-dawn,
(I told the night, and that at the wind of dawn,)

sans bruit, comme une larme il s'évapore.
without noise, like a tear it itself-evaporate.
(noiselessly, it evaporate like a tear.)

Je veux que le jour le proclame l'amour qu'au
I want that the day it proclaim the-love that-to-the
(I want the day to proclaim the love that I hid from the)

matin j'ai caché, et sur mon coeur ouvert,
morning I-have hidden, and on my heart open,
(morning, and over my open heart,)

penché, comme un grain d'encens, il l'enflamme.
bent, like a grain of-incense, it it-inflame.
(bent, like a grain of incense, inflame it.)

Je veux que le couchant l'oublie,
I want that the setting-sun it-forget,
(I want the setting sun to forget it,)

le secret que j'ai dit au jour, et l'emporte avec mon amour,
the secret that I-have said to-the day, and it-carry-away with my love,
(the secret that I told the day, and carry it away with my love,)

aux plis de sa robe pâlie!
to-the folds of its gown pallid!
(in the folds of her pale gown!)

Fauré

Le Voyageur

The Voyager

Voyageur, où vas-tu, marchant dans l'or vibrant
Voyager, where go-you, marching in the-gold vibrant
(Traveler, where are you going, walking in the vibrant gold)

de la poussière? "Je m'en vais au soleil couchant,
of the dust? "I myself-from-here go to-the sun setting
(Of the dust? "I am going to the setting sun)

pour m'endormir dans la lumière.
for me-to-sleep in the light.
(to sleep in the light.)

Car j'ai vécu n'ayant qu'un Dieu,
For I-have lived not-having but-one God,
(Because I have lived having only one God,)

l'astre qui luit et qui féconde,
the-star which shines and which feeds,
(the star which shines and which feeds,)

et c'est dans son linceul de feu
and it-is in its shroud of fire
(and it is in its shroud of fire)

que je veux m'en aller du monde!"
that I want myself-from-here to-go from-the world!"
(that I want to leave the world!")

Voyageur, presse donc le pas:
Voyager, press then the step:
(Traveler, hasten then your step:)

L'astre vers l'horizon décline.
The-star toward the-horizon declines.
(The star descends on the horizon.)

"Que m'importe, j'irai plus bas,
"What to-me-imports, I-will-go more low,
("What does it matter to me, I will go lower,)

L'attendre au pied de la colline.
It-to-await at-the foot of the hill.
(To await it at the foot of the hill.)

Et lui montrant mon coeur ouvert,
And to-it showing my heart open,
(And showing my open heart to it,)

saignant de son amour fidèle, je lui dirai:
bleeding from its love faithful, I it will-tell:
(bleeding from its faithful love, I will tell it:)

j'ai trop souffert, soleil! emporte-moi loin d'elle!"
I-have too-much suffered, sun! carry-me far from-her!"
(I have suffered too much, sun! take me far from her!")

Fauré

Les Berceaux

The Cradles

Le long du quai les grands vaisseaux,
The length of-the quay the great vessels,
(All along the quay the great ships,)

Que la houle incline en silence,
That the surge inclines in silence,
(That the surge inclines in silence,)

Ne prennent pas garde aux berceaux
Not take not guard of-the cradles
(Pay no mind to the cradles)

Que la main des femmes balance.
That the hand of women rocks.
(Which women's hands rock.)

Mais viendra le jour des adieux,
But will-come the day of-the farewells,
(But the day of farewells will come,)

Car il faut que les femmes pleurent,
Because it is-necessary that the women cry,
(Because women must cry,)

Et que les hommes curieux
and that the men curious
(and curious men)

Tentent les horizons qui leurrent.
Attempt the horizons which entice.
(Must attempt the enticing horizons.)

Et ce jour-là les grands vaisseaux,
And that day-there the great vessels,
(And on that day the great ships,)

Fuyant le port qui diminue,
Fleeing the port which diminishes,
(Fleeing the diminishing port,)

Sentent leur masse retenue
Feel their mass retained
(Feel their bulk held back)

Par l'âme des lointains berceaux.
By the-soul of-the far-away cradles.
(By the soul of the faraway cradles.)

Fauré

Les Matelots

The Sailors

Sur l'eau bleue et profonde nous allons voyageant,
On the-water blue and deep we go voyaging,
(On the deep blue water we go travelling,)

environnant le monde d'un sillage d'argent,
surrounding the world of-a track of-silver,
(encircling the world with a silver track,)

des îles de la Sonde, de l'Inde au ciel brûlé,
from-the isles of the Sunda, from the-India of-the heaven burned,
(from the Sunda Isles, from India with its burning skies,)

jusqu'au pôle gelé ...
until-to-the pole frozen...
(to the frozen pole...)

Nous pensons à la terre que nous fuyons toujours
We think to the earth that we flee always
(We think of the land that we flee, always)

à notre vieille mère, à nos jeunes amours;
to our old mother, to our young loves;
(of our old mother, of our young loves;)

mais la vague légère avec son doux refrain
but the wave light with its soft refrain
(but the light wave with its soft refrain)

endort notre chagrin. Existence sublime!
puts-to-sleep our sorrow. Existence sublime!
(puts our sorrow to sleep. Sublime existence!)

Bercés par notre nid, nous vivons sur l'abîme,
Rocked by our nest, we live on the-abyss,
(Cradled by our nest, we live on the abyss,)

au sein de l'infini, des flots rasant la cîme,
at-the breast of the-infinity, of-the waves grazing the peak,
(in the heart of infinity, on the waves grazing the peak,)

Dans le grand désert bleu nous marchons avec Dieu!
In the great desert blue we walk with God!
(In the great blue desert we walk with God!)

Fauré

Les Présents

The Presents

Si tu demandes, quelque soir, le secret de mon coeur malade,
If you ask, some evening, the secret of my heart sick,
(If you ask, some evening, the secret of my sickly heart,)

Je te dirai, pour t'émouvoir, une très ancienne ballade.
I to-you will-tell, for you-to-move, a very ancient ballad.
(I will tell, to move you, a very old ballad.)

Si tu me parles de tourment, d'espérance désabusée,
If you to-me speak of torment, of-hope disabused,
(If you speak to me of torment, of unfulfilled hope,)

j'irai te cueillir seulement des roses pleines de rosée.
I-will-go you to-gather only some roses full of dew.
(I will simply go gather for you roses full of dew.)

Si, pareille à la fleur des morts, qui fleurit dans l'exil
If, like to the flower of-the dead, that flowers in the-exile
(If, like flowers for the dead, that flower in the exile)

des tombes, tu veux partager mes remords! ...
of-the tombs, you wish to-share my remorses! ...
(of tombs, you wish to share my remorse! ...)

je t'apporterai des colombes.
I to-you-will-bring some doves.
(I will bring you doves.)

Les Roses d'Ispahan
The Roses of-Isfahan

Les roses d'Ispahan dans leur gaine de mousse,
The roses of-Isfahan in their sheath of moss,
(The roses of Isfahan in their sheath of moss,)

les jasmins de Mossoul, les fleurs de l'oranger
the jasmines of Mosul, the flowers of the-orange-tree
(the jasmines of Mosul, the flowers of the orange-tree)

ont un parfum moins frais, ont une odeur moins douce,
have a perfume less fresh, have a scent less sweet,
(have a perfume less fresh, have a scent less sweet,)

o blanche Leïlah! que ton souffle léger.
oh white Leilah! than your breath light.
(oh white Leilah! than your light breath.)

Ta lèvre est de corail, et ton rire léger sonne mieux
Your lip is of coral, and your laugh light sounds better
(Your lip is of coral, and your light laugh rings clearer)

que l'eau vive et d'une voix plus douce.
than the-water alive and of-a voice more sweet.
(than running water and in a sweeter voice.)

Mieux que le vent joyeux qui berce l'oranger,
Better than the wind joyous that rocks the-orange-tree,
(Better than the joyous wind that rocks the orange tree,)

mieux que l'oiseau qui chante au bord d'un nid de mousse.
better than the-bird that sings at-the border of-a nest of moss.
(better than the bird that sings at the edge of a nest of moss.)

O Leïlah! depuis que de leur vol léger tous les baisers
Oh Leilah! since that from their flight light all the kisses
(Oh Leilah! since all your kisses with their light flight)

ont fui de ta lèvre si douce, il n'est plus de parfum
have fled from your lip so sweet, if not-is more of perfume
(have fled from your lip so sweet, there is no more perfume)

dans le pâle oranger, ni de céleste arome aux roses
in the pale orange-tree, nor of celestial aroma to-the roses
(in the pale orange tree, nor heavenly aroma from the roses)

dans leur mousse. Oh! que ton jeune amour, ce papillon léger,
in their moss. Oh! that your young love, that butterfly light,
(in their moss. Oh! may your young love, that light butterfly,)

revienne vers mon coeur d'une aile prompte et douce,
return toward my heart of-a wing prompt and sweet,
(return toward my heart with a wing prompt and sweet,)

et qu'il parfume encor les fleurs de l'oranger,
and that-it perfume again the flowers of the-orange-tree,
(and may it perfume again the flowers of the orange tree,)

les roses d'Ispahan dans leur gaine de mousse!
the roses of-Isfahan in their sheath of moss!
(the roses of Isfahan in their sheath of moss!)

Madrigal de Shylock
Madrigal of Shylock

Celle que j'aime a de beauté Plus que
The-one whom I-love has of beauty More than
(The one whom I love is more beautiful than)

Flore et plus que Pomone, Et je sais,
Flora and more than Pomona, And I know,
(Flora and more than Pomona, And I know,)

pour l'avoir chanté, Que sa bouche est le soir d'automne,
for her-to-have sung, That her mouth is the evening of-autumn,
(from having sung for her, That her mouth is the autumn evening,)

Et son regard la nuit d'été.
And her glance the night of-summer.
(And her glance the summer night.)

Pour marraine elle eut Astarté,
For god-mother she had Astarté,
(She had Astarté for godmother,)

Pour patronne elle a la Madone,
For patron-saint she has the Madonna,
(She has the Madonna for a patron saint,)

Car elle est belle autant que bonne Celle que j'aime.
For she is beautiful as-much that good The-one whom I-love.
(For she is as beautiful as she is good The one I love.)

Elle écoute, rit et pardonne, N'écoutant que par charité:
She listens, laughs and pardons, Not-listening but by charity:
(She listens, laughs and pardons, Listening only out of charity:)

Elle écoute, mais sa fierté N'écoute ni moi ni personne,
She listens, but her pride Not-listens neither me nor anyone,
(She listens, but her pride does not listen to me nor anyone,)

Et rien encore n'a tenté Celle que j'aime.
And nothing yet not-has tempted The one whom I-love.
(And nothing yet has tempted The one I love.)

Fauré
Mai
May

Puisque mai tout en fleurs dans les prés nous reclame, viens!
Since May all in flowers in the meadows us reclaims, come!
(Since May, all in flower, calls us back to the meadows, come!)

ne te lasse pas de mêler à ton âme la campagne,
not yourself weary not of to-mix to your soul the countrysides,
(Do not weary of mixing your soul with the country,)

les bois, les ombrages charmants,
the woods, the shades charming,
(the woods, the charming shade,)

les larges clairs de lune au bord
the large lights of moon at-the border
(the great moonlight at the edge)

des flots dormants, le sentier qui finit où le chemin commence,
of-the billows sleeping, the path that ends where the road begins,
(of the sleeping clouds, the path that ends where the road begins,)

et l'air et le printemps et l'horizon immense,
and the-air and the spring and the-horizon immense,
(and the air and the spring and the immense horizon,)

l'horizon que ce monde attache humble et joyeux
the-horizon that this world attaches humble and joyous
(the horizon that this world humbly and joyously attaches)

comme une lèvre au bas de la robe des cieux!
like a lip at-the base of the gown of-the heavens!
(like a lip at the hem of the gown of the heavens!)

Viens! et que le regard des pudiques étoiles
Come! and that the glance of-the chaste stars
(Come! and may the glance of the chaste stars)

qui tombe sur la terre à travers tant de voiles,
which fall on the earth to traverse so-many of veils,
(which fall on the earth across so many veils,)

que l'arbre pénétré de parfums et de chants,
that the-tree penetrated of perfumes and of songs,
(may the tree imbued with perfumes and songs,)

que le souffle embrasé de midi dans les champs,
that the breeze aflame of noon in the fields,
(may the burning breeze of noontime in the fields,)

et l'ombre et le soleil, et l'onde et la verdure,
and the-shadow and the sun, and the-wave and the verdure,
(and the shadow and the sun, and the wave and the verdure,)

et le rayonnement de toute la nature fassent épanouir,
and the radiance of all the nature make to-blossom,
(and the radiance of all nature, make blossom,)

comme une double fleur, la beauté sur ton front
like a double flower, the beauty on your face
(like a double flower, the beauty in your face)

et l'amour dans ton coeur!
and the-love in your heart!
(and the love in your heart!)

Fauré

Mandoline

Mandolin

Les donneurs de sérénades Et les belles écouteuses
The givers of serenades And the beautiful listeners
(The serenaders and the beautiful listeners)

Échangent des propos fades Sous les ramures chanteuses.
Exchange some words insipid under the branches singers.
(Exchange insipid words under the singing branches.)

C'est Tircis et c'est Aminte, Et c'est l'éternel Clitandre,
It-is Tricis and it-is Aminte, And it-is the-eternal Clitandre,
(It's Tircis and Aminte, and the eternal Clitandre,)

Et c'est Damis qui pour mainte
And it-is Damis who for many
(And Damis who for many a)

Cruelle fait maint vers tendre.
Cruel-woman makes many verse tender.
(Cruel woman writes many tender verses.)

Leurs courtes vestes de soie, Leurs longues robes à queues,
Their short vests of silk, Their long gowns to trains,
(Their short silk coats, Their long gowns with trains,)

Leur élégance, leur joie Et leurs molles ombres bleues.
Their elegance, their joy And their soft shadows blue.
(Their elegance, their joy and their soft blue shadows.)

Tourbillonnent dans l'extase D'une lune rose et grise,
Swirl in the-ecstasy Of-a moon pink and grey,
(Swirl in the ecstasy Of a pink and grey moon,)

Et la mandoline jase Parmi les frissons de brise.
And the mandolin chatters Among the shivers of breeze.
(And the mandolin chatters Among the shivering breeze.)

Fauré
Mirages
Mirages

Cygne sur l'Eau
Swan on the-Water

Ma pensée est un cygne harmonieux et sage,
My thought is a swan harmonious and sage,
(My thought is a harmonious and wise swan,)

qui glisse lentement aux rivages d'ennui sur les ondes
which glides slowly to-the shores of-ennui on the waves
(gliding slowly to the shores of boredom on the bottomless)

sans fond du rêve,
without bottom of-the dream,
(waves of dream,)

du mirage, de l'écho, du brouillard,
of-the mirage, of the-echo, of-the fog,
(of mirage, of echo, of fog,)

de l'ombre, de la nuit. Il glisse, roi hautain,
of the-shadow, of the night. It glides, king haughty,
(of shadow, of night. It glides, haughty king,)

fendant un libre espace, poursuit un reflet
plowing a free space, pursues a reflection
(plowing a free space, pursues a vain reflection,)

vain, précieux et changeant,
vain, precious and changing,
(precious and changing,)

et les roseaux nombreux s'inclinent
and the reeds numerous themselves-incline
(and numerous reeds bend)

quand il passe, sombre et muet,
when it passes, somber and mute,
(when it passes, somber and mute,)

au seuil d'une lune d'argent;
at-the threshold of-a moon of-silver;
(on the threshold of a silvery moon;)

et des blancs nénuphars chaque
and of-the white water-lilies each
(and each round petal of the water lilies)

corolle ronde tour-à-tour a fleuri
corolla round turn-to-turn has flowered
(has in turn flowered)

de désir et d'espoir ... mais plus avant toujours, sur la brume
of desire and of-hope... but more ahead always, on the mist
(with desire and hope...but ever onward, in the mist)

et sur l'onde, vers l'inconnu fuyant,
and on the-wave, toward the-unknown fleeing,
(and on the wave, fleeing toward the unknown,)

glisse le cygne noir. Or j'ai dit,
glides the swan black. Now I-have said,
(the black swan glides. Now I have said,)

"Renoncez, beau cygne chimérique, à ce voyage lent
"Renounce, beautiful swan chimerical, to this voyage slow
("Renounce, beautiful imaginary swan, that slow voyage)

vers de troubles destins: nul miracle chinois, nulle étrange
toward of troubled destinies: no miracle Chinese, no strange
(toward troubled destinies: no Chinese miracle, no strange)

Amérique ne vous accueilleront en des havres certains; les golfes
America not you will-greet in some havens certain; the gulfs
(America will greet you in some safe harbor; the scented)

embaumés, les îles immortelles ont pour vous, cygne noir,
fragrant, the isles immortal have for you, swan black,
(gulfs, the immortal isles have for you, black swan,)

des récifs périlleux, demeurez sur les lacs
some reefs perilous, remain on the lakes
(perilous reefs, remain on the lakes)

où se mirent, fidèles,
where themselves mirror, faithful,
(which faithfully reflect,)

ces nuages, ces fleurs, ces astres, et ces yeux."
these clouds, these flowers, these stars, and these eyes."
(these clouds, these flowers, these stars, and these eyes.")

Fauré
Mirages
Mirages

Reflets dans l'Eau
Reflections in the-Water

Etendue au seuil du bassin, dans l'eau plus froide
Lying at-the edge of-the basin, in the-water more cold
(Lying at the edge of the pool, in water colder)

que le sein des vierges sages,
than the breast of-the virgins sage,
(than the breasts of sensible virgins,)

j'ai reflété mon vague ennui, mes yeux profonds,
I-have reflected my vague boredom, my eyes deep,
(I reflected my vague boredom, my deep,)

couleur de nuit et mon visage. Et dans ce miroir incertain
color of night and my face. And in this mirror uncertain
(night-colored eyes and my face. And in this uncertain mirror)

j'ai vu de merveilleux matins...
I-have seen some marvellous mornings...
(I have seen marvellous mornings...)

J'ai vu des choses pâles
I-have seen some things pale
(I have seen pale things)

comme des souvenirs sur l'eau que ne saurait
as some remembrances on the-water that not could-know
(as memories on the water that no morose wind)

ternir nul vent morose. Alors au fond du Passé bleu,
to-tarnish no wind morose. Then at-the bottom of-the Past blue,
(could deaden. Then at the bottom of the blue Past,)

mon corps mince n'était qu'un peu d'ombre mouvante,
my body slender not-was but-a little of-shadow moving,
(my slender body was nothing but a small moving shadow,)

sous les lauriers et les cyprès.
under the laurels and the cypresses.
(under the laurels and the cypresses.)

J'aimais la brise au souffle frais qui nous évente...
I-loved the breeze to-the breath fresh that us fans...
(I loved the breeze of the fresh breath that fans us...)

J'aimais vos caresses de soeur, vos nuances, votre douceur,
I-loved your caresses of sister, your nuances, your sweetness,
(I loved your sisterly caresses, your nuances, your sweetness,)

aube opportune; et votre pas souple et rythmé,
dawn opportune; and your step supple and rhythmic,
(opportune dawn; and your supple and rhythmic step,)

nymphes au rire parfumé, au teint de lune;
nymphs with-the laughter perfumed, to-the tint of moon;
(nymphs with scented laughter, moonlit complexions;)

et le galop des aegypans;
and the gallop of-the seahorses;
(and the gallop of seahorses;)

et la fontaine qui s'épand en larmes fades...
and the fountain that itself-flows in tears insipid...
(and the fountain that flows in insipid tears...)

par les bois secrets et divins j'écoutais frissonner
by the woods secret and divine I-listened to-shiver
(in secret and divine woods I have listened to the ceaseless)

sans fin l'hamadryade. O cher Passé mystérieux
without end the-woodnymph. O dear Past mysterious
(shivering of the woodnymph. O dear mysterious Past)

qui vous reflétez dans mes yeux comme un nuage,
that yourself reflect in my eyes like a cloud,
(that is reflected in my eyes like a cloud,)

il me serait plaisant et doux.
it to-me would-be pleasant and sweet.
(it would be pleasant and sweet to me.)

Passé, d'essayer avec vous le long voyage! ...
Past, of-to-try with you the long voyage! ...
(Past, to undertake the long voyage with you! ...)

Si je glisse, les eaux feront un rond fluide ...
If I slip, the waters will-make a circle fluid ...
(If I slip, the waters will make a fluid circle ...)

un autre rond, un autre à peine ...
an other circle, an other to pain ...
(another circle, just barely another ...)

Et puis le miroir enchanté reprendra
And then the mirror enchanted will-take-back
(And then the enchanted mirror will take back)

sa limpidité froide et sereine.
its limpidity cold and serene.
(its cold and serene limpidity.)

Mirages
Mirages

Jardin Nocturne
Garden Nocturnal
(Nocturnal Garden)

Nocturne jardin tout rempli de silence,
Nocturnal garden all filled of silence,
(Nocturnal garden all filled with silence,)

voici que la lune ouverte se balance
here-is that the moon open itself balances
(Behold the open moon that wavers)

en des voiles d'or fluides et légers;
in some veils of-gold fluid and light;
(among wispy, fluid veils of gold;)

elle semble proche et cependant lointaine...
it seems near and yet far-away...
(it seems near and yet faraway...)

Son visage rit au coeur de la fontaine
Its visage laughs to-the heart of the fountain
(Its face laughs in the heart of the fountain)

et l'ombre pâlit sous les noirs orangers.
and the-shadow pales under the black orange-trees.
(and the shadows pale under the black orange trees.)

Nul bruit, si ce n'est le faible bruit
No noise, if that not-is the feeble noise
(No noise, except the faint sound)

de l'onde fuyant goutte à goutte au bord
of the-wave fleeing drop to drop on-the shore
(of the wave fleeing drop by drop to the edge)

des vasques rondes, ou le bleu frisson
of-the basins round, or the blue shiver
(of the round basins, or the blue shiver)

(cont.)

d'une brise d'été, furtive parmi des palmes invisibles ...
of-a breeze of-summer, furtive among some palms invisible...
(of a summer breeze, furtive among invisible palms...)

Je sais, ô jardin, vos caresses sensibles,
I know, o garden, your caresses sensitive,
(I know, o garden, your sensitive caresses,)

et votre languide et chaude volupté!
and your languid and warm voluptuousness!
(and your languid and warm voluptuousness!)

Je sais votre paix délectable et morose,
I know your peace delectable and morose,
(I know your delectable and morose peace,)

vos parfums d'iris, de jasmins et de roses,
your perfumes of-irises, of jasmines and of roses,
(your perfumes of iris, jasmin and rose,)

vos charmes troublés de désirs et d'ennui ...
your charms troubled of desires and of-ennui...
(your charms troubled by desires and boredom...)

O jardin muet! L'eau des vasques s'égoutte
O garden mute! The-water of-the basins itself-drips
(O mute garden! The water of the basins drips)

avec un bruit faible et magique ...
with a noise feeble and magic...
(with a faint and magic sound...)

J'écoute ce baiser qui chante aux lèvres de la nuit.
I-listen-to that kiss which sings to-the lips of the night.
(I listen to that kiss which sings on the lips of night.)

Mirages
Mirages

Danseuse
Dancer

Soeur des Soeurs tisseuses de violettes,
Sister of-the Sisters weavers of violets,
(Sister of the violet-weaving Sisters,)

une ardente veille blémit tes joues...Danse!
an ardent vigil blemishes your cheeks...Dance!
(an ardent vigil pales your cheeks...Dance!)

et que les rythmes aigus dénouent tes
and that the rhythms sharp untie your
(and let the sharp rhythms untie your)

bandelettes. Vase svelte, fresque mouvante et souple,
ribbons. Vessel slender, fresco moving and supple,
(ribbons. Slender vessels, moving and supple fresco,)

danse, danse, paumes vers nous tendues,
dance, dance, palms toward us stretched,
(dance, dance, palms stretched toward us,)

pieds étroits fuyant tels des ailes nues
feet narrow fleeing like some wings nude
(narrow feet fleeing like nude wings)

qu'Eros découple...sois la fleur multiple un peu
that-Eros loosens...be the flower multiple a little
(that Eros loosens...be the multiple flower)

balancée, sois l'écharpe offerte au désir qui change,
balanced, be the-scarf offered to-the desire that changes,
(balanced a little, be the scarf offered to changing desire,)

sois la lampe chaste, la flamme étrange,
be the lamp chaste, the flame strange,
(be the chaste lamp, the strange flame,)

(cont.)

sois la pensée! Danse, danse au chant
be the thought! Dance, dance to-the song
(be the thought! Dance, dance to the song)

de ma flûte creuse. Soeur des Soeurs divines.
of my flute hollowed. Sister of-the Sisters divine.
(of my hollow flute. Sister of the divine Sisters.)

La moiteur glisse, baiser vain le long de ta hanche lisse ...
The moistness glides, kiss vain the length of your haunch smooth
(The moistness glides, a vain kiss on the length of your smooth hip)

Vaine danseuse!
Vain dancer!
(Vain dancer!)

Fauré

Nell

Nell

Ta rose de pourpre, à ton clair soleil,
Your rose of purple, to your bright sun,
(Your purple rose, in your bright sun,)

ô juin étincelle enivrée; penche aussi vers moi
Oh June sparkles drunken; bend also toward me
(Oh June; sparkles drunkenly; bend toward me also)

ta coupe dorée: mon coeur à ta rose est pareil.
your cup golden: my heart to your rose is parallel.
(Your golden cup: my heart is like your rose.)

Sous le mol abri de la feuille ombreuse
Under the soft refuge of the leaf shady
(Under the soft refuge of the shady leaf)

monte un soupir de volupté; plus d'un ramier
rises a sigh of voluptuousness; more of-one dove
(rises a sigh of voluptuousness; more than one dove)

chante au bois écarté, ô mon coeur, sa plainte amoureuse.
sings to-the woods pushed-away, o my heart, its complaint loving.
(sings in the lonely woods, o my heart, its loving complaint.)

Que ta perle est douce au ciel enflammé,
That your pearl is sweet to-the heaven inflamed,
(How sweet is your pearl in the inflamed heaven,)

étoile de la nuit pensive!
star of the night pensive!
(star of the pensive night!)

Mais combien plus douce est la clarté vive
But how-much more sweet is the light living
(But how much sweeter is the living light)

qui rayonne en mon coeur charmé! La chantante mer,
that shines in my heart charmed! The singing sea,
(that shines in my charmed heart! The singing sea,)

(cont.)

le long du rivage, taira son murmure éternel,
the length of-the shore, will-quiet its murmur eternal,
(the length of the shore, will quiet its eternal murmur,)

avant qu'en mon coeur, chère amour, ô Nell,
before that-in my heart, dear love, o Nell,
(before, in my heart, dear love, o Nell,)

ne fleurisse plus ton image!
not flourishes more your image!
(your image no longer flourishes!)

Fauré

Nocturne

Nocturne

La nuit, sur le grand mystère, entr'ouvre ses écrins bleus;
The night, on the great mystery, between-opens its jewel-boxes blue;
(Night, on the great mystery, opens its blue jewel boxes;)

autant de fleurs sur la terre que d'étoiles dans les cieux.
as-many of flowers on the earth that of-stars in the heavens.
(as many flowers on earth as stars in the heavens.)

On voit ses ombres dormantes s'éclairer à tous moments
One sees its shadows sleeping themselves-to-shine at all moments
(One sees its sleeping shadows shine at every moment)

autant par les fleurs charmantes que par les astres charmants.
as-much by the flowers charming that by the stars charming.
(as much from charming flowers as from charming stars.)

Moi, ma nuit au sombre voile n'a pour charme et pour clarté
Me, my night to-the somber veil not-has for charm and for clarity
(Me, my night with its somber veil has for charm and for clarity)

qu'une fleur et qu'une étoile, mon amour et ta beauté!
but-a flower and but-a star, my love and your beauty!
(only a flower and a star, my love and your beauty!)

Noël
Christmas

La nuit descend du haut des cieux,
The night descends from-the height of-the heavens,
(The night descends from the sky above,)

le givre au toit suspend ses franges.
the frost to-the roof suspends its fringes.
(the frost on the roof suspends its fringe.)

Et, dans les airs, le vol des anges éveille
And, in the airs, the flight of-the angels awakens
(And, in the wind, the flight of angels awakens)

un bruit mystérieux.
a noise mysterious.
(a mysterious noise.)

L'étoile qui guidait les mages s'arrête enfin dans les nuages,
The-star that guided the magi itself-arrests at-last in the clouds,
(The star that guided the magi stops at last in the clouds,)

et fait briller un nimbe d'or sur la chaumière où Jésus dort.
and makes to-shine a halo of-gold on the hut where Jesus sleeps.
(and makes a halo of gold shine on the stable where Jesus sleeps.)

Alors, ouvrant ses yeux divins, l'enfant couché dans l'humble crèche,
Then, opening his eyes divine, the-infant lying in the-humble crib,
(Then, opening his divine eyes, the child lying in the humble crib,)

de son berceau de paille fraîche, sourit aux nobles pèlerins.
from his cradle of straw fresh, smiles at-the noble pilgrims.
(from his cradle of fresh straw, smiles at the noble pilgrims.)

Eux s'inclinant, lui disent: Sire, reçois l'encens,
They themselves-bowing, to-him say: Sire, receive the-incense,
(Bowing down, they say to him: Lord, receive our incense,)

l'or et la myrrhe, et laisse-nous, ô doux Jésus,
the-gold and the myrrh, and let-us, oh sweet Jesus,
(gold and myrrh, and let us, oh sweet Jesus,)

baiser le bout de tes pieds nus.
to-kiss the tip of your feet nude.
(kiss the tip of your naked feet.)

Comme eux, ô peuple, incline-toi, imite leur pieux exemple,
Like them, oh people, incline-yourself, imitate their pious example,
(Like them, oh people, bow down, imitate their pious example,)

car cette étable, c'est un temple, et cet enfant sera ton roi!
for this stable, it-is a temple, and this infant will-be your king!
(for this stable is a temple, and this child will be your king!)

Fauré

Notre Amour

Our Love

Notre amour est chose légère Comme les parfums que le vent
Our love is thing light Like the perfumes that the wind
(Our love is a light thing like the perfumes that the wind)

Prend aux cimes de la fougère Pour qu'on les
Takes to-the tops of the fern For that-one them
(Takes to the top of the fern so one may)

respire en rêvant.
breathe in dreaming.
(breathe them in dreaming.)

Notre amour est chose légère. Notre amour est chose charmante,
Our love is thing light. Our love is thing charming,
(Our love is a light thing. Our love is a charming thing,)

Comme les chansons du matin Où nul regret ne se lamente,
Like the songs of-the morning Where no regret not itself laments,
(Like the songs of morning Where no regret laments,)

Où vibre un espoir incertain. Notre amour est chose charmante.
Where vibrates a hope uncertain. Our love is thing charming.
(Where vibrates an uncertain hope. Our love is a charming thing.)

Notre amour est chose sacrée Comme le mystère des bois
Our love is thing sacred Like the mystery of-the woods
(Our love is a sacred thing Like the mystery of the woods)

Où tressaille une âme ignorée, Où les silences
Where shudders a soul ignored, Where the silences
(Where an unknown soul shudders, Where silence)

ont des voix.
have some voices.
(has a voice.)

Notre amour est chose sacrée. Notre amour est chose infinie,
Our love is thing sacred. Our love is thing infinite,
(Our love is a sacred thing. Our love is an infinite thing,)

Comme le chemin des couchants Où la mer,
Like the path of-the setting-suns Where the sea,
(Like the setting sun's path Where the sea,)

aux cieux réunie,
to-the heavens reunited,
(united with the sky,)

S'endort sous les soleils penchants.
Itself-sleeps under the suns inclined.
(Goes to sleep under the inclined sun.)

Notre amour est chose infinie.
Our love is thing infinite.
(Our love is an infinite thing.)

Notre amour est chose éternelle Comme tout ce
Our love is thing eternal Like all this
(Our love is an eternal thing like everything)

qu'un Dieu vainqueur
that-a God vanquishing
(which a victorious God)

A touché du feu de son aile. Comme tout ce qui
Has touched of-the fire of his wing. Like all that which
(Has touched with the fire of his wing. Like everything which)

vient du coeur,
comes from-the heart,
(comes from the heart,)

Notre amour est chose éternelle.
Our love is thing eternal.
(Our love is an eternal thing.)

Fauré

Poème d'un Jour

Poem of-a Day

Rencontre

Meeting

J'étais triste et pensif quand je t'ai recontrée;
I-was sad and pensive when I you-have met;
(I was sad and pensive when I met you;)

Je sens moins, aujourd'hui, mon obstiné tourment.
I feel less, today, my obstinate torment.
(Today I feel less of my obstinate torment.)

O dis-moi, serais-tu la femme inespérée
O tell-me, might-be-you the woman unexpected
(O tell me, might you be the unexpected woman)

et le rêve idéal poursuivi vainement?
and the dream ideal pursued vainly?
(and the ideal dream vainly pursued?)

O passante aux doux yeux, serais-tu donc l'amie
O passerby to-the sweet eyes, might-be-you thus the-friend
(O passerby with sweet eyes, might you be the love)

qui rendrait le bonheur au poète isolé?
that would-return the happiness to-the poet isolated?
(that would return to bliss the lonely poet?)

Et vas-tu rayonner, sur mon âme affermie
And are-going-you to-shine, on my soul firmed
(And will you shine on my hardened heart)

comme le ciel natal sur un coeur d'exilé?
like the heaven natal on a heart of-exiled?
(like the native sky on an exile's heart?)

Ta tristesse sauvage, à la mienne pareille,
Your sadness savage, to the mine parallel,
(Your savage sadness, like mine,)

aime à voir le soleil décliner sur la mer!
loves to to-see the sun to-decline on the sea!
(loves to watch the sun set on the sea!

Devant l'immensité ton extase s'eveille,
Before the-immensity your ecstasy itself-awakes,
(Before its immensity your ecstasy awakens,)

et le charme des soirs à ta belle âme est cher.
and the charm of-the evenings to your beautiful soul is dear.
(and the charm of evening is dear to your beautiful soul.)

Une mystérieuse et douce sympathie
A mysterious and sweet sympathy
(A mysterious and sweet sympathy)

déjà m'enchaine à toi comme un vivant lien,
already me-enchains to you like a living bond,
(already enchains me to you like a living bond,)

et mon âme frémit, par l'amour envahie,
and my soul trembles, by the-love invaded,
(and my soul trembles, invaded by love,)

et mon coeur te chérit sans te connaître bien.
and my heart you cherishes without you to-know well.
(and my heart cherishes you without knowing you well.)

Fauré

Poème d'un Jour
Poem of-a Day

Toujours
Always

Vous me demandez de me taire; de fuir loin de vous pour jamais
You me ask of myself to-silence; of to-flee far from you for never
(You ask me to be silent; to flee far from you forever)

et de m'en aller, solitaire, sans me rappeler
and of myself-from-here to-go, solitary, without me to-recall
(and to go away, alone, without remembering)

j'aimais! Demandez plutôt aux étoiles de tomber dans l'immensité;
whom I-loved! Ask rather to-the stars of to-fall in the-immensity;
(whom I loved! Ask rather for the stars to fall into the vastness;)

à la nuit de perdre ses voiles, au jour de perdre sa clarté;
to the night of to-lose its veils, to-the day of to-lose its brightness;
(for the night to lose its veils, for the day to lose its brightness;)

Demandez à la mer immense de dessécher ses vastes flots,
Ask to the sea immense of to-dry its vast floats,
(Ask the immense sea to dry its vast waves,)

et, quand les vents sont en démence, D'apaiser ses sombres sanglots!
and, when the winds are in insanity, Of-to-appease its somber sobs
(and when the winds are in torment, To quiet their somber sobs!)

Mais n'espérez pas que mon âme s'arrache
But not-hope not that my soul itself-breaks-away
(But do not hope that my soul will break away)

à ses âpres douleurs,
to its harsh sorrows,
(from its harsh sorrows,)

et se dépouille de sa flamme comme le printemps de ses fleurs!
and itself throws-off of its flame like the spring of its flowers!
(and throw off its flame like the spring its flowers!)

Fauré

Poème d'un Jour
Poem of-a Day

Adieu
Farewell

Comme tout meurt vite, la rose déclose,
As all dies quickly, the rose unclosed,
(How everything dies quickly, the blooming rose,)

et les frais manteaux diaprés des prés;
and the fresh mantles dappled of-the meadows;
(and the fresh dappled cloak of the meadows;)

Les longs soupirs, les bien-aimées, fumées!
The long sighs, the well-loved-ones, smokes!
(Long sighs, loved-ones, vain hopes!)

On voit, dans ce monde léger, changer plus vite
One sees, in this world light, to-change more quickly
(One sees, in this fickle world, more quickly change)

que les flots des grèves, nos rêves;
than the floats of-the beaches, our dreams;
(than the waves of the beaches, our dreams;)

Plus vite que le givre en fleurs, nos coeurs;
More quickly than the hoar-frost in flower, our hearts;
(More quickly than the flowering hoar-frost, our hearts;)

A vous l'on se croyait fidèle,
To you the-one oneself believed faithful,
(To you one believed one would be faithful,)

Cruelle, mais hélas!
Cruel-one, but alas!
(Cruel one, but alas!)

les plus longs amours sont courts!
the more long loves are short!
(the longest loves are short!)

Et je dis en quittant vos charmes, sans larmes,
And I say in leaving your charms, without tears,
(And I say upon taking leave of your charms, without tears,)

presqu'au moment de mon aveu, adieu!
almost-at-the moment of my avowal, farewell!
(almost at the moment of my vow, farewell!)

Fauré

Prison

Prison

Le ciel est, par-dessus le toit, si bleu, si calme!
The sky is, above the roof, so blue, so calm!
(The sky is, above the roof, so blue, so calm!)

Un arbre, par-dessus le toit, berce sa palme, la cloche,
A tree, above the roof, cradles its palm, the bell,
(A tree, above the roof, cradles its palm, the bell,)

dans le ciel qu'on voit, doucement tinte.
in the sky that-one sees, softly chimes.
(in the sky that one sees, softly chimes.)

Un oiseau sur l'arbre qu'on voit chante sa plainte.
A bird on the-tree that-one sees sings its plaint.
(A bird on the tree that one sees sings its lament.)

Mon Dieu, mon Dieu, la vie est là, simple et tranquille.
My God, my God, the life is there, simple and tranquil.
(My God, my God, life is there, simple and tranquil.)

Cette paisible rumeur-là vient de la ville.
That peaceful noise-there comes from the town.
(That peaceful noise comes from the town.)

Qu'as-tu fait, ô toi que voilà pleurant sans cesse,
What-have-you done, oh you that there is crying without cease,
(What have you done, oh you there crying ceaselessly,)

dis, qu'as-tu fait, toi que voilà, de ta jeunesse?
say, what-have-you done, you that there is, with your youth?
(say, what have you done, you there, with your youth?)

Puisqu'ici-bas
Since-here-down
(Since down here)

Puisqu'ici-bas toute âme donne à quelqu'un sa musique,
Since-here-down all soul gives to someone its music,
(Since down here each soul gives someone its music,)

sa flamme, ou son parfum; puisqu'avril donne aux chênes
its flame, or its perfume; since-April gives to-the oaks
(its flame, or its perfume; since April gives the oaks)

un bruit charmant; Puisqu'ici toute chose donne toujours
a noise charming; Since-here all thing gives always
(a charming sound; Since here everything always gives)

son épine ou sa rose à ses amours que la nuit donne aux peines
its thorn or its rose to its loves that the night give to-the pains
(its thorn or its rose to its loves may the night give to sorrows)

l'oubli dormant. Puisque, lorsqu'elle arrive, s'y reposer,
the-oblivion sleeping. Since, when-it arrives, itself-there to-repose,
(a sleeping oblivion. Since, when it arrives, to rest there,)

l'onde amère à la rive donne un baiser; je te donne à cette heure,
the-wave bitter to the shore gives a kiss; I you give to this hour,
(the bitter wave gives the shore a kiss; in that hour, I give to you,)

penché sur toi, la chose la meilleure que j'aie en moi!
bent-over on you, the thing the best that I-have in me!
(bent over you, the best thing I have in me!)

Reçois donc ma pensée triste d'ailleurs, qui, comme une rosée,
Receive then my thought sad of-elsewhere, that, like a dew,
(Receive then my sad thoughts in addition, that, like the dew,)

t'arrive en pleurs! Mes transports pleins d'ivresse,
to-you-arrives in tears! My raptures full of-drunkeness,
(come to you in tears! My raptures full of elation,)

purs de soupçons. Reçois mes voeux sans nombres, ô mes amours!
pure of suspicions. Receive my vows without numbers, o my loves!
(with no suspicions. Receive my innumberable vows, o my love!)

Reçois la flamme ou l'ombre de tous mes jours!
Receive the flame or the-shadow of all my days!
(Recieve the flame or shadow of all my days!)

Et toutes les caresses de mes chansons!
And all the caresses of my songs!
(And all the caresses of my songs!)

Mon esprit qui sans voile vogue au hasard,
My spirit which without sail drifts at random,
(My spirit which drifts randomly without sail,)

et qui n'a pour étoile que ton regard;
and which not-has for star but your face;
(whose only star is your face;)

recois, mon bien céleste, ô ma beauté!
receive, my good heavenly, o my beauty!
(receive my heavenly joy, o my beauty!)

Mon coeur dont rien ne reste, l'amour ôté!
My heart of-which nothing not remains, the-love taken!
(My heart where nothing remains, when love is taken away!)

Fauré

Rêve d'Amour

Dream of-Love

S'il est un charmant gazon que le ciel arrose,
If-it is a charming grass that the heaven waters,
(If there is a charming lawn that heaven waters,)

où naisse en toute saison quelque fleur éclose,
where is-born in every season some flower bloomed,
(where some flower blooms in every season,)

où l'on cueille à pleine main lys, chèvre-feuille et jasmin,
where the-one gathers to full hand lilies, honeysuckle and jasmine,
(where one may gather handfuls of lilies, honeysuckle and jasmine,)

j'en veux faire le chemin où ton pied se pose!
I-of-it want to-make the path where your foot itself places!
(I want to make it the path where your foot walks!)

S'il est un sein bien aimant dont l'honneur dispose,
If-it is a breast well loving of-which the-honor disposes,
(If there is a very loving breast of which honor disposes,)

dont le tendre dévouement n'ait rien de morose,
of-which the tender devotion not-has nothing of moroseness,
(whose tender devotion knows no moroseness,)

si toujours ce noble sein bat pour un digne dessein,
if always this noble breast beats for a deserving design,
(if this noble breast always beats for a deserving design,)

j'en veux faire le coussin où ton front se pose!
I-of-it want to-make the cushion where your face itself places!
(I want to make it the cushion where your face rests!)

S'il est un rêve d'amour, parfumé de rose,
If-it is a dream of-love, perfumed of rose,
(If there is a dream of love, perfumed with roses,)

où l'on trouve chaque jour quelque douce chose,
where the-one finds every day some sweet thing,
(where one finds something sweet everyday,)

un rêve que Dieu bénit, où l'âme à l'âme s'unit,
a dream that God blesses, where the-soul to the-soul itself-unites,
(a dream that God blesses, where soul unites with soul,)

Oh! j'en veux faire le nid où ton coeur se pose.
Oh! I-of-it want to-make the nest where your heart itself places.
(Oh! I want to make it the nest where your heart is.)

Sérénade Toscane
Serenade Tuscan

O toi que berce un rêve enchanteur,
O you whom cradles a dream enchanting,
(O you who an enchanting dream cradles,)

tu dors tranquille en ton lit solitaire.
you sleep tranquil in your bed solitary.
(you sleep quietly alone in your bed.)

Éveille-toi! Regarde le chanteur, esclave de tes yeux,
Wake-you! Watch the singer, slave of your eyes,
(Wake up! Look at the singer, slave of your eyes,)

dans la nuit claire! Éveille-toi mon âme, ma pensée!
in the night bright! Wake-you my soul, my thought!
(in the bright night! Wake, my soul, my thought!)

Entends ma voix par la brise emportée, entends ma voix chanter!
Hear my voice by the breeze carried, hear my voice to-sing!
(Hear my voice carried by the breeze, hear my voice sing!)

Entends ma voix pleurer dans la rosée!
Hear my voice to-weep in the dew!
(Hear my voice weep in the dew!)

Sous ta fenêtre en vain ma voix expire,
Under your window in vain my voice expires,
(Under your window my voice expires in vain,)

et chaque nuit je redis mon martyre sans autre abri
and every night I resay my martydom without other shelter
(and every night I repeat my martydom with no other shelter)

que la voûte étoilée, le vent brise ma voix
than the arch starred, the wind breaks my voice
(than the starry canopy, the wind breaks my voice)

et la nuit est glacée,
and the night is frozen,
(and the night is cold,)

mon chant s'éteint en un accent suprême,
my song itself-extinguishes in an accent supreme,
(my song dies with a final accent,)

ma lèvre tremble en murmurant--je t'aime.
my lip trembles in murmuring--I you-love.
(My lips tremble in murmuring--I love you.)

Je ne peux plus chanter! Ah! daigne te montrer!
I not can more to-sing! Ah! deign you to-show
(I can sing no more! Ah! deign to show yourself!)

daigne apparaître! Si j'étais sûr que tu ne veux paraitre
deign to-appear! If I-was sure that you not want to-appear
(deign to appear! If I were sure that you did not want to appear)

je m'en irais, pour t'oublier, demander au sommeil
I me-from-there would-go for you-to-forget, to-ask of-the slumber
(I would go away to forget you, to ask slumber)

de me bercer jusqu'au matin vermeil, de me bercer
of me to-soothe until-to-the morning vermillion, of me to-cradle
(to soothe me until the crimson morning, to cradle me)

jusqu'à ne plus t'aimer!
until-to not more you-to-love!
(until I love you no more!)

Seule
Alone

Dans un baiser, l'onde au rivage dit ses douleurs;
In a kiss, the-wave to-the shore tells its sorrows;
(In a kiss, the wave tells its sorrows to the shore;)

pour consoler la fleur sauvage, l'aube a des pleurs;
for to-console the flower wild, the-dawn has some tears;
(to console the wild flower, the dawn has tears;)

le vent du soir conte sa plainte au vieux cyprès,
the wind of-the evening recounts its complaint to-the old cypress,
(the evening wind tells its lament to the old cypress,)

la tourterelle au térébinthe ses longs regrets.
the dove to-the terebinth its long regrets.
(the dove, its long regrets to the turpentine-tree.)

Aux flots dormants, quand tout repose, hors la douleur,
To-the billows sleeping, when all rests, outside-of the sorrow,
(To the sleeping billows, when all rests, except sorrow,)

la lune parle, et dit la cause de sa paleur.
the moon speaks, and tells the cause of its pallor.
(the moon speaks, and tells the cause of its pallor.)

Ton dôme blanc, Sainte-Sophie, parle au ciel bleu,
Your dome white, Saint-Sophie, speaks to-the heaven blue,
(Your white dome, Saint-Sophie, speaks to the blue heaven,)

et, tout rêveur le ciel confie son rêve à Dieu.
and, all dreamer the heaven confides its dream to God.
(and, heaven, all dreaming, confides its dream to God.)

Arbre ou tombeau, colombe ou rose. Onde ou rocher, tout,
Tree or tomb, dove or rose. Wave or crag, all,
(Tree or tomb, dove or rose. Wave or crag, all,)

ici-bas, a quelque chose pour s'épancher ... Moi, je suis seule,
here-down, has some thing for itself-to-reveal ... Me, I am alone,
(down here, has something to reveal ... Myself, I am alone,)

et rien au monde ne me répond,
and nothing at-the world not me answers,
(and nothing in the world answers me,)

rien que ta voix morne et profonde,
nothing but your voice mournful and profound,
(Nothing but your voice mournful and profound,)

sombre Hellespont!
sombre Hellespont!
(dark Hellepont!)

Soir
Evening

Voici que les jardins de la nuit vont fleurir.
Here-is that the gardens of the night go to-flower.
(Behold the gardens of night begin to flower.)

Les lignes, les couleurs, les sons deviennent vagues.
The lines, the colors, the sounds become vague.
(The lines, the colors, the sounds become vague.)

Vois! le dernier rayon agonise à tes bagues.
Look! the last ray agonizes at your rings.
(Look! the last ray dies on your rings.)

Ma soeur, entends-tu pas quelque chose mourir?
My sister, hear-you not some thing to-die?
(My sister, do you not hear something dying?)

Mets sur mon front tes mains fraîches comme une eau pure,
Place on my face your hands fresh like a water pure,
(Place your fresh hands on my face like pure water,)

mets sur mes yeux tes mains douces comme des fleurs.
place on my eyes your hands sweet like some flowers.
(place your sweet hands on my eyes like flowers.)

Et, que mon âme où vit le goût secret des pleurs,
And, that my soul where lives the taste secret of-the tears,
(And, let my soul in which lives the secret taste of tears,)

soit comme un lys fidèle et pâle à ta ceinture!
be like a lily faithful and pale at your belt!
(be like a faithful and pale lily at your waist!)

C'est la Pitié qui pose ainsi son doigt sur nous,
It-is the Pity who places thus its finger on us,
(It is Pity who places thus its finger on us,)

et tout ce que la Terre a de soupirs qui montent,
and all this that the Earth has of sighs that rise,
(and of all the rising sighs the Earth has,)

il semble qu'à mon coeur enivré le racontent tes yeux,
it seems that-to my heart intoxicated them recount your eyes,
(it seems that to my intoxicated heart, your eyes speak,)

levés au ciel, si tristes et si doux.
raised to-the heaven, so sad and so sweet.
(raised to heaven, so sad and so sweet.)

Spleen
Spleen

Il pleure dans mon coeur Comme il pleut sur la ville;
It weeps in my heart Like it rains on the town;
(It weeps in my heart Like it rains on the city;)

Quelle est cette langueur Qui pénètre mon coeur?
What is this languor That penetrates my heart?
(What is this languor That penetrates my heart?)

O bruit doux de la pluie Par terre et sur les toits!
O noise soft of the rain On earth and on the roofs!
(O soft noise of the rain On the ground and on the roofs!)

Pour un coeur qui s'ennuie O le chant de la pluie!
For a heart that itself-wearies O the song of the rain!
(O the song of the rain for a weary heart!)

Il pleure sans raison Dans ce coeur qui s'écoeure.
It weeps without reason In this heart that itself-disheartens.
(It weeps without reason In this dejected heart.)

Quoi! nulle trahison?...Ce deuil est sans raison.
What! no treason?...This mourning is without reason.
(What! no treason?...This mourning is without reason.)

C'est bien la pire peine De ne savoir pourquoi
It-is well the worst pain Of not to-know why
(It's the worst pain To not know why)

Sans amour et sans haine Mon coeur a tant de peine!
Without love and without hate My heart has so-much of pain!
(Without love and without hate My heart has so much pain!)

Fauré
Sylvie
Sylvia

Si tu veux savoir ma belle,
If you want to-know my beauty,
(If you want to know, my beauty,)

où s'envole à tire d'aile,
where itself-flies by pull of-wing,
(where on the wing flies,)

l'oiseau qui chantait sur l'ormeau? Je te le dirai,
the-bird that sang on the-elm? I you it will-tell,
(the bird that sang on the elm? I will tell you,)

ma belle, il vole vers qui l'appelle.
my beautiful-one, it flies toward who it-calls.
(my beautiful one, it flies toward whoever calls it.)

Vers celui-là qui l'aimera!
Toward that-one-there who it-will-love!
(Toward the one who will love it!)

Si tu veux savoir, ma blonde,
If you want to-know, my blonde-one,
(If you want to know, my blonde one,)

pourquoi sur terre et sur l'onde
why on earth and on the wave
(why on the earth and on the wave)

la nuit tout s'anime et s'unit?
the night all itself-animates and itself-unites?
(at night everything comes alive and comes together?)

Je te le dirai, ma blonde,
I you it will-tell, my blonde-one,
(I will tell you, my blonde-one,)

c'est qu'il est une heure au monde où,
it-is that-it is an hour at-the world where
(it is because there is an hour in the world,)

loin du jour, veille l'amour!
far from-the day, keeps-vigil the-love!
(far from day, where love keeps vigil!)

Si tu veux savoir
If you want to-know
(If you want to know)

Sylvie, pourquoi j'aime à la folie tes yeux brillants et langoureux?
Sylvie, why I-love to the folly your eyes shining and languorous?
(Sylvie, why I madly love your shining and languorous eyes?)

Je te le dirai, Sylvie--C'est que sans toi dans la vie
I you it will-tell, Sylvie--It-is that without you in the life
(I will tell you, Sylvie--It's that without you in life)

tout pour mon coeur n'est que douleur!
all for my heart not-is but sorrow!
(all to my heart is nothing but sorrow!)

Tarentelle
Tarentelle

Aux cieux la lune monte et luit,
At-the heavens the moon rises and shines,
(The moon rises and shines in the heavens,)

Il fait grand jour en plein minuit!
It makes great day in full midnight!
(It turns midnight into full day!)

Viens avec moi, me disait-elle,
Come with me, to-me said-she,
(Come with me, she said,)

viens sur le sable grésillant,
come on the sand sizzling,
(come on the sizzling sand,)

où saute et brille en frétillant, la Tarentelle.
where leaps and shines in quivering, the Tarantella.
(where quivering, the Tarantella leaps and shines.)

Sus! sus! les danseurs, en voici deux, foule sur l'eau,
Up! up! the dancers, of-them here-are two, crowd on the-water,
(Get up! get up! dancers, here are two of them, crowd on the water,)

foule autour d'eux! L'homme est bien fait, la fille est belle;
crowd around of-them! The-man is well made, the girl is beautiful;
(crowd around them! The man is handsome, the girl is beautiful;)

mais gare à vous, sans y penser, c'est jeu d'amour
but beware to you, without of-it to-think, it-is game of-love
(but you beware, without thinking of it, it's a game of love)

que de danser la Tarentelle! Doux est le bruit du tambourin!
that of to-dance the Tarantella! Sweet is the noise of-the tambourine!
(to dance the Tarantella! Sweet is the noise of the tambourine!)

Si j'étais fille de marin et toi pêcheur, me disait-elle,
If I-was daughter of sailor and you fisherman, to-me said-she,
(If I were a sailor's daughter and you a fisherman, she said,)

toutes les nuits, joyeusement,
all the nights, joyously,
(every night, joyously,)

nous danserions en nous aimant la Tarentelle!
we would-dance in each-other loving the Tarantella!
(we would dance the Tarantella and love each other!)

Tristesse
Sadness

Avril est de retour. La première des roses,
April is of return. The first of-the roses,
(April has returned. The first of the roses,)

de ses lèvres mi-closes, rit au premier beau jour;
from its lips half-closed, laughs at-the first beautiful day;
(with its lips half-closed, laughs at the first beautiful day;)

la terre bienheureuse s'ouvre et s'épanouit;
the earth well-happy itself-opens and itself-blossoms;
(the happy earth opens and blooms;)

tout aime, tout jouit. Hélas!
all loves, all enjoys. Alas!
(everything loves, everything enjoys. Alas!)

j'ai dans le coeur une tristesse affreuse.
I-have in the heart a sadness frightful.
(I have in my heart a frightful sadness.)

Les buveurs en gaité, dans leurs chansons vermeilles,
The drinkers, in gaity, in their songs vermillion,
(The drinkers, happily in their ruddy songs,)

célèbrent sous les treilles le vin et la beauté;
celebrate under the trellises the wine and the beauty;
(celebrate wine and beauty under the trellises;)

la musique joyeuse, avec leur rire clair,
the music joyous, with their laughter bright,
(joyous music, with their bright laughter,)

s'éparpille dans l'air. Hélas! j'ai dans le coeur
itself-scatters in the-air. Alas! I-have in the heart
(scatters in the air. Alas! I have in my heart)

une tristesse affreuse! En déshabillés blancs les jeunes
a sadness frightful! In dishabilles white the young
(a frightful sadness! In white dishevelment the young)

demoiselles s'en vont sous les tonnelles
maidens themselves-from-here go under the arbors
(maidens pass under the arbors)

au bras de leurs galants;
at-the arm of their sweethearts;
(on the arms of their sweethearts;)

la lune langoureuse argente leurs baisers longuement appuyés.
the moon languorous silvers their kisses lengthily placed.
(the languorous moon silvers their kisses, lengthily placed.)

Hélas! j'ai dans le coeur une tristesse affreuse.
Alas! I-have in the heart a sadness frightful.
(Alas! I have in my heart a frightful sadness.)

Moi; je n'aime plus rien, ni l'homme ni la femme,
Me; I not-love more nothing, neither the-man nor the woman,
(Myself; I no longer love anything, neither man nor woman,)

ni mon corps, ni mon âme. Pas même mon vieux chien.
nor my body, nor my soul. Not even my old dog.
(nor my body, nor my soul. Not even my old dog.)

Allez dire qu'on creuse,
Go to-say that-one hollows,
(Go tell them to dig,)

sous le pâle gazon, une fosse sans nom. Hélas!
under the pale grass, a grave without name. Alas!
(under the pale grass, an unmarked grave. Alas!)

j'ai dans le coeur une tristesse affreuse.
I-have in the heart a sadness frightful.
(I have in my heart a frightful sadness.)

Ballade de la Reine Morte d'Aimer
Ballad of the Queen Dead of-to-Love
(Of the Queen who Died of Love)

En Bohême était une Reine
In Bohemia was a Queen
(In Bohemia there was a Queen)

Douce soeur du Roi de Thulé,
Sweet sister King of-the Thulé,
(Sweet sister of the King of Thulé

Belle entre toutes les Reines,
Beautiful among all the Queens,
(Beautiful among all Queens,)

Reine par sa toute Beauté.
Queen by her all Beauty.
(Queen because of her supreme Beauty.)

Le grand Trouvère de Bohême
The great Troubadour of Bohemia
(The great Troubadour of Bohemia)

Un soir triste d'automne roux
One night sad of-autumn red
(One sad, red autumn night)

Lui murmura le vieux: "Je t'aime"!
To-her murmered the old: "I you-love"!
(Murmured to her the old line: "I love you"!

Ames folles et coeurs si fous!...
Souls mad and hearts so mad!...
(Foolish souls and hearts so foolish!...)

Et la Très Belle toute blanche
And the Very Beautiful-One all white
(And the all-white Very Beautiful One)

Le doux Poète tant aima
The gentle Poet so-much loved
(Loved the gentle Poet so much)

Que sur l'heure son âme blanche
That on the-hour her soul white
(That on the hour her white soul)

Vers les étoiles s'exhala...
Toward the stars itself-exhaled...
(Exhaled toward the stars...)

Les grosses cloches de Bohême
The fat bells of Bohemia
(The great bells of Bohemia)

Et les clochettes de Thulé
And the little-bells of Thulé
(And the little bells of Thulé)

Chantèrent l'Hosanna suprême
Sang the-Hosanna final
(Sang the final Hosanna)

De la Reine morte d'aimer.
Of the Queen dead of-to-love
(Of the Queen who died of love.)

Ravel
Cancion Española
Song Spanish
(Spanish Song)

Adios meu homiño, adios,
Goodbye my man, goodbye,
(Goodbye my man, goodbye,)

Ja qui te marchas pr'a guerra
Since that you marched for-to war
(Since you marched away to war)

Non t'olvides d'aprendina
Not you-forget to-learn
(Don't you forget)

Quiche qued' a can'a terra.
That stays to nothing-to earth.
(That nothing remains on earth.)

La la la la...
La la la la...
(La la la la...)

Castellanos de Castilla
Castilians from Castile
(Castilians from Castile)

Tratade ben os galegos:
Triumph well to-the Galicians
(Triumph the Galicians well)

Cando van, van comos rosas,
When they-go, they-go like roses,
(When they go, they go like roses,)

Cando ven, ven como negros.
When they-return, they-return like blacks.
(When they return, they return hardened.)

La la la la....
La la la la....
(La la la la....)

Ravel

Canzone Italiana

Song Italian

(Italian Song)

M'affaccio la finestra e vedo l'onde,
Myself-show the window and I-see the-waves,
(I stand at the window and see the waves,)

Vedo le mie miserie che sò granne!
I-see the my miseries that so great!
(I see my miseries so large!)

Chiamo l'amòre mio, nun m'arrisponde!
I-call the-love mine, no-one me-answers!
(I call to my love, no one answers me!)

Chiamo l'amòre mio, nun m'arrisponde!
I call the-love mine, no-one me-answers!
(I call to my love, no one answers me!)

Chanson Espagnole
Song Spanish
(Spanish Song)

Adieu, va, mon homme, adieu,
Goodbye, go, my man, goodbye,
(Goodbye, go, my husband, goodbye,)

Puisqu'ils t'ont pris pour la guerre
Since-they you-have taken for the war
(Since they have taken you to war)

Il n'est désormais sur terre,
There not-is henceforth on earth,
(There is on earth, henceforth,)

Las! pour moi, ni ris, ni jeu!
Alas! for me, neither laughter, nor play!
(Alas! for me, neither laughter, nor play!)

La la la la...
La la la la...
(La la la la...)

Castille, prends nos garçons Pour faire triompher ta cause,
Castile, take our boys For to-make to-triumph your cause,
(Castile, take our boys To triumph your cause,)

S'en vont aussi doux que roses,
They-from-here go as sweet that roses,
(They go away as sweet as roses,)

Reviennent durs comme chardons.
Return hard like thistles.
(Return hard like thistles.)

La la la la....
La la la la....
(La la la la....)

Chanson Française
(Chant Populaire Limousin)
Song French
(Song Popular Limousin)

Jeneta ount anirem gardar,
Jenny where we-shall-go to-watch,
(Jenny, where shall we go to watch,)

Qu'ajam buon tems un'oura? Lan la!
That-we-have good times an-hour? Lan la!
(That we may enjoy ourselves for an hour? Lan la!)

Aval, aval, al prat barrat;
There, there, to-the meadow barred;
(There, there, to the striped meadow;)

la de tan belas oumbras! Lan la!
the-one of many beautiful shadows! Lan la!
(that it has so many beautiful shadows! Lan la!)

Lou pastour quita soun mantel,
The shepherd leaves his cloak,
(The shepherd takes off his cloak,)

Per far siere Janetan. Lan la!
To make sit Jenny. Lan la!
(To have Jenny sit. Lan la!)

Janeta a talamen jougat,
Jenny has so-much played,
(Jenny has played so much,)

Que se ies oublidada, Lan la!
That she has forgotten, Lan la!
(That she has forgotten herself, Lan la!)

Chanson Française
(Chant Populair limousin)
Song French
(Song Popular Limousin)

Jeanneton où irons-nous garder,
Jenny where shall-we-go to-guard,
(Jenny, where shall we go to watch,)

Qu'ayons bon temps une heure? Lan, la!
That-have good times an hour? Lan, la!
(That we may enjoy ourselves for an hour? Lan, la!)

Là-bas, là-bas, au pré barré;
There-down, there-down, at-the meadow barred;
(Over there, over there, in the striped meadow;)

Y'a de tant belles ombres! Lan la!
There-is of so-many beautiful shadows! Lan la!
(There are so many beautiful shadows! Lan la!)

Le pasteur quitte son manteau,
The shepherd leaves his cloak,
(The shepherd takes off his cloak,)

Et fait seoir Jeannette. Lan la!
And makes to-sit Jenny. Lan la!
(And has Jenny sit. Lan la!

Jeannette a tellement joué,
Jenny has so-much played,
(Jenny has played so much,)

Que s'y est oubliée, Lan la!
That herself-there is forgotten, Lan la!
(That she has forgotten herself, Lan la!)

Chanson Italienne - Romaine
Song Italian - Roman
(Italian Song - Roman)

Penchée à ma fenêtre, j'écoute l'onde,
Bended at my window, I-listen-to the-wave,
(Leaning at my window, I listen to the waves.)

J'écoute ma misère si profonde!
I-listen-to my misery so deep!
(I listen to my misery so deep!)

Je clame mon amour, nul qui réponde!
I cry my love, no-one who answers!
(I cry out my love, but no one answers!)

Je clame mon amour, nul qui réponde!
I cry my love, no-one who answers!
(I cry out my love, but not one answers!)

Chansons Madécasses
Songs Madagascan
(Madagascan Songs)

I

Nahandove
Nahandove

Nahandove, ô belle Nahandove! L'oiseau nocturne a commencé
Nahandove, oh beautiful Nahandove! The-bird nocturnal has begun
(Nahandove, oh beautiful Nahandove! The nocturnal bird)

ses cris, la pleine lune brille sur ma tête, et la rosée
its cries, the full moon shines on my head, and the dew
(cries, the full moon shines on my head, and the new-born dew)

naissante humecte mes cheveux. Voici l'heure; qui
nascent moistens my hair. Here-is the-hour; who
(moistens my hair. Here the hour is come; who

peut t'arrêter, Nahandove, ô belle Nahandove! Le lit
can you-to-stop, Nahandove, oh beautiful Nahandove! The bed
(can stop you, Nahandove, oh beautiful Nahandove! The bed)

de feuilles est préparé; je l'ai parsemé de fleurs
of leaves is prepared; I it-have strewn with flowers
(of leaves is prepared; I have strewn it with flowers)

et d'herbes odoriféantes; il est digne de tes charmes,
and with-herbs sweet-smelling; it is worthy of your charms,
(and with sweet-smelling herbs; it is worthy of your charms,)

Nahandove, ô belle Nahandove! Elle vient.
Nahandove, oh beautiful Nahandove! She comes.
(Nahandove, oh beautiful Nahandove! She comes.)

J'ai reconnu la respiration précipitée que donne
I-have recognized the breathing precipitated that gives
(I recognized the rapid breathing caused by)

une marche rapide; j'entends le froissement
a walk rapid; I-hear the rustle
(a brisk walk; I hear the rustle)

de la pagne qui l'enveloppe; c'est elle,
of the loin-cloth which her-envelops, it-is she,
(of the loin-cloth which envelops her; it is she,

c'est Nahandove, la belle Nahandove!
it-is Nahandove, the beautiful Nahandove!
(it is Nahandove, the beautiful Nahandove!)

Reprends haleine, ma jeune amie; repose-toi sur mes genoux.
Re-take breath, my young love; rest-yourself on my knees.
(Catch your breath, my young love; rest on my knees.)

Que ton regard est enchanteur! Que le mouvement
That your glance is enchanting! That the movement
(How enchanting is your glance! How the movement)

de ton sein est vif et délicieux sous la main
of your breast is alive and delicious under the hand
(of your breast is alive and delicious under the hand)

qui le presse! Tu souris, Nahandove, ô belle Nahandove!
which it presses! You smile, Nahandove, oh beautiful Nahandove!
(which presses it! You smile, Nahandove, oh beautiful Nahandove!)

Tes baisers pénètrent jusqu'à l'âme; tes caresses brûlent
Your kisses penetrate until-to the-soul; your caresses burn
(Your kisses penetrate my soul; your caresses burn)

tous mes sens; arrête, ou je vais mourir. Meurt-on
all my senses; stop, or I am-going to-die. Does-one-die
(all my senses; stop, or I shall die. Does one die)

de volupté, Nahandove, ô belle Nahandove!
of voluptuousness, Nahandove, oh beautiful Nahandove!
(of voluptuousness, Nahandove, oh beautiful Nahandove!)

Le plaisir passe comme un éclair. Ta douce haleine
The pleasure passes like a flash. Your sweet breath
(Pleasure passes like a flash of lightening. Your sweet breath)

s'affaiblit, tes yeux humides se referment,
itself-falters, your eyes humid themselves re-close,
(falters, your moist eyes close again,)

ta tête se penche mollement, et tes transports
your head itself bends softly, and your ecstasies
(your head bends softly, and your ecstasies)

s'éteignent dans la langueur. Jamais tu ne fus
themselves-extinguish in the languor. Never you not were
(melt into languor. Never were you)

si belle, Nahandove, ô belle Nahandove! Tu pars,
so beautiful Nahandove, oh beautiful Nahandove! You leave
(more beautiful Nahandove, oh beautiful Nahandove! You leave)

et je vais languir dans les regrets et les désirs.
and I am-going to-languish in the regrets and the desires.
(and I will languish in regrets and desires.)

Je languirai jusqu'au soir. Tu reviendras ce soir,
I will-languish until-to-the evening. You will-return this evening,
(I will languish until evening. You will return this evening,)

Nahandove, ô belle Nahandove!
Nahandove, oh beautiful Nahandove!
(Nahandove, oh beautiful Nahandove!)

Chansons Madécasses
Songs Madagascan
(Madagascan Songs)

II

Aoua!
Aoua!

Méfiez-vous des Blancs, habitants du rivage.
Distrust-you of-the whites, inhabitants of-the shore.
(Inhabitants of the shore, beware of the white man.)

Du temps de nos pères, des Blancs descendirent
From-the times of our fathers, some whites descended
During the time of our fathers, some whites descended)

dans cette île. On leur dit: Voila des terres,
on this isle. One to-them said: Here-are of-the lands,
(on this island. We told them: Here are lands,)

que vos femmes les cultivent; soyez justes, soyez bons,
that your wives them cultivate; be just, be good,
(may your wives cultivate them; be just, be good,)

et devenez nos frères. Les Blancs promirent,
and become our brothers. The whites promised,
(and become our brothers. The whites promised,)

et cependant ils faisaient des retranchements.
and yet they made some entrenchments.
(and yet they built entrenchments.)

Un fort menaçant s'eleva; le tonnerre fut renfermé
A fort menacing itself-arose; the thunder was enclosed
(A menacing fort arose; the thunder was closed)

dans des bouches d'airain; leurs prêtres voulurent
in some mouths of-brass; their priests wanted
(in mouths of brass; their priests wanted)

nous donner un Dieu que nous ne connaissons pas,
us to-give a God that we not knew not,
(to give us a God that we did not know,)

ils parlèrent enfin d'obéissance et d'esclavage.
they spoke finally of-obedience and of-slavery.
(they spoke at last of obedience and of slavery.)

Plûtot la mort. Le carnage fut long et terrible;
Rather the death. The carnage was long and terrible;
(Death sooner. The carnage was long and terrible;)

mais malgré la foudre qu'ils vomissaient, et qui écrasait
but despite the thunder that-they vomited, and that crushed
(but despite the thunder that they vomited, and that destroyed)

des armées entières, ils furent tous exterminés.
some armies entire, they were all exterminated.
(entire armies, they were all exterminated.)

Aoua: Méfiez-vous des Blancs. Nous avons vu de nouveaux
Aoua: Distrust-you of-the whites. We have seen some new
(Aoua: Beware of the white man. We have seen new)

tyrans, plus forts et plus nombreux, planter leur
tyrants, more strong and more numerous, to-plant their
(tyrants, stronger and more numerous, planting their)

pavillon sur le rivage. Le ciel a combattu pour nous.
pavillion on the shore. The sky has combatted for us.
(flag on the shore. The sky has fought for us.)

Il a fait tomber sur eux les pluies, les tempêtes
It has made to-fall on them the rains, the tempests
(It has made rain fall on them, tempests)

et les vents empoisonnés. Ils ne sont plus, et nous
and the winds poisoned. They not are more, and we
(and poisoned winds. They are no more, and we)

(cont.)

vivons, et nous vivons libres. Aoua! Méfiez-vous
live, and we live free. Aoua! Distrust-you
(live, and we live free. Aoua!)

des Blancs, habitants du rivage.
of-the whites, inhabitants of-the shore.
(inhabitants of the shore, beware of the white man.)

Chansons Madécasses
Songs Madagascan
(Madagascan Songs)

III

Il est doux
It is sweet

Il est doux de se coucher, durant la chaleur,
It is sweet of oneself to-lie-down, during the heat
(It is sweet to rest, during the heat,)

sous un arbre touffu, et d'attendre que le vent du soir
under a tree tufted, and of to-wait that the wind of-the evening
(under a leafy tree, and to wait for the evening wind)

amène la fraîcheur. Femmes, approchez. Tandis que
brings the freshness. Women, approach. While that
(to bring its freshness. Women, approach. While)

je me repose ici sous un arbre touffu, occupez
I myself rest here under a tree tufted, occupy
(I rest under a leafy tree, occupy)

mon oreille par vos accents prolongés. Répétez la chanson
my ear by your accents prolonged. Repeat the song
(my ear with your prolonged accents. Repeat the song)

de la jeune fille, lorsque ses doigts tressent la natte
of the young girl, when her fingers weave the plait
(of the young girl, when her fingers weave the plait)

ou lorsqu'assise auprès du riz, elle chasse les
or when-sitting beside of-the rice, she chases the
(or when sitting beside the rice, she chases away the)

oiseaux avides. Le chant plaît à mon âme. La danse
birds greedy. The song is-pleasing to my soul. The dance
(greedy birds. The song pleases my soul. The dance)

est pour moi presqu'aussi douce qu'un baiser. Que vos
is for me almost-as sweet that-a kiss. That your
(is for me almost as sweet as a kiss. May your)

pas soient lents; qu'ils imitent les attitudes du plaisir
steps be slow; that-they imitate the attitudes of-the pleasure
(steps be slow; may they imitate the attitudes of pleasure)

et l'abandon de la volupté. Le vent du soir;
and the-abandon of the voluptuousness. The wind of-the evening
(and abandon of voluptuousness. The evening wind)

se lève; la lune commence à briller au travers des arbres
itself rises; the moon begins to to-shine to-the through of-the trees
(rises, the moon begins to shine through the trees)

de la montagne. Allez, et preparez le repas.
of the mountain. Go, and prepare the repast.
(of the mountain. Go, and prepare the feast.)

Cinq Mélodies Populaires Grecques
Five Melodies Popular Greek
(Five Greek Popular Melodies)

I

Le Réveil de la Mariée
The Awakening of the Bride

Réveille-toi, perdrix mignonne,
Awake-you, partridge pretty,
(Wake up, pretty partridge,)

Ouvre au matin tes ailes.
Open to-the morning your wings.
(Open your wings to the morning.)

Trois grains de beauté
Three spots of beauty
(Three beauty marks)

Mon coeur en est brûlé.
My heart of-them has burned.
(Have inflamed my heart.)

Vois le ruban d'or que je t'apporte
See the ribbon of-gold that I you-bring
(See the golden ribbon that I bring you)

Pour le nouer autour de tes cheveux.
For it to-tie around of your hair.
(To tie around your hair.)

Si tu veux, ma belle, viens nous marier!
If you wish, my beauty, come us to-marry!
(If you wish, my beauty, come let us be married!)

Dans nos deux familles tous sont alliés.
In our two families all are allied.
(In our two families all are kindred.)

Là-bas, Vers l'Eglise
Over-there, Toward the-Church

Là-bas, vers l'église,
Over-there, toward the-church,
(Over there, toward the church,)

Vers l'église Ayio Sidéro,
Toward the-church St. Sidéro,
(Toward the St. Sidéro church,)

L'église, O Vierge Sainte,
The-church, O Vigin Saint,
(The church, O Holy Virgin,)

L'église Ayio Constanndino,
The-church St. Constantine,
(The St. Constantine church,)

Se sont réunis,
Themselves are reunited,
(They are gathered,)

Rassemblés en nombre infini,
Reassembled in number infinite,
(Assembled in infinite number,)

Du monde, O Vierge Sainte,
In-the world, O Virgin Saint,
(People, O Holy Virgin,)

Du monde tous les plus braves!
In-the world all the most brave!
(All the bravest in the world!)

Quel Galant!
What Gallant!

Quel galant m'est comparable
What gallant to-me-is comparable
(What suitor is comparable to me)

D'entre ceux qu'on voit passer?
Of-among those who-one sees to-pass?
(Among those one sees passing?)

Dis, Dame Vassiliki?
Say, Lady Vassiliki?
(Tell me, Lady Vassiliki?)

Vois, pendus à ma centure
See, hung on my belt
(See, hung on my belt)

Pistolets et sabre aigu...
Pistols and saber sharp...
(Pistols and sharp saber...)

Et c'est toi que j'aime.
And it-is you whom I-love.
(And it is you whom I love.)

Chanson des Cueilleuses de Lentisques
Song of-the Gatherers of Lentisks

O joie de mon âme, joie de mon coeur,
O joy of my soul, joy of my heart,
(O joy of my soul, joy of my heart,)

Trésor qui m'est si cher;
Treasure who to-me-is so dear;
(Treasure so dear to me;)

Joie de l'âme et du coeur,
Joy of the-soul and of-the heart,
(Joy of the soul and of the heart,)

Toi que j'aime ardemment,
You whom I-love ardently,
(You whom I love ardently,)

Tu est plus beau qu'un ange.
You are more beautiful than-an angel.
(You are more beautiful than an angel.)

O lorsque tu parais, ange si doux,
O when you appear, angel so sweet,
(O when you appear, angel so sweet,)

Devant nos yeux,
Before our eyes,
(Before our eyes,)

Comme un bel ange blond
Like a beautiful angel blond
(Like a beautiful blond angel)

Sous le clair soleil,
Under the bright sun,
(Under the bright sun,)

Hélas, tous nos pauvres coeurs soupirent!
Alas, all our poor hearts sigh!
(Alas, all our poor hearts sigh!)

Tout Gai!
All Gay!

Tout gai,
All gay,
(All gay,)

Ah, tout gai;
Ah, all gay;
(Ah, all gay;)

Belle jambe, tireli qui danse,
Beautiful leg, tireli that dances,
(Beautiful leg, tireli that dances,)

Belle jambe, la vaiselle danse.
Beautiful leg, the pottery dances.
(Beautiful leg, the pottery dances.)

Tra-la-la.
Tra-la-la.
(Tra-la-la.)

Deux Epigrammes de Clément Marot
Two Epigrams of Clement Marot

I.

...D'Anne qui luy jecta de la neige
...Of Anne who him threw of the snow
(...Of Anne who threw snow at him)

Anne par jeu me jecta de la neige,
Anne in play me threw of the snow,
(Anne in play threw snow at me,)

Que je cuidoys froide, certainement:
Which I thought cold, certainly:
(Which I thought cold, certainly:)

Mais c'estoit feu, l'expérience en ay je,
But it-was fire, the experience of-it have I,
(But it was fire, which I experienced,)

Car embrasé je fuz soubdainement.
Because afire I was suddenly.
(Because afire I suddenly was.)

Puisque le feu loge secretement
Since-that the fire lodges secretly
(Since the fire lodges secretly)

Dedans la neige, où trouveray je place
Inside the snow, where will-find I place
(In the snow, where will I find a place)

Pour n'ardre point? Anne, ta seule grâce
For not-to-burn at-all? Anne, your only grace
(To burn no more? Anne, only your grace)

Estaindre peut le feu que je sens bien,
To-quench can the fire that I feel well,
(Can quench the fire that I deeply feel,)

Non point par eau, par neige ne par glace,
Not none by water, by snow nor by ice,
(Not by water, nor snow nor ice,)

Mais par sentir ung feu pareil au mien.
But by to-feel a fire equal to-the mine.
(But by feeling a fire equal to mine.)

Ravel
Deux Epigrammes
Two Epigrams

II

...D'Anne jouant de l'espinette
...Of-Anne playing of the-spinet
(...Of Anne playing at the spinet)

Lorsque je voy en ordre la brunette,
When I see in order the brunette,
(When I see all neat the brunette,)

Jeune, en bon point, de la ligne des Dieux,
Young, in good style, of the line of-the Gods,
(Young, in good style, descended from the Gods,)

Et que sa voix, ses doits et l'espinette
And that her voice, her fingers and the-spinet,
(And her voice, her fingers and the spinet,)

Meinent ung bruyct doulx et mélodieux,
Make a sound sweet and melodious
(Make a sweet and melodious sound,)

J'ay du plaisir, et d'oreilles et d'yeulx
I-have of-the pleasure, and of-ears and of-eyes
(I have the pleasure both of ears and eyes)

Plus que les sainctz en leur gloire immortelle,
More than the saints in their glory immortal,
(More than the saints in their immortal glory,)

Et autant qu'eulx je deviens glorieux
And as-much-as that-them I become glorious
(And I become as glorious as them)

Dès que je pense estre un peu aymé d'elle.
As-soon that I think to-be a little loved of-her.
(When I think I am a little loved by her.)

Ravel
Deux Melodies Hébraïques
Two Melodies Hebraic

I.

Kaddisch
Kaddish

Que ta gloire, O Roi des Rois, soit exaltée;
That your glory, O King of-the Kings, be exalted;
(Let your glory, O King of Kings, be exalted;)

O toi qui doit renouveler le monde et ressusciter les morts.
O you who must to-renew the world and to-resuscitate the deads.
(O you who renews the world and revives the dead.)

Que ton règne, Adonäi, soit proclamé par nous, fils d'Israël,
That your reign, Lord, be proclaimed by us, sons of Israel,
(Let your reign, Lord, be proclaimed by us, sons of Israel,)

aujourd'hui, demain, à jamais. Disons tous: Amen.
today, tomorrow, to ever. Let-us-say all: Amen.
(today, tomorrow, forever. Let all say: Amen.)

Qu'il soit aimé, qu'il soit chéri, loué,
That-it be loved, that-it be cherished, lauded,
(Let your radiant name be loved, let it be cherished, lauded)

glorifié, ton nom radieu.
glorified, your name radiant.
(glorified, your radiant name.)

Qu'il soit béni, sanctifié, adoré,
That-it be blessed, sanctified, adored,
(Let it be blessed, sanctified, adored,)

ton nom qui plane sur les cieux, sur nos louanges,
your name which soars on the heavens, on our praises,
(your name which soars in the heavens, in our praises,)

sur nos hymnes, sur toutes nos bénédictions.
on our hymns, on all our benedictions.
(in our hymns, in all our blessings.)

Que le ciel clément nous accorde le calme,
That the heaven clement us accord the calm,
(Let merciful heaven accord us calm,)

la paix, le bonheur. Disons tous: Amen.
the peace, the happiness. Let-us-say all: Amen.
(peace, happiness. Let all say: Amen.)

Ravel
Deux Melodies Hébraïques
Two Melodies Hebraic

II.

L'énigme éternelle
The enigma eternal
(The eternal enigma)

Monde tu nous interroges: Tra la tra la...
World you us question: Tra la tra la...
(World you question us: Tra la tra la...)

L'on répond: Tra la la la...
The-one responds: Tra la la la...
(We reply: Tra la la la...)

Si l'on peut te répondre Tra la la la...
If the-one can you to-answer Tra la la la...
(If we can answer you Tra la la la...)

Monde tu nous interroges Tra la la la....
World you us question Tra la la la...
(World you question us Tra la la la...)

Ravel

Don Quichotte à Dulcinée

Don Quixote to Dulcinea

Chanson Romanesque

Song Romanesque

(Romanesque Song)

Si vous me disiez que la terre
If you to-me said that the earth
(If you told me that the earth)

A tant tourner vous offensa,
To so-much to-turn you offended,
(Offended you with so much turning,)

Je lui dépêcherais Pança:
I to-it would-dispatch Panza:
(I would dispatch Panza:)

Vous la verriez fixe et se taire.
You it would-see fixed and itself to-silence.
(You would see it motionless and silent.)

Si vous me disiez que l'ennui
If you to-me said that the-boredom
(If you told me that your boredom comes)

Vous vient du ciel trop fleuri d'astres,
To-you comes from-the sky too flowered of-stars,
(From the sky too flowered with stars,)

Déchirant les divins cadastres,
Tearing the divine cadaster,
(Destroying the divine order,)

Je faucherais d'un coup la nuit.
I would-mow-down of-a blow the night.
(With a blow I would cut them from the night.)

Si vous me disiez que l'espace
If you to-me said that the-space
(If you told me that space)

Ainsi vidé ne vous plaît point,
Thus emptied not you pleases at-all,
(Thus emptied does not please you at all,)

Chevalier dieu, la lance au poing,
Knight god, the lance at-the fist,
(God-like knight, with lance in hand,)

J'étoilerais le vent qui passe.
I-would-bestar the wind which passes.
(I would bestar the passing wind.)

Mais si vous disiez que mon sang
But if you said that my blood
(But if you said that my blood)

Est plus à moi qu'à vous, ma Dame,
Is more to me than-to you, my Lady,
(Is more mine than yours, my Lady,)

Je blêmirais dessous le blâme
I would-pale under the blame
(I would pale under the blame)

Et je mourrais, vous bénissant.
And I would-die, you blessing.
(And I would die, blessing you.)

O Dulcinée.
O Dulcinea.
(O Dulcinea.)

Ravel
Don Quichotte à Dulcinée
Don Quixote to Dulcinea

Chanson Epique
Song Epic
(Epic Song)

Bon Saint Michel qui me donnez loisir
Good Saint Michael who to-me gives leisure
(Good Saint Michael who gives me leisure)

De voir ma Dame et de l'entendre,
Of to-see my Lady and of her-to-hear,
(To see my Lady and to hear her,)

Bon Saint Michel qui me daignez choisir
Good Saint Michael who me deigns to-choose
(Good Saint Michael who deigns to choose me)

Pour lui complaire et la défendre,
For to-her please and her defend,
(To please her and defend her,)

Bon Saint Michel veuillez descendre
Good Saint Michael may-you-wish to-descend)
(Good Saint Michael please descend)

Avec Saint Georges sur l'autel
With Saint George upon the-altar
(With Saint George upon the altar)

De la Madone au bleu mantel.
Of the Madonna at-the blue mantle.
(Of the Madonna of the blue mantle.)

D'un rayon du ciel bénissez ma lame
Of-a ray from-the heaven bless my blade
(With a ray from heaven bless my sword)

Et son égale en pureté
And its equal in purity
(And its equal in purity)

Et son égale en piété
And its equal in piety
(And its equal in piety)

Comme en pudeur et chasteté: Ma Dame.
As in modesty and chastity: My Lady.
(As in modesty and chastity: My Lady.)

(O grands Saint Georges et Saint Michel)
(O great Saint George and Saint Michael)
((O great Saint George and Saint Michael))

L'ange qui veille sur ma veille,
The-angel who watches on my vigil,
(The angel who watches over my vigil,)

Ma douce Dame si pareille
My sweet Lady so similar
(My sweet Lady so much like)

A vous, Madone au bleu mantel!
To you, Madonna of-the blue mantle!
(You, Madonna of the blue mantle!)

Amen.
Amen.
(Amen.)

Don Quichotte à Dulcinée
Don Quixote to Dulcinea

Chanson à Boire
Song at to-Drink
(Drinking Song)

Foin du bâtard, illustre Dame,
Hay of-the bastard, illustrious Lady,
(Enough of the bastard, illustrious Lady,)

Qui pour me perdre à vos doux yeux,
Who for me to-lose to your sweet eyes,
(Who spoils me in your sweet eyes,)

Dit que l'amour et le vin vieux
Says that the-love and the wine old
(Saying that love and old wine)

Mettent en deuil mon coeur, mon âme!
Put in mourning my heart, my soul!
(Put grief in my heart, my soul!)

Je bois à la joie! La joie est le seul but
I drink to the joy! The joy is the only goal
(I drink to joy! Joy is the only goal)

Où je vais droit...lorsque j'ai bu!
Where I go straight...when I-have drunk!
(To which I go straight...when I've been drinking!)

Foin du jaloux, brune maîtresse,
Hay of-the jealous-one, brunette mistress,
(Enough of the jealous one, brunette mistress,)

Qui geind, qui pleure et fait serment
Who whines, who cries and makes oath
(Who whines, who cries and swears)

D'être toujours ce pâle amant
Of-to-be always this pale lover
(To always be this pale lover)

Qui met de l'eau dans son ivresse!
Who puts of the-water in his inebriation!
(Who waters down his drunken state!)

Je bois à la joie! La joie est le seul but
I drink to the joy! The joy is the only goal
(I drink to joy! Joy is the only goal)

Où je vais droit...lorsque j'ai bu!
Where I go straight...when I-have drunk!
(To which I go straight...when I've been drinking!)

Ravel
Histoires Naturelles
Histories Natural
(Natural Histories)

Le Paon
The Peacock

Il va sûrement se marier aujourd'hui.
He goes surely himself to-marry today.
(He is surely going to be married today.)

Ce devait être pour hier.
It must to-be for yesterday.
(It was supposed to be yesterday.)

En habit de gala, il était prêt.
In clothes of gala, he was ready.
(In gala attire, he was ready.)

Il n'attendait que sa fiancée.
He not-waited but his fiancée.
(He waited only for his fiancée.)

Elle n'est pas venue.
She not-is not come.
(She did not come.)

Elle ne peut tarder.
She not can to-delay.
(She cannot be long.)

Glorieux, il se promène avec une allure de prince indien
Glorious, he himself promenades with an allure of prince Indian
(Glorious, he struts with the allure of an Indian prince)

et porte sur lui les riches présents d'usage.
and carries on him the rich presents of-usage.
(And carries with him the usual rich presents.)

L'amour avive l'éclat de ses couleurs
The-love revives the-flash of his colors
(Love revives the brightness of his colors)

et son aigrette tremble comme une lyre.
and his crest trembles like a lyre.
(and his crest trembles like a lyre.)

La fiancée n'arrive pas.
The fiancée not-arrives not.
(The fiancée does not arrive.)

Il monte au haut du toit et regarde du côté du soleil.
He mounts to-the top of-the roof and looks-at of-the side of-the sun.
(He climbs on top of the roof and looks toward the sun.)

Il jette son cri diabolique: Léon! Léon!
He throws his cry diabolic: Léon! Léon!
(He throws his diabolical cry: Léon! Léon!)

C'est ainsi qu'il appelle sa fiancée.
It-is thus that-he calls his fiancée.
(It is like this that he calls his fiancée.)

Il ne voit rien venir et personne ne répond.
He not sees nothing to-come and no-one not responds.
(He sees nothing coming and no one answers.)

Les volailles habituées ne lèvent même point la tête.
The fowls accustomed not lift even at-all the head.
(The accustomed fowls don't even raise their heads.)

Elles sont lasses de l'admirer.
They are tired of him-to-admire.
(They are tired of admiring him.)

Il redescend dans la cour, si sûr d'être beau
He re-descends into the courtyard, so sure of-to-be beautiful
(He climbs down again into the coutyard, so sure of being beautiful)

qu'il est incapable de rancune.
that-he is incapable of rancor.
(that he is incapable of bitterness.)

Son mariage sera pour demain.
His marriage will-be for tomorrow.
(His marriage will be tomorrow.)

Et, ne sachant que faire du reste de la journée,
And, not knowing that to-do of-the rest of the day,
(And, not knowing what to do for the rest of the day,)

il se dirige vers le perron.
he himself directs toward the steps.
(he heads toward the steps.)

Il gravit les marches, comme des marches de temple,
He ascends the steps, like some steps of temple,
(He ascends the steps, like steps of a temple,)

d'un pas officiel.
of-a step official.
(with an official step.)

Il relève sa robe à queue toute lourde des yeux
He re-raises his robe to tail all heavy of-the eyes
(He lifts his tail, all heavy with eyes)

qui n'ont pu se détacher d'elle.
that not-have been-able themselves to-detach from-it.
(that could not detach themselves from it.)

Il répète encore une fois la cérémonie.
He repeats again one time the ceremony.
(Once more he practices the ceremony.)

Ravel

Histoires Naturelles
Histories Natural
(Natural Histories)

Le Grillon
The Cricket

C'est l'heure où, las d'errer,
It-is the-hour where, tired of-to-wander,
(It is the hour when, tired of wandering,)

l'insecte nègre revient de promenade
the-insect black returns from promenade
(the black insect returns from its stroll)

et répare avec soin le désordre de son domaine.
and repairs with care the disorder of his domain.
(and carefully tidies the disorder of its home.)

D'abord il ratisse ses étroites allées de sable.
At-first he rakes his narrow alleys of sand.
(At first he rakes his narrow alleys of sand.)

Il fait du bran de scie qu'il écarte au
He makes some bran of saw that-he spreads at-the
(He makes some sawdust which he spreads at the)

seuil de sa retraite.
threshold of his retreat.
(threshold of his retreat.)

Il lime la racine de cette grande
He files the root of this tall
(He files the root of this tall)

herbe propre à le harceler. Il se repose.
grass proper to him to-harrass. He himself reposes.
(grass which might harrass him. He rests.)

Puis il remonte sa minuscule montre.
Then he rewinds his minuscule watch.
(Then he rewinds his minuscule watch.)

A-t-il fini? est-elle cassée?
Has-he finished? is-it broken?
(Has he finished? is it broken?)

Il se repose encore un peu.
He himself reposes again a little.
(He rests again for a little.)

Il rentre chez lui et ferme sa porte.
He re-enters to-the-house-of his and closes his door.
(He goes in again and closes his door.)

Longtemps il toure sa clef dans la serrure délicate.
Longtime he turns his key in the lock delicate.
(For a long time he turns his key in the delicate lock.)

Et il écoute: Point d'alarme dehors.
And he listens: No of-alarm outside.
(And he listens: No alarm outside.)

Mais il ne se trouve pas en sûreté.
But he not himself finds not in security.
(But he does not feel safe.)

Et comme par une chaînette dont la poulie grince,
And like by a little-chain whose the pulley creaks,
(And like a creaking pulley with a little chain,)

il descend jusqu'au fond de la terre.
he descends until-to-the bottom of the earth.
(he descends to the depths of the earth.)

On n'entend plus rien.
One not-hears more nothing.
(One hears nothing more.)

Dans le campagne muette, les peupliers se dressent
In the countryside mute, the poplars themselves stand-up)
(In the silent countryside, the poplars rise)

comme des doigts en l'air et désignent la lune.
like some fingers in the-air and designate the moon.
(like fingers in the air pointing at the moon.)

Ravel

Histoires Naturelles
Histories Natural
(Natural Histories)

Le Cygne
The Swan

Il glisse sur le bassin, comme un traîneau blanc,
It glides on the basin, like a sleigh white,
(It glides on the pond, like a white sleigh,)

de nuage en nuage.
from cloud in cloud.
(from cloud to cloud.)

Car il n'a faim que des nuages floconneux
For it not-has hunger but of-the clouds flaky
(Because it hungers only for flaky clouds)

qu'il voit naître, bouger,
that-he sees to-be-born, to-move,
(that he sees being born, moving,)

et se perdre dans l'eau.
and themselves to-lose in the-water.
(and vanishing in the water.)

C'est l'un d'eux qu'il désire.
It-is the-one of-them that-he desires.
(It is one of these which he desires.)

Il le vise du bec,
He it aims of-the beak,
(He takes aim with his beak,)

et il plonge tout à coup son col vêtu de neige.
and he plunges all at blow his neck vested of snow.
(and suddenly plunges with his snowy neck.)

Puis, tel un bras de femme sort d'une manche,
Then, like an arm of woman goes-out from-a sleeve,
(Then, like a woman's arm emerging from a sleeve,)

il le retire. Il n'a rien.
it it retires. He not-has nothing.
(it draws it back. He has nothing.)

Il regarde: les nuages effarouchés ont disparu.
It looks: the clouds startled have disappeared.
(It looks: the startled clouds have disappeared.)

Il ne reste qu'un instant désabusé,
There not remains but-an instant disabused,
(There remains but a disillusioned instant,)

car les nuages tardent peu à revenir,
for the clouds delay little to to-return,
(because the clouds delay little their return,)

et là-bas, où meurent les ondulations
and there-down, where die the undulations
(and over there, where the waves)

de l'eau, en voici un qui se reforme.
of the-water, of-them here-is one that itself reforms.
(in the water die, there is one re-forming.)

Doucement, sur son léger coussin de plumes,
Softly, on its light cushion of feathers,
(Softly, on its light cushion of feathers,)

le cygne rame et s'approche.
the swan paddles and itself-approaches.
(the swan paddles and approaches.)

Il s'épuise à pêcher de vains reflets
It itself-exhausts to to-fish of vain reflections
(It exhausts itself by fishing for vain reflections)

et peut-être qu'il mourra
and perhaps that-he will-die
(and perhaps will die)

victime de cette illusion, avant d'attraper
victim of this illusion, before of-to-trap
(a victim of this illusion, before trapping)

un seul morceau de nuage.
a single morsel of cloud.
(a single morsel of clouds.)

Mais qu'est-ce que je dis?
But what-is-this that I say?
(But what am I saying?)

Chaque fois qu'il plonge,
Each time that-he plunges,
(Each time he plunges,)

il fouille du bec la vase nourrisante
he digs of-the beak the mud nourishing
(he digs into the nourishing mud with his beak)

et ramène un ver. Il engraisse comme une oie.
and brings-back a worm. He grows-fat like a goose.
(and brings out a worm. He is growing fat like a goose.)

Histoires Naturelles
Histories Natural
(Natural Histories)

Le Martin-Pêcheur
The King-Fisher

Ça n'a pas mordu ce soir,
That not-has not bitten this evening,
(Not a bite all evening,)

mais je rapporte une rare émotion.
but I bring-back a rare emotion.
(but I had a rare experience.)

Comme je tenais ma perche de ligne tendue,
As I held my rod of line extended,
(As I held my rod with its line cast out,)

un martin-pêcheur est venu s'y poser.
a king-fisher is come himself-there to-perch.
(a king-fisher came and perched there.)

Nous n'avons pas d'oiseau plus éclatant.
We not-have not of-bird more brilliant.
(We have no bird more brilliant.)

Il semblait une grosse fleur bleue au bout d'une longue tige.
He seemed a large flower blue at-the end of-a long stalk.
(He resembled a large blue flower at the end of a long stalk.)

La perche pliait sous le poids. Je ne respirais plus,
The rod bent under the weight. I not breathed more,
(The rod bent under its weight. I held my breath,)

tout fier d'être pris pour un arbre par un martin-pêcheur.
all proud of-to-be taken for a tree by a king-fisher.
(proud of being taken for a tree by a king-fisher.)

Et je suis sûr qu'il ne s'est pas envolé de peur,
And I am sure that-he not himself-is not flown of fear,
(And I am sure that he did not fly away in fear,)

mais qu'il a cru qu'il ne faisait que passer
but that-he has believed that-he not made but to-pass
(but that he believed that he was only moving)

d'une branche à une autre.
from-one branch to an other.
(from one branch to another.)

Ravel
Histoires Naturelles
Histories Natural
(Natural Histories)

La Pintade
The Guinea-Fowl

C'est la bossue de ma cour.
She-is the hunchback of my courtyard.
(She is the hunchback of my courtyard.)

Elle ne rêve que plaies à cause de sa bosse.
She not dreams but wounds by cause of her hump.
(She dreams of nothing but evil because of her hump.)

Les poules ne lui disent rien:
The fowls not to-her say nothing:
(The fowls say nothing to her:)

Bruquement, elle se précipite et les harcèle.
Brusquely, she herself darts and them harasses.
(Brusquely, she throws herself at them and harasses them.)

Puis elle baisse la tête, penche le corps,
Then she lowers the head, leans the body,
(Then she lowers her head, leans her body,)

et de toute la vitesse de ses pattes maigres,
and of all the speed of her paws skinny,
(and with all the speed of her skinny feet,)

elle court frapper de son bec dur,
she runs to-hit of her beak hard,
(she runs hitting with her hard beak,)

juste au centre de la roue d'une dinde.
just at-the center of the tail of-a turkey.
(just at the center of a turkey's tail.)

Cette poseuse l'agaçait.
This poseur her-bothered.
(This poseur bothered her.)

Ainsi, la tête bleue, ses barbillons à vif,
Thus, the head blue, her wattles to lively,
(Thus, with blue head, lively wattles,)

cocardière, elle rage du matin au soir.
showy, she rages from-the morning to-the evening.
(being showy, she rages from morning to evening.)

Elle se bat sans motif, peut-être parce
She herself beats without motive, perhaps by-that
(She fights without cause, perhaps because)

qu'elle s'imagine toujours qu'on se moque
that-she herself-imagines always that-one itself mocks
(she always imagines that they laugh)

de sa taille, de son crâne chauve et de sa queue basse.
of her figure, of her head bald and of her tail low.
(at her figure, at her bald head and her low tail.)

Et elle ne cesse de jeter un cri discordant
And she not ceases of to-throw a cry discordant
(And she constantly utters her discordant cry)

qui perce l'air comme une pointe.
which pierces the-air like a point.
(which pierces the air like a bullet.)

Parfois elle quitte la cour et disparaît.
At-times she quits the courtyard and disappears.
(At times she leaves the courtyard and disappears.)

Elle laisse aux volailles pacifiques un moment de répit.
She leaves the fowls pacifistic a moment of respite.
(She leaves the peaceful fowls a moment of respite.)

Mais elle revient plus turbulente et plus criarde.
But she returns more turbulent and more clamorous.
(But she returns more turbulent and more clamorous.)

Et, frénétique, elle se vautre par terre.
And, frenetic, she herself wallows on earth.
(And, frantic, she wallows in the ground.)

Qu'a-t-elle donc?
What-has-she then?
(What is wrong with her?)

La sournoise fait une farce.
The sneak makes a farce.
(The sneak plays a prank.)

Elle est allée pondre son oeuf à la campagne.
She is gone to-lay her egg at the country.
(She has gone to lay her egg in the country.)

Je peux le chercher si ça m'amuse.
I can it to-search if that myself-amuses.
(I can search for it if I like.)

Et elle se roule dans la poussière comme une bossue.
And she herself rolls in the dust like a hunchback.
(And she rolls in the dust like a hunchback.)

La Chanson du Rouet
The Song of-the Spinning-wheel

O mon cher rouet, ma blanche bobine,
Oh my dear spinning-wheel, my white bobin,
(Oh my dear spinning wheel, my white bobin,)

Je vous aime mieux que l'or et l'argent!
I you love better than the-gold and the-silver!
(I love you more than gold and silver!)

Vous me donnez tout, lait, beurre et farine,
You me give all, milk, butter and flour,
(You give me everything, milk, butter and flour,)

Et le gai logis, et le vêtement.
And the happy lodging, and the vestments.
(And a happy home, and clothing.)

Vous chantez dès l'aube avec les oiseaux;
You sing from the-dawn with the birds;
(You sing from sun-up with the birds;)

Eté comme hiver, chanvre ou laine fine,
Summer like winter, hemp or wool fine,
(Summer and winter, hemp or fine wool,)

Par vous, jusqu'au soir, charge les fuseaux.
By you, until-to-the evening, load the spindles.
(You load the spindles until evening.)

Vous me filerez mon suaire étroit,
You me will-spin my shroud narrow,
(You will spin me my narrow shroud,)

Quand, près de mourir, et courbant l'échine,
When, close of to-die, and bending the-spine,
(When, close to dying, and with spine bent,)

Je ferai mon lit éternel et froid.
I will-make my bed eternal and cold.
(I make my eternal and cold bed.)

Les Grands Vents Venus d'Outre-Mer

(The Great Winds that Come from Overseas)

Les grands vents venus d'outre-mer
The great winds come from-over-sea
(The great winds that come from overseas)

Passent par la Ville, l'hiver,
Pass by the Town, the-winter,
(Pass through the Town, in winter,)

Comme des étrangers amers.
Like some foreigners bitter.
(Like bitter foreigners.)

Ils se concertent, braves et pâles,
They themselves gather, brave and pale,
(They gather, brave and pale,)

Sur les places, et leurs sandales
On the squares, and their sandals
(On the town squares, and their sandals)

Ensablent le marbre des dalles.
Cover-with-sand the marble of-the flagstones.
(Cover the marble flagstones with sand.)

Comme des crosses à leurs mains fortes
Like some gun-butts to their hands strong
(As if with the butt of a gun in their strong hands)

Ils heurtent l'auvent et la porte
They strike the-porch-roof and the door
(They strike at the porch roof and the door)

Derrière qui l'horloge est morte;
Behind whom the-clock is dead;
(Behind which the clock is dead;)

Et les adolescents amers
And the adolescents bitter
(And the bitter youths)

S'en vont avec eux vers la Mer!
Themselves-from-it go with them toward the Sea!
(Go with them to the Sea!)

Ravel
Manteau de Fleurs
Cloak of Flowers

Toutes les fleurs de mon jardin sont roses,
All the flowers of my garden are pink,
(All the flowers of my garden are pink,)

Le rose sied à sa beauté.
The pink becomes to her beauty.
(Pink becomes her beauty.)

Les primevères sont les premières écloses,
The Primulas are the first-ones bloomed,
(The Primulas are the first to bloom,)

Puis viennent les tulipes et les jacinthes roses,
Then come the tulips and the hyacinths pink,
(Then come the tulips and the pink hyacinths,)

Les jolis oeillets, les si belles roses,
The pretty pinks, the so beautiful roses,
(The pretty pinks, the roses so beautiful,)

Toute la variété des fleurs si roses,
All the variety of-the flowers so pink,
(All the varieties of flowers so pink,)

Du printemps et de l'été!
Of-the sping and of the-summer!
(Of spring and of summer!)

Le rose sied à sa beauté!
The pink becomes to her beauty!
(Pink becomes her beauty!)

Toutes mes pivoines sont roses,
All my peonies are pink,
(All my peonies are pink,)

Roses aussi sont mes glaieuls,
Pink also are my gladiolas
(Pink also are my gladiolas.)

Roses mes géraniums; seuls,
Pink my geraniums; alone,
(Pink my geraniums; alone,)

Dans tout ce rose un peu troublant,
In all this pink a little troubling,
(In all this somewhat troubling pink,)

Les lys ont le droit d'etre blancs.
The lilies have the right of-to-be white.
(Do the lilies have the right to be white.)

Et quand elle passe au milieu des fleurs
And when she passes in-the middle of-the flowers
(And when she passes amidst the flowers)

Emperlées de rosée en pleurs,
Pearled of dew in tears,
(Pearled with weeping dew,)

Dans le parfum grisant des roses,
In the perfume intoxicating of-the roses,
(In the intoxicating perfume of the roses,)

Et sous la caresse des choses
And under the caress of-the things
(And under the caress of things)

Toute grâce, amour, pureté!
All grace, love, purity!
(All grace, love, purity!)

Les fleurs lui font un manteau rose
The flowers for-her make a cloak pink
(The flowers make a pink cloak for her)

Dont elle pare sa beauté!
Of which she adorns her beauty!
(With which she adorns her beauty!)

Mayerke - Chanson Hébraïque
Mayerke - Song Hebraic
Mayerke - Hebrew Song

Mayerke, mon fils, O, Mayerke, mon fils,
Mayerke, my son, Oh, Mayerke, my son,
(Mayerke, my son, Oh, Mayerke, my son,)

Devant qui te trouves-tu là?
Before whom yourself find-you there?
(Before whom do you stand?)

"Devant lui, Roi des Rois, et seul Roi," père mien.
"Before him, King of-the Kings, and only King," father mine.
("Before him, Kings of Kings, and King alone," my father.

Et que lui demandes-tu là?
And what him ask-you there?
(And what do you ask of him?)

"Des enfants, longue vie et mon pain," père mien.
"Some children, long life and my bread," father mine
(Children, long life and my bread," father mine.

Mais me dis, pourquoi des enfants?
But to-me tell, why some children?
(But tell me, why children?

"Aux enfants on apprend la Thora," père mien.
"To-the children one learns the Torah," father mine.
("To children one teaches the Torah," my father.)

Mais me dis, pourquoi longue vie?
But to-me tell, why long life?
(But tell me, why long life?)

"Ce qui vit chante gloire au Seigneur," père mien.
"All that lives sings glory to-the Lord," father mine.
("All that lives sings glory to the Lord," my father.)

Mais tu veux encore du pain?
But you wish still some bread?
(But do you still wish bread?)

"Prends ce pain, nourris-toi, bénis-le" père mien.
"Take this bread, nourish-yourself, bless-it," father mine.
(Take this bread, nourish yourself, bless it," my father.

Nicolette

Nicolette

Nicolette, à la vesprée, S'allait promener au pré,
Nicolette, to the vespers, Herself-was-going to-walk to-the field,
(Nicolette, one evening, Went to walk in the field,)

Cueillir la pâquerette, la jonquille et le muguet.
(To-gather the daisy, the jonquil and the lily-of-the-valley.
(To gather daisies, jonquils and lilies-of-the-valley.)

Toute sautillante, toute guillerette, Lorgnant ci, là,
All skipping, all perky, Ogling here, there,
(Skipping, lively, Looking here, there,)

de tous les côtés. Rencontra vieux loup grognant, Tout hérissé,
of all the sides. She-met old wolf growling, All bristly,
(on all sides. She met an old growling wolf, All hairy,)

l'oeil brillant: "Hé là! ma Nicolette, viens-tu pas
the-eye shining: "Hey there! my Nicolette, come-you not
(with shining eye: "Hey there! my Nicolette, won't you come)

chez Mère-Grand?" A perte d'haleine, s'enfuit Nicolette,
to-house Mother-Grand?" To loss of-breath, herself-flew Nicolette,
(to Grandmother's house?" Till out of breath, Nicolette ran away,)

Laissant là cornette et socques blancs. Rencontra page joli,
Leaving there cornet and clogs white. She-met page pretty,
(Leaving cornet and white clogs there. She met a handsome page,)

Chausses bleues et pourpoint gris: "Hé là! ma Nicolette,
Pants blue and doublet gray: "Hey there! my Nicolette,)
(with blue pants and gray doublet: "Hey there! my Nicolette,)

veux-tu pas d'un doux ami?" Sage, s'en retourna,
want-you not of-a sweet friend?" Sage, herself-from-it returned,
(don't you want a sweet friend?" Wise, she turned away,)

pauvre Nicolette, Très lentement, le coeur bien marri.
poor Nicolette, Very slowly, the heart well sorry.
(poor Nicolette, Very slowly, her heart very heavy.)

Rencontra seigneur chenu, Tors, laid, puant et ventru:
She-met lord gray-headed, Twisted, ugly, stinking and stomached:
(She met a gray-haired lord, Twisted, ugly, stinking and fat:)

"Hé là! ma Nicolette, veux-tu pas tous ces écus?"
"Hey there! my Nicolette, wish-you not all these coins?"
("Hey there! my Nicolette, don't you want all these coins?")

Vite fut en ses bras, bonne Nicolette...
Quickly was in his arms, good Nicolette...
(Quickly she flew into his arms, good Nicolette...)

Jamais au pré n'est plus revenue.
Never to-the field not-is more returned.
(Never to return to the field again.)

Ravel
Noël des Jouets
Christmas of-the Toys
(The Toy's Christmas)

Le troupeau verni des moutons
The flock varnished of-the sheep
(The painted flock of sheep)

Roule en tumulte vers la crèche.
Rolls in tumult toward the creche.
(Rolls in tumult toward the creche.)

Les lapins tambours, brefs et rêches,
The rabbit drummers, brief and rough,
(The rabbit drummers, short and rough,)

Couvrent leurs aigres mirlitons.
Cover their harsh reed-pipes.
(Cover their harsh reed pipes.)

Vierge Marie, en crinoline,
Virgin Mary, in crinoline,
(The Virgin Mary, in crinoline,)

Ses yeux d'émail sans cesse ouverts,
Her eyes of-enamel without cease open,
(Her enamel eyes forever open,)

En attendant Bonhomme hiver
In waiting-for Goodman winter
(Waiting for Old Man winter)

Veille Jésus qui se dodine.
Watches Jesus who himself dozes.
(Watches over the dozing Jesus.)

Car, près de là, sous un sapin,
Because, close to there, under a fir,
(Because, close by, under a fir-tree,)

Furtif, emmitouflé dans l'ombre,
Furtive, muffled in the-shadow,
(Furtively, muffled in the wood's shadow,)

Du bois, Belzébuth, le chien sombre,
Of-the wood, Beelzebub, the dog sombre,
(Beelzebub, the somber dog,)

Guette l'Enfant de sucre peint.
Awaits the-Infant of sugar painted.
(Awaits the sugar-painted child.)

Mais les beaux anges incassables
But the beautiful angels unbreakable
(But the beautiful unbreakable angels)

Suspendus par des fils d'archal
Suspended by some wires of-brass
(Suspended by brass wires)

Du haut de l'arbuse hiémal
From-the height of the-bush winter
(From the top of the Christmas tree)

Assurent la paix des étables.
Assure the peace of-the stables.
(Insure the peace of the stables.)

Et leur vol de clinquant vermeil
And their flight of flashy crimson
(And their flight of crimson tinsel)

Qui cliquette en bruits symétriques
Which jingles in noises symmetrical
(Which jingles in symmetrical noises)

S'accorde au bétail mécanique
Themselves-accord with-the livestock mechanical
(Harmonizes with the mechanical beasts)

Dont la voix grêle bêle: "Noël! Noël! Noël!"
Whose the voice shrill bleats: "Noël! Noël! Noël!"
(Whose shrill voices bleat: "Noël! Noël! Noël!")

Placet futile
Petition futile
(Futile Petition)

Princesse! à jalouser le destin d'une Hébé
Princess! to to-envy the destiny of-a Hébé
(Princess! to envy the destiny of a Hébé)

Qui point sur cette tasse au baiser de vos lèvres,
Which rises on this cup to-the kiss of your lips,
(Which rises on this cup at the kiss of your lips,)

J'use mes feux mais n'ai rang discret que d'abbé
I-use my fires but not-have rank discreet but of abbé
(I enjoy my desires but have only the discreet rank of abbé)

Et ne figurerai même nu sur le Sèvres.
And not will-appear likewise nude on the Sèvres.
(And likewise will not appear nude on the Sèvres.)

Comme je ne suis pas ton bichon embarbé,
Like I not am not your lap-dog bearded,
(As I am not your bearded lap-dog,)

Ni la pastille ni du rouge, ni Jeux mièvres
Nor the lozenge nor of-the rouge, nor Games maudlin
(Nor lozenge nor rouge, nor maudlin Games)

Et que sur moi je sais ton regard clos tombé,
And that on me I know your glance closed fallen,
(And since I know that your closed glance has fallen upon me,)

Blonde dont les coiffeurs divins sont des orfèvres!
Blond-one whose the hairdressers divine are some goldsmiths!
(Blond one whose divine hairdressers are goldsmiths!)

Nommez-nous...toi de qui tant de ris framboisés
Name us...you from whom so-much of laughter raspberried
(Name us...you from whom so much raspberried laughter)

Se joignent en troupeau d'agneaux apprivoisés
Themselves join in flock of-lambs tamed
(Joins together in a flock of tamed lambs)

Chez tous broutant les voeux et bêlant aux délires,
At everyone grazing the wishes and bleating to-the deliriums,
(Grazing their wishes everywhere and bleating into delirium,)

Nommez-nous...pour qu'Amour ailé d'un éventail
Name us...for that-Love winged of-a fan
(Name us...so that Love winged with a fan)

M'y peigne flûte aux doigts endormant ce bercail,
Me-there paints flute to-the fingers sleeping this sheepfold,
(Paints me there flute in fingers lulling this sheepfold,)

Princesse, nommez-nous berger de vos sourires.
Princess, name us shepherd of your smiles.
(Princess, name us shepherd of your smiles.)

Ravel
Rêves
Dreams

Un enfant court Autour des marbres...
A child runs Around the marbles...
(A child runs around the marble...)

Une voix sourd Des hauts parages...
A voice deaf of-the high latitudes...
(A high muffled voice...)

Les yeux si graves De ceux qui t'aiment
The eyes so heavy of those who you-love
(The eyes so heavy of those who love you)

Songent et passent Entre les arbres...
Dream and pass Between the trees...
(Dream and pass between the trees...)

Aux grandes orgues De quelque gare
To-the large organs Of some station
(The wave of past departures)

Gronde la vague Des vieux departs...
Rumbles the wave of-the old departures...
(Rumbles to the large organs of some station...)

Dans un vieux rêve Au pays vague
In an old dream To-the countries vague
(In an old dream in the faint countries)

Des choses brèves Qui meurent sages...
Of-the things brief which die wise...
(Of brief things which die wise...)

Ronde

Round

(Les Vieilles:) (The Old-Women:)

N'allez pas au bois d'Ormonde, Jeunes filles,
Not-go not to-the woods of-Ormonde, Young girls,
(Do not go to the woods of Ormonde, Young girls,)

n'allez pas au bois: Il y a plein de satyres,
not-go not to-the woods: It there has full of satyrs,
(do not go to the woods: There are many satyrs,)

de centaures, de malins sorciers, Des farfadets et des incubes,
of centaurs, of evil sorcerers, Some leprechauns and some incubuses,
(centaurs, evil sorcerers, leprechauns and incubuses,)

Des ogres, des lutins, Des faunes, des follets, des lamies,
Some ogres, some imps, Some fauns, some sprites, some lamias,
(ogres, imps, fauns, sprites, lamias,)

Diables, diablets, diablotins, Des chèvre-pieds, des gnomes,
Devils, little-devils, crackers, Some goat-footed-satyrs, some gnomes,
(ogres, little devils, crackers, goat-footed satyrs, gnomes,)

des démons, Des loups-garous, des elfes, des myrmidons,
some devils, Some werewolves, some elves, some myrmidons,
(some devils, werewolves, elves, myrmidons,)

Des enchanteurs et des mages, des stryges, des sylphes,
Some enchanters and some magi, some stryges, some sylphs,
(enchanters and magi, stryges, sylphs,)

des moines-bourrus, des cyclopes, des djinns, gobelins,
some monks-surly, some cyclopses, some genies, goblins,
(peevish monks, cyclopses, genies, goblins,)

korrigans, nécromans, kobolds...Ah!
elves, necromans, kobolds...Ah!
(elves, necromans, kobolds...Ah!)

(Les Vieux:) (The Old-Men:)

N'allez pas au bois d'Ormonde, Jeunes garçons,
Not-go not to-the woods of-Ormonde, Young boys,
(Do not go to the woods of Ormonde, Young boys,)

n'allez pas au bois: Il y a plein de faunesses,
not-go not to-the woods: It there has full of faunesses,
(do not go to the woods: There are many faunesses,)

De bacchantes et de males fées, Des satyresses, des ogresses,
Of bacchantes, and of evil fairies, Some satyresses, some ogresses,
(bacchantes, and evil fairies, satyresses, ogresses,)

Et des babaïagas, Des centauresses et des diablesses,
And some babaiagas, Some centauresses and some she-devils,
(And of babaiagas, centauresses and she-devils,)

Goules sortant du sabbat, Des farfadettes et des démones,
Ghouls going-out from-the sabbath, Some elves and some demons,
(Ghouls coming from their sabbath, elves and demons,)

Des larves, des nymphes, des myrmidones, Hamadryades, dryades,
Some ghosts, some nymphs, some myrmidons, Woodnymphs, dryads,
(Of ghosts, of nymphs, of myrmidons, Woodnymphs, dryads,)

naïades, ménades, thyades, follettes, lémures, gnomides, succubes,
naiads, maenads, thyads, sprites, lemures, gnomes, succubus,
(naiads, maenads, thyads, sprites, lemures, gnomes, succubus,)

gorgones, gobelines...Ah!
gorgons, goblins...Ah!
(gorgons, goblins...Ah!)

(Les Filles et Les Garçons:) (The Girls and The Boys:)

N'irons plus au bois d'Ormonde, -Hélas! plus jamais
Not-we-shall-go more to-the woods of-Ormonde, -Alas! more never
(We shall go no more to the woods of Ormonde, -Alas! never again)

n'irons au bois. -Il n'y a plus de satyres,
not-we-shall-go to-the woods. -It not-there has no-more of satyres,
(we shall not go to the woods. -There are no more satyres,)

-plus de nymphes ni de males fées. -Plus de farfadets,
-no-more of nymphs nor of evil fairies. -No-more of leprechauns,
(no more nymphs nor evil fairies. -No more leprechauns,)

plus d'incubes, Plus d'ogres, de lutins, De faunes, de follets,
no-more of-incubuses, No-more of-ogres, of imps, Of fauns, of sprites,
(no more incubuses, No more ogres, imps, Fauns, sprites,)

de lamies, Diables, diablots, diablotins, De chèvre-pieds,
of lamias, Devils, little-devils, crackers, Of goat-footed-satyres,
(lamias, Devils, little devils, crackers, Goat-footed satyres,)

de gnomes, de démons, De loups-garous, ni d'elfes, de myrmidons,
of gnomes, of demons, Of werewolves, nor of-elves, of mirmidons,
(gnomes, demons, Werewolves, nor elves, mirmidons,)

Plus d'enchanteurs, ni de mages, de stryges, de sylphes,
More of-enchanters, nor of mages, of stryges, of sylphs,
(No more enchanters, nor mages, stryges, sylphs,)

de moines-bourrus, de cyclopes, de djinns, de diabloteaux,
of monks-surly, of cyclops, of genies, of imps,
(peevish monks, cyclops, genies, imps,)

d'éfrits, d'aegypans, de sylvains, gobelins, korrigans,
of-efrits, of-aegypans, of sylphs, goblins, elves,
(efrits, aegypans, sylphs, goblins, elves,)

nécromans, kobolds...Ah! Les malavisés vieilles,
necromancers, kobolds...Ah! The ill-advised old-women,
(necromancers, kobolds...Ah! The ill-advised old women,)

les malavisés vieux les ont affarouchés -Ah!
the ill-advised old-men them have scared-away -Ah!
(the ill-advised old men have scared them away -Ah!)

Ronsard à son Ame

Ronsard to his Soul

Amelette Ronsardelette, Mignonnelette, doucelette,
Little-soul of-Little-Ronsard, Little-Darling, little-sweet-one
(Little soul of Little Ronsard, Little Darling, little sweet one)

Très-chère hostesse de mon corps, Tu descens là-bas, faiblelette,
Very-dear hostess of my body, You go-down there, slightly-weak,
(Dearest hostess of my body, You go down there, slightly weak,)

Pasle, maigrelette, seulette, Dans le froid royaume des mors;
Pale, little-thin, little-alone, In the cold realm of-the dead;
(Pale, thin, alone, Into the cold realm of the dead;)

Toutesfois simple, sans remors De meurtre, poison,
Nevertheless simple, without remorse of murder, poison
(Nevertheless simple, without remorse for murder, poison,)

et rancune. Méprisant faveurs et trésors, Tant enviez
and bitterness. Scorning favors and treasures, so-much envied
(and bitterness. Scorning favors and treasures, so much envied)

par la commune. Passant, j'ay dit: suy ta fortune,
by the common. Passing, I-have said: follow your fortune,
(by the common. Passing, I said: follow your fortune,)

Ne trouble mon repos, je dors.
Not trouble my repose, I sleep.
(Do not trouble my rest, I am sleeping.)

Sainte

Saint

A la fenêtre recélant Le santal vieux qui se dédore
At the window hiding the sandalwood old that itself ungolds
(At the recessed window the old fading sandalwood)

De sa viole étincelante Jadis avec flûte ou mandore,
Of her viol sparkling Once with flute or mandora,
(Of her once sparkling viol with flute or mandora,)

Est la Sainte pâle, étalant Le livre vieux qui se déplie
Is the Saint pale, displaying the book old that itself unfolds
(Is the pale Saint, displaying the old book that lies open)

Du Magnificat ruisselant Jadis selon vêpres
Of-the magnificat glistening Once according-to vespers
(To the once glistening magnificat according to vespers

et complie: A ce vitrage d'ostensoir Que frôle
and compline: At this glass of-monstrance That brushes
(and compline: At this monstrance glass That, brushed)

une harpe par l'Ange Formée avec son vol du soir
a harp by the-Angel Formed with his flight of-the evening
(by the Angel's harp Formed with his evening flight)

Pour la délicate phalange Du doigt que, sans le vieux
For the delicate phalanx Of-the finger that, without the old
(For the delicate phalanx Of the finger that, without the old)

santal Ni le vieux livre, elle balance Sur le
sandalwood Nor the old book, she balances On the
(sandalwood Nor the old book, she balances On the)

plumage instrumental, Musicienne du silence.
plumage instrumental, Musician of-the silence.
(instrumental plumage, Musician of the silence.)

Ravel
Shéhérazade
Scheherazade

Asie
Asia

Asie, Asie, Asie,
Asia, Asia, Asia,
(Asia, Asia, Asia,)

Vieux pays merveilleux des contes de nourrice,
Ancient land marvelous of-the tales of nursemaid,
(Ancient marvelous land of fairy tales,)

Où dort la fantaisie comme une impératrice,
Where sleeps the fantasy like an empress,
(Where fantasy sleeps like an empress,)

En sa forêt tout emplie de mystère.
In its forest all filled of mystery.
(In its forest full of mystery.)

Asie, Je voudrais m'en aller avec la goëlette
Asia, I would-like me-from-it to-go with the schooner
(Asia, I would like to go there with the schooner)

Qui se berce ce soir dans le port,
Which itself rocks this night in the port,
(Which rocks tonight in the port,)

Mystérieuse et solitaire,
Mysterious and solitary,
(Mysterious and solitary,)

Et qui déploie enfin ses voiles violettes,
And which deploys at-last its sails violet,
(And which at last spreads its violet sails,)

Comme un immense oiseau de nuit dans le ciel d'or.
Like an immense bird of night in the sky of-gold.
(Like an immense bird of night in the golden heaven.)

(cont.)

Je voudrais m'en aller vers des îles de fleurs,
I would-like me-from-it to-go toward some islands of flowers,
(I would like to go toward the islands of flowers,)

En écoutant chanter la mer perverse,
In listening to-sing the sea perverse,
(While listening to the perverse sea sing,)

Sur un vieux rythme ensorceleur.
On an old rhythm bewitching.
(On an old bewitching rhythm.)

Je voudrais voir Damas et les villes de Perse,
I would-like to-see Damascus and the villages of Persia,
(I would like to see Damascus and the towns of Persia,)

Avec des minarets légers dans l'air.
With some minarets light in the-air.
(With airy minarets in the sky.)

Je voudrais voir de beaux turbans de soie,
I would-like to-see some beautiful turbans of silk,
(I would like to see beautiful turbans of silk,)

Sur des visages noirs aux dents claires.
On some faces black to-the teeth bright.
(Above black faces with bright teeth.)

Je voudrais voir des yeux sombres d'amour,
I would-like to-see some eyes somber of-love,
(I would like to see eyes somber with love,)

Et des prunelles brillantes de joie,
And some pupils brilliant of joy,
(And pupils brilliant with joy,)

En des peaux jaunes comme des oranges.
In some skins yellow like some oranges.
(In skins yellow as oranges.)

Je voudrais voir des vêtements de velours
I would-like to-see some vestments of velvet
(I would like to see clothes of velvet)

Et des habits à longues franges.
And some robes to long fringes.
(And robes with long fringes.)

Je voudrais voir des calumets, entre des bouches
I would-like to-see some calumets, between some mouths
(I would like to see calumets, between lips)

Tout entourées de barbe blanche.
All encircled of beard white.
(All encircled by white beard.)

Je voudrais voir d'âpres marchands aux regards louches,
I would-like to-see some-bitter merchants to-the glances suspicious,
(I would like to see rough merchants with suspicious glances,)

Et des cadis, et des vizirs
And some cadis, and some viziers
(And cadis, and viziers)

Qui d'un seul mouvement de leur doigt qui se penche,
Who of-a single movement of their finger which itself leans,
(Who with a single movement of their bent finger,)

Accordent vie ou mort, au gré de leur désir.
Accord life or death, to-the wish of their desire.
(Grant life or death, at the whim of their desire.)

Je voudrais voir la Perse, et l'Inde, et puis la Chine,
I would-like to-see the Persia, and the-India, and then the-China,)
(I would like to see Persia, and India, and then China,)

Les mandarins ventrus sous les ombrelles,
The mandarins stomached under the umbrellas,
(The corpulant mandarins under their parasols,)

Et les princesses aux mains fines,
And some princesses of-the hands fine,
(And princesses with delicate hands,)

Et les lettrés qui se querellent
And the scholars who themselves quarrel
(And scholars who quarrel among themselves)

Sur la poésie et sur la beauté.
On the poetry and on the beauty.
(Over poetry and beauty.)

Je voudrais m'attarder un palais enchanté,
I would-like myself-to-linger a palace enchanted,
(I would like to linger at an enchanted palace,)

Et comme un voyageur étranger
And like a voyager foreign
(And like a foreign traveler)

Contempler à loisir des paysages peints
To-contemplate at leisure some countrysides painted
(To contemplate at leisure the countrysides painted)

Sur des étoffes en des cadres de sapin,
On some stuff in some frames of fir,
(On fabric in fir-wood frames,)

Avec un personnage au milieu d'un verger.
With a personage at-the midst of-an orchard.
(With a figure in the midst of an orchard.)

Je voudrais voir des assassins souriant
I would-like to-see some assasins smiling
(I would like to see assasins smiling)

Du bourreau qui coupe un cou d'innocent,
Of-the executioner who cuts a neck of-innocent,
(At the executioner who cuts off an innocent head,)

Avec son grand sabre courbé d'Orient.
With his large saber curved of-Orient.
(With his large curved Oriental saber.)

Je voudrais voir des pauvres et des reines,
I would-like to-see some poor and some queens,
(I would like to see the poor and queens,)

Je voudrais voir des roses et du sang,
I would-like to-see some roses and some blood,
(I would like to see roses and blood,)

Je voudrais voir mourir d'amour ou bien de haine.
I would-like to-see to-die of-love or well of hate.
(I would like to see someone die for love or else for hate.)

Et puis m'en revenir plus tard
And then myself-from-it to-return more late
(And then returning later)

Narrer mon aventure aux curieux de rêves,
To-narrate my adventure to-the curious of dreams,
(To tell my adventure to those curious about dreams,)

En élevant comme Sindbad ma vielle tasse arabe
In raising like Sinbad my old cup Arab
(Raising, like Sinbad, my old Arabic cup)

De temps en temps jusqu'à mes lèvres,
From time in time until-to my lips,
(From time to time to my lips,)

Pour interrompre le conte avec art....
For to-interrupt the tale with art....
(To interrupt the tale with art....)

Ravel
Shéhérazade
Scheherazade

La Flûte Enchantée
The Flute Enchanted
(The Enchanted Flute)

L'ombre est douce et mon maître dort
The-shadow is soft and my master sleeps
(The shadows are soft and my master sleeps)

Coiffé d'un bonnet conique de soie,
Capped of-a bonnet conical of silk,
(Capped with a conical silk bonnet,)

Et son long nez jaune en sa barbe blanche.
And his long nose yellow in his beard white.
(And his long yellow nose in his white beard.)

Mais moi, je suis éveillée encor
But me, I am awake still
(But I, I am still awake)

Et j'écoute au dehors
And I-listen at-the outside
(And outside I hear)

Une chanson de flûte où s'épanche
A song of flute where itself-pours-out
(The song of a flute which pours out)

Tour à tour la tristesse ou la joie.
Turn to turn the sadness or the joy.
(In turn sadness or joy.)

Un air tour à tour langoureux ou frivole
An air turn to turn languorous or frivolous
(An air in turn languorous or frivolous)

Que mon amoureux chéri joue.
That my lover dear plays.
(That my dear lover plays.)

Et quand je m'approche de la croisée,
And when I myself-approach to the crossing,
(And when I approach the window,)

Il me semble que chaque note s'envole
It to-me seems that each note itself-flies
(It seems to me that each note flies)

De la flûte vers ma joue,
From the flute toward my cheek,
(From the flute toward my cheek,)

Comme un mystérieux baiser.
Like a mysterious kiss.
(Like a mysterious kiss.)

Ravel
Shéhérazade
Scheherazade

L'Indifférent
The-Indifferent-One

Tes yeux sont doux comme ceux d'une fille,
Your eyes are sweet like those of-a girl,
(Your eyes are soft like a girl's,)

Jeune étranger, et la courbe fine
Young stranger, and the curve fine
(Young stranger, and the delicate curve)

De ton beau visage de duvet ombragé,
Of your beautiful face of down shaded,
(Of your beautiful face, shaded with down,)

Est plus séduisante encore de ligne.
Is more seductive still of line.
(Is still more seductive in its line.)

Ta lèvre chante sur le pas de ma porte
Your lip sings on the step of my door
(On my doorstep your lips sing)

Une langue inconnue et charmante,
A language unknown and charming,
(An unknown and charming language,)

Comme une musique fausse.
Like a music false.
(Like false music.)

Entre! Et que mon vin te réconforte...
Enter! And that my wine you recomfort...
(Enter! And let my wine refresh you...)

Mais non, tu passes,
But no, you pass,
(But no, you pass by,)

Et de mon seuil je te vois t'éloigner,
And from my threshold I you see yourself-to-distance,
(And from my theshold I see you leaving,)

Me faisant un dernier geste avec grâce,
To-me making a last gesture with grace,
(With a last graceful gesture to me,)

Et la hanche légèrement ployée
And the hip lightly bent
(And your hips lightly swaying)

Par ta démarche féminine et lasse....
By your gait feminine and languid....
(With your feminine and languid gait....)

Si Morne!
So Mournful!
(So Bleak!)

Se replier sur soi-même, si morne!
Oneself to-refold on oneself, so mournful!
(Thrown back on oneself, so bleak!)

Comme un drap lourd, qu'aucun dessin de fleur n'adorne.
Like a drape heavy, that-no design of flower not-adorns.
(Like a heavy cloth, that no flower pattern adorns.)

Se replier, s'appesantir et se tasser
Itself to-re-fold, to-make-heavy and to settle
(Thrown back on itself, becoming heavy and settled)

Et se toujours, en angles noirs et mats, casser.
And itself always, in angles black and matte, to-break.
(And always, in black and matte angles, breaking.)

Si morne! et se toujours interdire l'envie
So mournful! and itself always to-interdict the-envy
(So bleak! and always forbidding the desire)

De tailler en drapeaux l'etoffe de sa vie.
Of to-tailor in flags the-fabric of its life.
(To cut up in flags the stuff of one's life.)

Tapir entre les plis ses mauvaises fureurs
To-hide between the folds its evil furors
(Cowering between the folds one's evil furors)

Et ses rancoeurs et ses douleurs et ses erreurs.
And its rancors and its sorrows and its errors.
(And one's rancors and one's sorrows and one's errors.)

Ni les frissons soyeux, ni les moires fondantes
Neither the shivers silky, nor the moires melting
(Neither the silky shivers, nor the melting moires)

Mais les pointes en soi des épingles ardentes.
But the points in itself of-the pins ardent.
(But the points of ardent pins within oneself.)

Oh! le paquet qu'on pousse ou qu'on jette à l'écart,
Oh! the packet that-one pushes or that-one throws to the-side
(Oh! the packet that one pushes away or throws to the side,)

Si morne et lourd, sur un rayon, dans un bazar.
So mournful and heavy, on a shelf, in a bazaar.
(So bleak and heavy, on a shelf, in a bazaar.)

Déjà sentir la bouche âcre des moisissures
Already to-feel the mouth acrid of-the-moulds
(Already feeling the mouth acrid of moulds)

Gluer, et les taches s'étendre en leurs morsures.
To-glue, and the stains themselves-to-spread in their morsels.
(Gumming up, and the stains spreading in their bites.)

Pourrir, immensément emmaillotté d'ennui;
To-rot, immensely swaddled of-ennui;
(Rotting, hugely swaddled in boredom;)

Etre l'ennui qui se replie en de la nuit.
To-be the-ennui that itself refolds in of the night.
(Being the boredom that folds back upon itself in the night.)

Tandis que lentement, dans les laines ourdies,
While that slowly, in the woolens warped,
(While slowly, in the warped woolens,)

De part en part, mordent les vers des maladies.
From part in part, bite the worms of-the maladies.
(Through and through, the worms of sickness bite.)

Soupir
Sigh

Mon âme vers ton front où rêve, ô calme soeur,
My soul toward your face where dreams, o calm sister,
(My soul toward your face where dreams, o calm sister,)

Un automne jonché de taches de rousseur,
An autumn strewn of stains of russet,
(An autumn strewn with freckles,)

Et vers le ciel errant de ton oeil angélique,
And toward the heaven wandering of your eye angelic,
(And toward the wandering heaven of your angelic eye,)

Monte, comme dans un jardin mélancolique,
Rises, like in a garden melancholy,
(Rises, like in a melancholy garden,)

Fidèle, un blanc jet d'eau soupire vers l'Azur!
Faithful, a white jet of-water sighs toward the-Azure!
(Faithful, a white fountain sighs toward the skies!)

Vers l'Azur attendri d'octobre pâle et pur
Toward the-Azure made-tender of-October pale and pure
(Toward the skies made tender by pale and pure October)

Qui mire aux grands bassins de sa langueur infinie
Which mirrors to-the great basins of its langor infinite
(Which mirrors its infinite languor in the great pools)

Et laisse, sur l'eau morte où la fauve agonie
And lets, on the-water dead where the savage agony
(And lets, on the dead water where the savage agony)

Des feuilles erre au vent et creuse un froid sillon,
Of-the leaves wanders to-the wind and hollows a cold furrow,
(Of leaves wanders in the wind and digs a cold furrow,)

Se traîner le soleil jaune d'un long rayon.
Itself to-drag the sun yellow of-a long ray.
(The yellow sun drag out in a long ray.)

Sur L'Herbe
On the-Grass

L'abbé divague. Et toi, marquis,
The-abbot rambles. And you, Marquis,
(The abbot rambles. And you, Marquis,)

Tu mets de travers ta perruque.
You put of across your wig.
(You put your wig on sideways.)

Ce vieux vin de Chypre est exquis
This old wine of Cyprus is exquisite
(This old wine from Cyprus is exquisite)

Moins, Camargo, que votre nuque.
Less, Camargo, than your neck.
(Though less, Camargo, than your neck.)

Ma flamme... Do, mi, sol, la si.
My flame...Do, mi, sol, la si
(My flame...Do, mi, sol, la si)

L'abbé, ta noirceur se dévoile.
The-abbot, your blackness itself unveils.
(Abbot, your baseness reveals itself.)

Que je meure, mesdames, si Je ne vous décroche une étoile!
That I die, my-ladies, if I not you un-hook a star!
(May I die, my ladies, if I don't get you a star!)

Je voudrais être petit chien! Embrassons nos bergères,
I would-like to-be little dog! Let-us-kiss our shepherdesses,
(I would like to be a little dog! Let's kiss our shepherdesses,)

l'une Après l'autre. Messieurs! eh bien?
the-one After the-other. Gentlemen, eh well?
(one After the other. Gentlemen, well?)

Do mi, sol. Hé! bonsoir, la Lune!
Do mi, sol. Hey! good-evening, the Moon!
(Do mi, sol. Hey! good evening, Moon!)

Surgi de la croupe et du bond
Risen from the crupper and from-the leap

Surgi de la croupe et du bond
Surged from the crupper and from-the bound
(Risen from the crupper and from the leap

D'une verrerie éphémère
Of-a glassware ephemeral
(Of a piece of ephemeral glassware)

Sans fleurir la veillée amère
Without to-flower the vigil bitter
(Without flowering the bitter vigil)

Le col ignoré s'interrompt.
The neck ignored itself-interrupted.
(The ignored neck is interrupted.)

Je crois bien que deux bouches n'ont
I believe well that two mouths not-have
(I well know that two mouths have not)

Bu, ni son amant ni ma mère,
Drunk, nor her lover nor my mother,
(Drunk, neither her love nor my mother,)

Jamais à la même Chimère,
Ever to the same Chimera,
(Ever to the same Chimera,)

Moi, sylphe de ce froid plafond!
Me, sylph of this cold ceiling!
(Me, sylph of this cold ceiling!)

Le pur vase d'aucun breuvage que l'inexhaustible veuvage
The pure mud of-no liquid that the-inexhaustible widowhood
(The pure mud of no liquid that inexhaustible widowhood)

Agonise mais ne consent,
Agonizes but not consents,
(Agonizes but does not consent,)

Naïf baiser des plus funèbres!
Naive kiss of-the most funereal!
(Naive and most funereal kiss!)

A rien expirer annonçant
To nothing to-breath announcing
(To breath out nothing announcing)

Une rose dans les ténèbres.
A rose in the shadows.
(A rose in the shadows.)

Ravel
Tripatos
Tripatos

Héryia pou dhen idhen ilyios
Hands have not seen sun
(Hands that have not seen the sun)

Poss ta pianoun è yiatri.
How them grasp the doctors.
(How do the doctors grasp them.)

Keénas meh ton alo léye
One to the other says
(One says to the other)

Poss dhen ine yia zoi?
How not is for life?
(How is it that this will not live?)

Tralilila lalalala lilili la,....
Tralilila lalalala lilili la,....
(Tralilila lalalala lilili la,....)

Ravel

Tripatos

Tripatos

Mains qui n'ont pas vu le soleil
Hands that not-have not seen the sun
(Hands that have not seen the sun)

Comment les prennent les médecins.
How them take the doctors.
(How do the doctors grasp them.)

Et l'un avec l'autre disent:
And the-one with the-other say:
(And one and another say:)

Comment se fait-il
How itself makes-it
(How does it happen)

Qu'elle ne soit pas destinée à vivre?
That she not is not destined to to-live?
(That she is not destined to live?)

Tralilila lalalala lilílili la,....
Tralilila lalalala lilílili la,....
(Tralilila lalalala lilílili la,....)

Trois beaux oiseaux du Paradis
Three beautiful birds of-the Paradise

Trois beaux oiseaux du Paradis,
Three beautiful birds of-the Paradise,
(Three beautiful birds of Paradise,)

(Mon ami z-il est à la guerre)
(My love he is at the war)
([My love is at war])

Trois beaux oiseaux du Paradis Ont passé par ici.
Three beautiful birds of-the Paradise Have passed by here.
(Three beautiful birds of Paradise Have passed by here.

Le premier était plus bleu que ciel,
The first was more blue than sky,
(The first was bluer than the sky,)

Le second était couleur de neige,
The second was color of snow,
(The second was the color of snow,)

Le troisième rouge vermeil.
The third red vermillion.
(The third was vermillion red.)

"Beaux oiselets du Paradis, Qu'apportez par ici?"
"Beautiful little-birds of-the Paradise, What-you-bring by here?"
("Beautiful little birds of Paradise, What do you bring here?")

"J'apporte un regard couleur d'azur.
"I-bring a glance color of-azure.
("I bring a glance the color of the sky.)

(Ton ami z-il est à la guerre")
(Your love he is at the war")
([Your love is at war"])

"Et moi, sur beau front couleur de neige,
"And me, on beautiful face color of snow,
("And I, on your beautiful snow-colored face,)

Un baiser dois mettre, encor plus pur."
A kiss must to-place, still more pure."
(Must place a kiss, still purer.")

"Oiseau vermeil du Paradis, Que portez-vous ainsi?"
"Bird vermillion of-the Paradise, What carry-you thus?"
("Vermillion bird of Paradise, What do you carry thus?")

"Un joli coeur tout cramoisi,"
"A pretty heart all crimson,"
("A happy heart all crimson,")

..."Ah! je sens mon coeur qui froidit...Emportez-le aussi."
..."Ah! I feel my heart which grows-cold...Take-this also."
(..."Ah! I feel my heart which grows cold...Take this also.")

Un Grand Sommeil Noir
A Great Sleep Black
(A Great Black Sleep)

Un grand sommeil noir Tombe sur ma vie:
A great sleep black Falls on my life;
(A great black sleep Falls upon my life:)

Dormez, tout espoir, Dormez, toute envie!
Sleep, all hope, sleep, all envy!
(Sleep, all hope, sleep, all longing!)

Je ne vois plus rien, Je perds la mémoire
I not see more nothing. I lose the memory
(I see nothing more, I lose my memory)

Du mal et du bien..., O la triste histoire!
Of-the evil and of-the good..., Oh the sad story
(Of evil and good..., Oh the sad story!)

Je suis un berceau Qu'une main balance
I am a cradle that-a hand rocks,
(I am a cradle that a hand rocks,)

Au creux d'un caveau: Silence, silence!
At-the hollow of-a vault: Silence, silence!
(In the hollow of a vault: Silence, silence!)

(Articles have been included in alphabetization)

Index of Song Titles

(Articles have been included in alphabetization)

(cont.)